CONVICTIONS

CONVICTIONS

My Life with a
Good Communist

Jo Langer

GRANTA

Granta Publications, 12 Addison Avenue, London W11 4QR

First published in Great Britain by André Deutsch Limited, 1979
This edition published by Granta Books, 2011

A CIP catalogue record for this book is available
from the British Library.

1 3 5 7 9 10 8 6 4 2

ISBN 978 1 84708 338 8

Printed in the UK by CPI William Clowes Beccles NR34 7TL

To Elizabeth and Brian Henderson

Foreword

In all the horrors and tragedies of Europe's twentieth century, the Czechoslovak political trials of the 1950s have a peculiar foulness of their own. This is not due to their scale; the central group of victims, in the so-called Slánský trials between 1951 and 1953, numbered no more than a few score, of whom eleven were hanged. By Soviet or Nazi standards, they were a small affair. And yet the Prague trials spread a poison that was to humiliate and paralyse the Czechs and Slovaks for over thirty years, and which revolted the rest of the world.

There were many reasons for this disgust. The first was the shameless fraudulence of the trials. The charges against the defendants were transparently absurd and untrue; their confessions and the statements of the prosecution witnesses were so grotesque that they had obviously been extorted by terror. The second reason was the cannibal spectacle of a Communist Party suddenly devouring its own leadership, in response to orders from Moscow – Rudolf Slánský had been the Secretary General of the Party. A third was the nauseous anti-Semitism pervading the proceedings. Eleven out of the fourteen Slánský defendants had secular Jewish origins, and the fictitious charges against them included plotting with Zionist agents abroad to recruit Czech and Slovak Jews in a conspiracy to overthrow the communist regime.

But a fourth reason, which only began to take effect years later, was that the survivors of these trials started to tell their stories. Some had already written memoirs after their release from prison, hiding them in desk drawers. The brief Prague Spring of 1968 allowed some of these accounts to reach the West and to be published, among them Artur London's *The Confession* (first published in France in1969), which was made into a devastating film by Costa-Gavras. These stories brought a new phase of revelations. It became clear, for instance, that the false confessions had not been extracted by appeals to the prisoners' loyalty to the communist cause (as Arthur Koestler had suggested in *Darkness at Noon*, his novel about the Moscow show trials in the 1930s), but by old-fashioned physical violence and torture, coupled with false promises that repeating a pack of self-accusing lies in court might save a defendant's life. It emerged that the Slánský trials had been directed and stage-managed by a special team of Soviet 'advisers', with the Czechs acting under their orders as jailers, interrogators and executioners.

The survivors' tales were not only about prisons and torture. Most of the victims had families, and some were married to foreigners. These women, educated and experienced, had almost all been loyal to the Party up to the moment of the trials. Now, after the arrests of their husbands, they found themselves expelled from their jobs, evicted from their homes, struggling to bring up children who were often thrown out of school as the offspring of 'traitors'. The lucky ones were 'transferred to production' in factories, which at least brought some money. Others stayed alive only through the kindness of friends who took the risk of bringing them food and fuel.

Several of them wrote heartbreaking accounts of their lives in these times. Among those women witnesses are Josefa Slánská, widow of the star victim (*Report on My Husband*: 1969); the late Marian Šlingová from New Zealand (*Truth Will Prevail*: 1968), whose husband Ota Šling was hanged in 1952; Rosemary Kavan (*Love and Freedom*: 1985), British-born, whose husband Pavel was sentenced to life imprisonment and died shortly after early release (but their son Jan was to become Foreign Minister of free Czechoslovakia). Jo Langer, in contrast, came originally from a Hungarian Jewish family in Budapest. She fell in love with Oscar Langer, also Jewish, when he was a young communist militant in his native Slovakia.

They emigrated to America during the Second World War, to escape both the Nazis and the Slovak fascists, and on their return Oscar Langer became a prominent figure in the new communist regime in Bratislava. It was here that disaster befell them in the years of Stalinist terror. Oscar was arrested, forced to give false evidence against Rudolf Slánský and then himself sentenced to twenty-two years' imprisonment. Like many other political prisoners, he served much of his sentence as a slave labourer in the north Bohemian uranium mines, working underground without proper nourishment or lighting, unprotected against heat, cold or the radioactive dust that penetrated his lungs and poisoned his internal organs.

Jo, with two young daughters, was flung from privileged nomenklatura status into the gutters of Slovak society without money, home or help. The story of how she survived, navigating between the callous stupidity of the authorities and the earthy kindness of ordinary Slovaks, is among the best descriptions of life under communism ever written. It is also a unique confession, composed in old age, of a passionate woman's changing feelings about lovers, husbands and causes.

Before the Second World War, the Czechoslovak Republic had been a small but prosperous democracy, well run and spared much of the turbulence and poverty that afflicted its neighbours in Central Europe. But in 1938 the self-confidence of its citizens was shattered when the western powers – Britain and France – betrayed Czechoslovakia to Hitler's territorial demands at Munich, allowing Nazi Germany to seize its northern Sudeten territories. A few months later, in March 1939, Germany invaded the rump of Czechoslovakia and broke up what was left of the Republic: the Czech lands became the Reich Protectorate of Bohemia and Moravia, while Slovakia became an 'independent' puppet state under a semi-fascist regime.

After the war, Czechoslovakia reappeared. The country had suffered relatively little damage or slaughter compared to Poland or Hungary, and the Czechs and Slovaks greeted the Red Army liberators with genuine enthusiasm – not least because they believed that the Soviet Union would have rescued them at the time of

Munich if only the French and British had stood firm. In the first post-war years, a centre-left coalition, including the Communist Party, seemed to be making a good job of reconstruction. Out of all the nations in Eastern and Central Europe occupied by Soviet forces, Czechoslovakia was the only one (with the exception of Germany) where the Communist Party at first enjoyed some genuine support in the industrial working class. While Soviet control over Poland, Hungary and Eastern Europe was being imposed by police terror and fraudulent elections, Czechoslovakia seemed to be holding to the framework of liberal democracy.

This changed in February 1948. The Communist Party, whose leader Klement Gottwald was an uncritical worshipper of the Soviet Union, had already taken control of the key ministries of defence and the interior. Now began a campaign to break up the coalition and drive the 'bourgeois' parties into opposition. In February, gigantic demonstrations in Prague – orchestrated, but with some genuine popular support – forced Gottwald's rivals out of power and replaced them with a government dominated by the communists and their allies.

Industry and trade were nationalized. In the countryside, a start was made on the total collectivization of agriculture; resistance from small farmers and peasants was crushed by police batons and jail sentences. Purges of non-communist officials began at once, but it was not until late 1949 that the first political trials began under the direction of Soviet security officers taking their orders from the Kremlin. At first, the victims were politicians from the 'bourgeois' opposition parties. But soon attention turned to supposed 'Slovak nationalists' and to officials who had spent the war years in Britain serving the government-in-exile. Many in both categories were loyal communists who had fought bravely against the Nazis: an ominous sign of the direction the political terror would now take.

One aspect of Stalin's paranoia was his mistrust of foreign communists. Another, often overlapping the first, was his hatred of 'cosmopolitan' Jews. After 1948, when Josip Broz Tito's Yugoslavia broke away from the Soviet bloc, Stalin seems to have concluded that all the Party leaderships in the Soviet-dominated zone of Europe should be purged in a series of show trials modelled on the monstrous Moscow trials of the 1930s. Men and women with intellectual backgrounds and experience of the outside world would be branded as spies and traitors, and replaced by more obedient cadres with no international contacts. Some satellite countries, such as Poland and East Germany, managed to evade this order until Stalin died in 1953. But the Czechoslovak communists carried it out with slavish enthusiasm. Rudolf Slánský and his ruling team were arrested and charged with Zionist-Titoist-revisionist treason. Traditional anti-Semitism was now distilled into a principle of the communist state, and Oscar Langer was tortured for days until he agreed to kneel and repeat a hundred times that he was 'of Jewish nationality'. The preparations for the trial, which meant battering defendants and witnesses into learning the parts scripted for them by the Soviet advisers, took a year.

Jo Langer shows how these purges privately appalled Party members in Slovakia. They knew many of these people, and knew they could not be traitors and spies. But fear, and faith in the Party's historic destiny, kept them quiet. As Oscar Langer said uneasily to Jo, not long before his own arrest: 'These men are perhaps not guilty in the everyday sense of the word. But just now the fate and interests of individuals are of secondary importance. Our whole future, maybe the future of mankind, is at stake.'

As she writes in this wonderful and recklessly revealing book, the 1956 upheavals against Stalinist tyranny in Poland and Hungary left Czechoslovakia almost untouched. It was not until 1960 that the show-trial prisoners were released, and Oscar came home. But, almost at once, the marriage began to fall apart. It had always been a difficult one, several times on the edge of divorce or separation. In his prison years, Oscar had clung to his rigid faith in the communist system, insisting that the real saboteurs and traitors to the Leninist ideal had been the security police. Jo, who had spent those years among ordinary factory workers and villagers, had long since rejected the whole regime and its ideology as incurably rotten. When Oscar died, his health shattered by prison, she respected his obstinate courage, unselfishness and 'purity', but also felt 'a sneaking sense of relief at no longer having to live up to something I could not cope with'.

Most of this book was written during the Prague Spring of 1968, in an interval of hope that Jo Langer could not entirely share. 'Socialism with a human face' was still too much like the old socialism for her, and she had ugly memories of the Stalinist pasts of some of those who were now preaching democracy and free speech. When the Soviet tanks rumbled into Bratislava that August, she was not really surprised, and a few days later escaped to Austria with her younger daughter. Some years later in Sweden, where she settled for the rest of her life, she wrote down her final reflections on what she and her family had gone through.

First published in 1979, ten years before the 'Velvet Revolution' overthrew the communist regime, Jo Langer's book remains intensely relevant. In the first place, it is a sharp reminder that 'history' is almost always a construction by a privileged minority. Jo writes that, after her expulsion from the elite, 'I belonged to the overwhelming majority of the population, including the workers with whose lives and attitudes I became closely acquainted . . . The feelings and lives of the non-writing majority of a period are then expressed in the reconstructions of historians . . . Hardly ever do they depend on accounts written by people who just tried to live in the time in question. And the silent majority is nowhere as silent as it is in a totalitarian state.'

Her real scorn is reserved for 'leftists' in western countries who were unwilling to believe the evidence of police terror in Soviet Europe, or who tried weakly to relativize it. In a very painful passage, she describes her failure to persuade her cousin, the great French actress Simone Signoret, to intervene on her husband's behalf. Signoret, who only a few years later was to play a magnificent part in *The Confession*, precisely about the Slánský trials, replied: 'But if you had stayed in New York, your husband, as a communist, would have met with very much the same fate.' Jo walked out of the room. It is only fair to add that Signoret grew bitterly ashamed of this remark, which, according to her own memoirs, seems to have marked a turning point in her own political outlook. A few years later, after the Soviet invasion and Jo's flight to Sweden, she reached out to her 'Bratislava cousin' and found something like forgiveness and affection. And in the 1980s it was Signoret who saw to the translation of *Convictions* into French and ensured that it became a best-seller in France.

This book is many things: a searching set of political reflections, a record of appalling bureaucratic hypocrisy and callousness, a tough and empathetic description of village life with Slovakia's Hungarian minority (a community still ignored and despised by many ethnic Slovaks). It is a rueful account of friendship – those 'best friends' who make themselves scarce when times get bad, and those unexpected, unpromising individuals who turn out to be rock-solid allies, ready to take any risk and share any windfall. It is a candid account of a bad marriage that was never quite loveless, of sex, loneliness and desire. But above all, *Convictions* is about what happens to people who know that something is becoming a disaster – a regime, a marriage, a creed – but decide to go on pretending that nothing is seriously wrong. It was only when Jo Langer hit bottom and realized that she had nothing left to lose – no career, no home, no beliefs, no hope – that she began to feel unafraid and at ease.

Neal Ascherson
London
December 2010

Author's Note

This book consists of material written in Czechoslovakia during the short-lived 'Prague Spring'; of some documents from the 'fifties; of passages from a diary which I kept when I was a young girl in Budapest; and of material written since I became a refugee in Sweden.

I fled from Czechoslovakia in August 1968, five days after the USSR invaded the country. Although the drive between Bratislava, where we lived, and the Austrian frontier takes little more than half an hour, on that day my younger daughter and I felt that it was much longer because the road was lined with Russian tanks. Fortunately the invaders let us pass, our own frontier guards were still sympathetic and the Austrians asked no questions.

Believing that our purpose would be less evident if our car was not full of luggage, we took nothing with us but two small bags. Mine was stuffed with typewritten pages, newspaper clippings, notes, and most of the letters I had exchanged with my husband during the ten years he had spent in jail. We were leaving a lot behind and we didn't know what would happen to us in exile, but once we were over the frontier I felt happy. I had my daughter and my papers; nothing else was important.

Hard, crowded benches. A suffocating stink of unwashed bodies and of undigested cheap drink. The lights are out. Out of order or switched off by somebody who does not feel the need to read on a long trip. Someone bold enough for that would be a person with a certain standing and therefore best to avoid an argument with, on the Prague–Bratislava night express in the year 1951.

The heat is unbearable, the windows are tightly shut. I begin to feel sick, but I am afraid to ask for air. I am afraid because I am alone. Crowded in among muttering, grumbling, sweating, snoring fellow-creatures, I am utterly alone in an unreal world of my own. As proof of life and reality I hear the whimpering of a baby, but even the baby belongs to a different world. There is their world, where things good, bad and even unexpected can happen; all somehow within the limits of the possible. In mine, the impossible, the absolutely illogical, the inconceivable has happened.

I am thirsty. I must, at least, get up and move about. But if I start to speak to my neighbours I might start crying, or even give away my secret. In the dark, I cannot see any faces. I crave for communication, but the least expression of sympathy from one is liable to provoke reactions from others that would make things even worse. The only one I could confide in is the baby. Babies do not read papers.

The man next to me puts his hand on my knee. How about snuggling up, little lady? Nausea, panic. Stumbling blindly over legs and peasant women's skirts and baskets, I manage to reach the corridor A single fly-specked bulb sheds its dirty yellow light over men hunched up on bundles or half stretched out on the floor. These, at least, have faces. I press my forehead against the cool window-pane. Sparks from the engine fly in a steady stream. Presently they begin to fade as the sky becomes grey with approaching dawn. A young man at my feet awakes and turns a sleepy but cheerful face up to me. – God, what a trip! But we are almost there. You going home too? Yes, I am going home. From a business trip to Prague that was supposed to last for a month. For me it ended after four days. Late in the evening my brother-in-law called me long-distance to tell me that Oscar, my husband, had been arrested. I said yes, I am coming. We both held on to the phone for a few seconds in complete silence, then hung up. The telephone was known as a sly, murderous monster.

My companions on the trip promised to pack and send my suit-case, a colleague got a taxi and helped me to catch the night-train. Shock, curiosity, sympathy, helpfulness, tearful embraces, yes. Not many words. Above all, no comments. We were six of us in the hotel room when the call came, all good friends. But at such a moment and in those times, who dared to trust five other people? Or, for that matter, the walls.

This happened four years after our return to Czechoslovakia from America. We belonged to the lucky few who had managed to escape in 1938 when, after the Anschluss, the Germans were already on the other side of the Danube. For me, America was at first a gratefully accepted, but strange and hard-to-get-used-to place of refuge. In the course of eight years, however, it gradually became my home, where my child, who was only a baby when we emigrated, would grow up, for better or worse, as an American. For Oscar, who was an ardent communist and a very homesick Slovak, America was no more than a place of temporary exile, to be grudgingly endured until the war was over and he would be given a chance to put his faith and talents at the service of his own country, where he would help to build up the best socialism of all.

When the war did finally come to an end, refugees in America began to receive their first personal news. No letters at first, only short communications through the Red Cross, published in alphabetical order in foreign-language papers. I scanned the Hungarian paper daily – I am Hungarian by birth – prepared for the worst, and yet hoping, alternately relieved and panicked when my name wasn't there. By the time it appeared, I was already so numbed by the horrors announced to others that my reaction to the message sent by a surviving uncle was inadequate to its contents.

'Mother suicide shortly before liberation, brother Károly perished work squadron USSR, wife back from concentration camp searching for children, Uncle Eugen, wife, daughter, grandson shot in their home, cousin George killed in Szálasi pogrom. Sorry. Hope you well. Write. Kornel.'

Presently, letters began to arrive from my husband's surviving relatives. His parents had died in the transit camp Teresin. His eldest sister, her husband and her two lovely young daughters were gassed in Auschwitz. His seventeen-year-old nephew had fought and fallen in the Slovak uprising. His younger brother survived, illogically enough, because he happened to be in jail for communist activities at the time of the worst deportations. Having broken out of jail, he joined the partisans and was now a high officer and editor-in-chief of the army's daily. Another brother and sister with their families managed to hide in the mountains, fed by genuinely helpful or willing-to-be-bribed Slovak villagers. The brothers' letters were full of hope, plans and enthusiasm.

Then the letter from the Party arrived. They were calling my husband home. He was needed as the talented economist and the trusted comrade they knew him to be. The letter bore the signature of Karol Bacílek who was to become a few years later head of the State Police; which gave him the privilege of delivering to the hangman eleven of his nearest and hundreds of less well-known old comrades.

As for me, once the war was over, there was nobody left to call me home from America. After eight years, I felt less of a stranger there than I would in Slovakia, where I had spent only three years in my early twenties, at the start of our marriage. Besides, I was just beginning to know English, while of Slovak I knew only a few words. I also loved my job. After two years of waitressing, an evening course and a couple of miserable office jobs, I had found work as a secretary to a redheaded self-educated Jew who owned a big bookshop on Michigan Avenue in Chicago, and when in 1944 he moved the business, we followed him to New York.

Our customers were mostly collectors of first editions and otherwise rare books, the business was conducted largely on a mail-order basis, very adroitly stimulated by avalanches of long, witty, excellently written and seemingly very personal letters which were really all the same letter sent with small changes to customers all over the country. In some ways, of course, this was a racket, but it was an innocent, intelligent, amusing one, in which I enjoyed participating. My boss, Ben, came to the States as a child from Lithuania. As a very young boy he already had to support himself, so instead of going to school, he started dusting shelves in a bookshop. He must have done a good deal more reading than dusting because when I met him as a middle-aged man, he knew almost all of Shakespeare and an unbelievable amount of both classic and modern literature by heart. It was this fantastic memory rather than a creative intellect that made his letters so good. Even the catalogues we issued resembled literary essays rather than ordinary information on what we had to sell. We sent genuine rare books to collectors, and parcels of more or less worthless junk, bought by weight at auctions, to the gullible would-be-intellectual rich, who were charmed by Ben. We even published poetry written (and well paid for) by moneyed elderly ladies. These prettily bound volumes we included in the parcels sent cash-on-delivery to our old customers who were sufficiently amused by Ben's letters to accept and pay for them without ever returning (or perhaps even reading) any of them. On the other hand, we also shipped many parcels of good reading matter for almost nothing to soldiers stranded at impossible garrisons, in Iceland or worse, and we wrote them long, encouraging epistles, full of quotations, home gossip and dirty limericks. In Chicago Ben was known to dye his own shirts in all the colours of the rainbow, and for other eccentricities, all of which served to attract people to the shop. Once they were in, they were sure to be talked into buying. Some afternoons we had authors there to sign their books, and I served tea. There was Christopher Morley and Richard Wright, and there was Henry Miller – although he did not sign anything because his books were banned. He came quite often. I don't know whether Ben and he were really friends or whether Ben knew him for the literary genius he is. He never said so, and the few smuggled-in copies of *Tropic of Cancer* we had were sent out on loan to customers who figured in our subject-files under P for pornography. Ben liked to mention that it was he who had discovered and found a publisher for John Steinbeck. Who knows, of the many stories he told, this might have been one with a grain of truth in it. Ben, bless his soul, was a fake in many ways, but a harmless one, and the best boss I ever had. He was also a diabetic who slowly but steadily drank himself to death. When sober, he could not dictate.

Thursdays I had off. But Wednesdays I had to stay after the customers and the staff had left. Ben placed a big bottle of gin on his desk (always gin, and never a drop for me) and started to dictate. At about midnight he removed his upper dental plate. Around two in the morning the bottle was empty, and his lower plate was out as well. At this point, I no longer got much of what he was mumbling, but this flustered me only while I was new. Later on I knew just about what he would write to whom, and there was a tacit understanding between us that I was free to add passages expressing his particular esteem or affection for the addressee according to my own fancy, in his style. Between Wednesdays I sorted out and completed the raw material thus jotted down. The resulting letters were then distributed, with minor individual adjustments according to the addressee, among the girls who typed them out and mailed them to remote corners of the States to various customers who would – we hoped – never meet and compare notes.

Once the bottle was empty and my notebook full, I put the dental plates into an envelope, Ben into a taxi, and delivered him safely to his wife. After this I had permission to use the taxi to take me home at his expense.

I loved the immense room with its tall shelves holding ever-changing exciting rows and rows of over forty thousand books

They formed something like a protective shield between me and the strange, raw, tough Chicago I was faced with as a newcomer.

When we arrived in the USA, the number of unemployed was eight million. I had no special qualifications and my husband didn't know English. We did bring some furniture, but all the money we had was what we got for a smuggled-out diamond, bought for the purpose and sold cheap in Paris where the market just then was naturally glutted with this particular commodity. It was urgent to start earning. The relatives who sent us our 'affidavit' were well-off but not rich, nor did we want more from them than their advice. According to them, to begin with it would be best for my husband to learn a trade, and for me who knew the language, to sell things. So my husband tried his hand at a different trade about once every fortnight, while I was going from door to door, from beauty-shop to beauty-shop and from all sorts of other places to other places, always with new kinds of samples in a little suitcase, without ever making a single sale. Both of us were complete failures. Thinking back, I can no longer tell whether all of this was hilarious or tragic, probably both.

What made me so hopelessly inefficient as a saleswoman was my firm conviction that if the persons I approached really needed the powder-puffs, magazines, brushes or whatever else I was supposed to talk them into buying, they would certainly already have these things. On the other hand, if they didn't have them, they evidently didn't need them. I was incapable of delivering sales talk and retreated at the first doubtful look before the prospective buyer even had a chance to say no. The end of this career came when I was carrying samples of ugly little table lamps to be sold to hotels On the first day, which was also to be the last, I picked a promising-looking hotel and went in through the main entrance. Since I had a suitcase and looked like a lady rather than like the wretched little disgusting, obtrusive insect I felt like, the bellboy came running, grabbed my samples and led me straight to the reception desk. Seeing the porter's beautiful obsequious smile fading when I started my explanation was the climax of many months of humiliation. I ended up in the nearest toilet crying my heart out. To this very day I can't understand the soul of a sales-man; and yet, everything seems to depend on the selling and buying of loads of things nobody really wants.

I was to be more successful as a waitress. Harder on the feet but easier on the mind: I was serving food to people who wanted to eat. By then my husband was working as an all-round helper in his cousin's business and slowly picking up English. I worked nights and took care of little Susie during the day, which meant total exhaustion. As I learned the trade and its tricks I began to make enough money to pay for a kindergarten, but I continued with night-work because drunk nocturnal customers and truck drivers at dawn were better tippers than white-collar lunchers. I don't know how things are for waitresses in the States nowadays, but then the salary itself was very low, representing only a fraction of a very good income. The great thing was to learn how to make tips. In the beginning, of course, I was uneasy, timid, eager to please and therefore easy to exploit, terrified of rude bosses and customers' vulgar advances. I had much to learn that was never taught at school. It took me quite some time to catch on to the fact that cooks had to be bribed if one wanted to be given – and thus be able to give – quick service resulting in tips. This was a circle both vicious and lucrative which one could not ignore or avoid. Some of the cooks I had to deal with still haunt my nightmares to this day. Most of them were big fat elderly Mediterranean men, and for one reason or another all of them were wildly hysterical. Perhaps this was the effect of stress, fumes and heat. They had blood-red sweating faces, and long sharp knives swooped about in their agitated hands as they screamed and swore at waitresses, helpers, customers and life in general in the foulest imaginable language. Possibly I associated them with Hell because of the impression the hot stinking kitchen made on me when I came run-ning from the icy air-conditioned cleanness of the dining-room to shout my orders.

I liked the sandwich-men, who were usually graceful, beautiful, smiling young Latin Americans. However, one particular kitchen drove even one of these mild creatures mad before my eyes. I can recall my intense love and sympathy going out to him on that

7

unforgettable occasion. A bunch of girls were hollering their orders at him through a little window, all at once, something like this: 'Ham on rye with lettuce, no without, toast it, two salami thin on white, no pickles, quick, I was first, three salmon on rye, no butter, get a move on, can you hear me, three fried eggs, turn them over, no, just see they're not runny, Pepito don't just stare, do you hear me . . .' Pepito went on working, but he was shaking. Suddenly he gave out a shriek which could have been a laugh or a sob, then he threw a platter full of sandwiches into the air, and as they fell, he started stamping them wildly into the floor. My understanding was mixed with envy. My background forebade running amok. His did not, and it must have given him the terrific relief I needed so badly.

In time I became a tough and efficient waitress, but an unhappy wife. My husband, who at home had risen to a rather high position at an unusually early age and who was used to being looked up to at work, among his political friends and by me, was now drifting from one badly paid manual job to another, rapidly losing his self-esteem. A man of the word, he was too proud to speak beginner's English, so he chose not to talk when English was needed, and he avoided fellow-refugees because most of them had turned in his eyes into despicable assimilants, obsessed with the dollar-chase. He became touchy, quarrelsome, indifferent to the child and critical of me, constantly pointing out dust under the bed and specks on potatoes although he knew very well how exhausted I was and how little experience I had as a cook and home-maker.

There was also tension between us in an area which had formerly been one of wholehearted agreement. For example, we had some German friends, Communist Party workers sentenced to death by the Nazis, whom we had helped to hide and feed while they were living illegally in Czechoslovakia, and who had managed to escape to England. At the beginning of the war I kept up a correspondence with them. Then came the time when Ribbentropp and Stalin signed their pact. The swastika started to fly over Moscow airport and the cream of the German Communist Party was handed over by the Russians to the Gestapo. Our friends, in not unnatural disgust, decided to leave the Party – and my husband asked me to stop writing to them. He was also scornful of books which made me shudder and start thinking: accounts available in America of the Moscow trials of the thirties. These my husband dismissed as primitive, mendacious capitalist propaganda. While I was beginning to suspect that Soviet Russia was not in fact the utopia we had both believed it to be, he was still absolutely loyal to his idea of Russian socialism.

He was, however, more shaken by the party line's eccentricities than he would admit, so in his free time he began writing articles justifying them. The New York Slovak communist paper was glad to publish them but could not afford to pay. Oscar spent many evenings at political meetings with local Slovak comrades, and my resentment increased.

That is not to say that I expressed, or even felt, outright opposition to Oscar's political ideas. On the contrary, I would have been glad if he could have removed my doubts. I loved my husband, admired his steadfastness, and was ashamed of my own bourgeois background, so when uncomfortable thoughts occurred to me I tried to suppress them, and I tried not to ask Oscar awkward questions. This was all the easier to do after the hateful imperialistic war turned into the Great Struggle for the Russian Motherland. Given the choice between Nazi Germany and the USSR, how could I do anything but side with the latter? But I cannot claim that these attempts to go on sharing my husband's outlook made me a lovable wife.

I was not only overworked, but was intellectually and socially just as frustrated as he was, longing for books and congenial friends, always desperate for a moment of rest. It is true that I was the family supporter, but I certainly rubbed it in. I made it quite clear that the time Oscar spent writing unpaid articles, and at meetings, was 'free' only because he was indifferent to his wife and child; that he was avoiding other refugees only because they, who *did* care for their families, were making better livings. I told him that at this rate he would never learn English well enough to get a decent job. In short, I did my best to confirm his own feelings of failure. And of course the meals I served, and our home, were more often than not a mess, especially after his attitude stopped me from even trying my poor best. It got so that the very sight of each other jarred our nerves.

I moved my bed into Susie's room and spent nights waiting for him to come to me, or to call me back, hoping for a reunion of the two people we once were. He did not come nor did he call me. He was lying next door with the same thoughts and hopes – but this he told me later, on the day Pearl Harbor was attacked and America entered the war.

This happened only twenty-four hours after we had agreed that it would be best to try a temporary separation. I had announced that I was moving to California. As a waitress I could support myself and the child very well, he would be spared my reproachful presence and my housekeeping, and I would be spared the Chicago climate which made me ill. He consented and we promised each other that we would live together again if and when we felt that we could. On Pearl Harbor day we fell into each other's arms, and at the bedside of our sleeping child we promised each other to start trying again here and now, to do our best for each other, and to stay together. For better or worse, we did.

I found it less hard than Oscar did to get used to America, but I did not find it easy. For a Central European, exile in Chicago was difficult to adjust to and almost impossible to like. One tends to forget the bad and remember more of the good, particularly regarding a country that saved one's life, besides which my memory is affected by comparisons with the subsequent years in Czechoslovakia; but even so, when I look through the diary I kept sporadically, I find that apart from the difficulties of making a living and our personal problems, there were plenty of shocks to be met.

First, as immigrants we were an anachronism. We were latecomers. Long before our arrival, great tracts of virgin land lay there ready to be worked by willing hands. Factories shot up overnight, crying out for human limbs and brains to make them run. There were mines to be dug, railroad tracks to be laid and skyscrapers to be raised. The bedraggled of the world came from abroad, and they were needed. They had a hard time at first, some made good, others did not, but if they were willing and able to work there was a place for them. People poked fun at greenhorns but nobody sent them home. We, the refugees, were made to feel unwelcome. There was a historical difference in the spirit of our coming and of our acceptance. As an old-timer customer of mine once exclaimed impatiently over his spaghetti: 'Refugees! Vat for you people go around calling yourselves fancy names! Ve vere yust immigrants and greenhorns, and that vas good enough . . . !'

When we arrived, millions were out of work. America was struggling with the same problems that brought about the war in Europe and her subsequent bloodstained prosperity was likely to be no more than an intermezzo. The Lady on Bedloe's Island had become a matron, and whatever children she was forced to bear now were liable to turn out reluctantly accepted misfits. Grotesquely enough, the same Americans who on the slightest provocation sent us back where we came from were just as quickly indignant at suspecting that some of us considered their country as a place of much-appreciated but only temporary refuge.

Our first impression of Chicago was smoke, clouds, dirt and oppressive crowds of people, all in a dreadful hurry, and apparently sad, angry or drunk. For a long time we seemed always to be saying the wrong thing at the wrong time to the wrong person; even our gestures were out of place. In our relations to the natives we wavered between the two extremes of megalomania (they were all uncouth fools) and inferiority complex (we were the fools). We found ourselves on a strange planet. However, most of my desperate notes complaining about America as it struck us then seem ridiculous now. Rudeness, grey uniformity of houses, the deafening impact of vulgar advertisements, ugly billboards defacing cities and the countryside, impolite children, mass-manufactured tasteless food gobbled up without sitting down, the cultural and aesthetic debasement of comic books, young women getting drunk in public, adolescents spending afternoons at the movies on weekdays instead of reading good books, the mutual hostility and name-calling between national and racial groups – all of this has come to Europe since then, while America seems to have acquired some of the features of European life we so missed at the time.

I adjusted more easily than my husband because eventually I found work I liked and I could always experience moments of intense happiness with my beautifully developing child; but even so, when news about the Nazi atrocities started coming through, something inside me went to pieces. We were already in New York, which was a great improvement on Chicago. Oscar was working as a public accountant, we were making a living and peace seemed to be in sight; but suddenly I found myself on the verge of insanity. I was tortured by the obsessive conviction that some dreadful price would be exacted by fate for our comparative safety and wellbeing. Every day, coming home from work, I expected to find my daughter mortally ill or dead. At night I lived through all of this and worse in nightmares from which I awoke in a cold sweat, only to lie awake with terror in my heart and thoughts even worse than the nightmares. At work I kept seeing ever-enlarging black spots before my eyes, and awakening in the dark, I dared not switch on the light because then I would know that I was already blind. My head, my heart and my throat were in the grip of ever-tightening iron rings. Both hoping and fearing that there was a physical cause for these things, I consulted several doctors, all of whom found nothing wrong with me except that I needed rest and possibly psychiatric help.

So I went to see a psychiatrist, paying for an hour what I earned in a week. I told him that when I heard the sound of an approaching plane I kept wishing for it to be a bomber trying to kill us. I asked him why, when others were being murdered in cold blood, our lives were safe simply because we happened to have a piece of paper, the affidavit my husband's cousin had sent years before without having been asked for it, just as an afterthought to a European visit and because we had felt a mutual erotic attraction. After listening to me for half an hour, the psychiatrist asked me if I had ever had premarital or extramarital sexual interests or affairs. I said yes, but that since the beginning of the war I had become uninterested in sex, in or outside marriage. Sex implied pleasure, and how could I allow myself that when my place was there with the others, in bombed cities and in the concentration camps? He asked me pointed questions about my husband. I assured him over and over that there was nothing wrong with my husband – that indeed his absolute normality in this respect was my only complaint against him and the only reason for my past extramarital affairs. The psychiatrist advised me to take a lover.

It was no use spending more money. I ended my sessions and went on going blind, suffocating and half-living in a self-made cell of darkness.

Around Christmas news of victories began to come from the front. We were happy to hear that twenty thousand Germans had been killed, delighted to know that so-and-so many thousands of bombs had been dropped on Berlin, Dresden and other cities. Did this have to happen to our moral values in order that 'Peace on Earth and good will to men' might return?

Somehow, with tremendous effort, I managed to go on with the pretence of living. When the Red Cross message came I didn't react with the healthy shock and sorrow of a sane person. It was just a fitting addition to the horrors I was already living with in my cell. I was guilty, mankind on both sides of the front was guilty, God's non-existence, or his guilt, was more certain than ever before. But since I didn't die I got better. Gradually, small translucent spots appeared on the walls of my cell, letting in occasional rays of light. On a sudden impulse, to my little daughter's delight and Oscar's dismay, I bought a cocker spaniel puppy. It cost only five dollars because its tail curled against all the cocker spaniel rules. It was Blackie's eyes, his innocence and devotion, that awakened my dead emotions, and his having eaten part of my dotted housecoat and leaving dotted droppings on the carpet afterwards brought on my first laugh. We lived on the northernmost tip of Manhattan, and obligatory walks with the puppy made us discover nearby Washington Park, Inwood Park with the Cloisters and the lovely evening view across the river to the Palisades. Blackie's innocent eyes made me take Susie on frequent visits to the little zoo in Central Park, where we spent hours, Susie on her rollerskates, with her ball and her skipping rope, and I in silent, meditative communication with the animals, in search of God, not finding him but perhaps learning to resent him less.

Susie remembers Blackie, the unicorn of the beautiful old

tapestry in the Cloisters, and the animals in Central Park as integral parts of the nostalgically recalled highlights of her American childhood. Perhaps they meant so much because they were connected with her mother's slow emergence from her cell, and this just when she was reaching the age when our parent–child relationship suddenly changed into a friendship between two persons, reacting, thinking, feeling in similar ways and talking about things on equal terms, getting very close to each other.

By the time the Party's letter arrived, and Oscar started making concrete plans for our return home, we were already American citizens. Susie was an American child, and I, surrounded by Ben's books and the bookish friends I had made by then, was beginning to feel at home. Even my accent had reached the point where people whose forefathers didn't exactly come over with the *Mayflower* occasionally took me for a Scotswoman. New York was already 'infected' with a bit of Europe. There were exciting small theatres, new literary magazines, and thanks to Viennese refugees, little shops with edible pastries and a few tables that could be used instead of cafés where, in the Central European manner, friends could be met and world problems could be solved. And, of course, at breakfast we drank as much orange juice as we liked, which – when told in Czechoslovakia later – was to become one of the most incredible legends about our whole stay in the States.

The first half of 1946 was a period of uncertainty blended with hopeful planning. In everyday life this meant an unrepaired door lock, a blocked kitchen sink and other minor domestic miseries which were not eliminated because we were 'leaving anyhow'. Money had to be saved for the trip home and to buy food-packages for the family and some friends. Although the sink was stinking and we were gradually selling the few saleable things we had, it was by no means certain that we would be leaving. A retarding moment was when first-hand news reached us of incipient pogroms in Slovakia against surviving Jews who, back from the death-camps or mountain hide-outs, had made claims to the homes from which they had been driven and to valuables 'hidden' for them by helpful gentile neighbours. To me this looked like one of many frighteningly accumulating signs indicating that the war had been fought in vain, but my husband, after the first shock, and encouraged by his brothers' frequent letters, interpreted it as one more reason for going back to help establish socialism, which would change these poor misguided people.

It was a slow, painful process, but in the end I gave in. I felt by then that I knew too much about Russia not to have doubts about socialism, but then I also knew America well enough to see the abyss between it and the ideas of its founders. I saw the world as a big chaos where nothing was what it was called and where evil always and everywhere outweighed good. However, aware of having been sick in my mind, I allowed that such a black view might well be a projection of my neurosis – as I had been taught to call my guilt feelings – and all that went with it. Because I was still struggling with darkness, Oscar's faith seemed like a light to follow.

After all, I was told, we were not going to live in Russia but in a European country that before the war had been ahead of the States as far as democracy and social justice were concerned. Now the task was to erase the interruption and effects of the war and to help this country ahead on the old road to an even better future.

Soon I was so well converted that I began to find my own personal motivations. What I most wanted was to see my husband working for what he believed in, which would make him again the man he used to be when I came to love and respect him. Becoming the man he once was, he too would return to loving me for what I was, and our marriage would be saved. I also desperately wished to have another child and at home I might be able to afford it. As for material hardships, I was sincerely willing to make do with only one pair of shoes if it meant that no one would go barefoot, and was quite prepared to exchange our modern, centrally heated flat on Manhattan, with its built-in refrigerator, for one in which I would have to carry coal, if it would contribute to getting others out of slums. If that was socialism, I was for it. By way of a curious logic, I also began longing to be where my nearest and dearest had been murdered even though I could neither revive nor avenge them. The future seemed safer in the very place where the horrors had been perpetrated. They were less likely to recur where people had seen them and could neither refuse to believe them nor ignore them, as did most Americans.

My husband flew ahead. Susie and I stayed on for two months, waiting for a boat. After a tearful farewell to Blackie, whom we left in the gentle hands of the bookshop's old Negro storeman, I said goodbye to everybody else and we boarded a small French freighter bound for Le Havre. The few passengers were all French citizens on their way home. Because of the danger of mines, the boat changed route for Bordeaux and the passage lasted a fortnight. This gave both grown-ups and children a chance to become friends. After a good dinner accompanied by lively conversation, anecdote-telling and laughter I suddenly became aware of the fact that all through my American years I had never once had a good laugh, one of those contagious, idiotic, tearful, sidesplitting group laughs that inevitably explode when Europeans sit together around bottles of good wine. Now that I'd had it again I was quite sure that we were on our way home. When the first contours of the old continent appeared on the horizon, I cried silently with the others.

***

The business trip from which I was called home five years later, in the summer of 1951, on the day of my husband's arrest, was one on which my colleagues and I had set out with melancholy feelings. They were sending us to Prague to train our successors.

Ever since the coup in February 1948 (subsequently to be commemorated every year by obligatory marches celebrating The Day of the Great February Events and our First Worker President, the Great Klement Gottwald), our national economy had been subjected to an almost ceaseless process of organization, re-organization and re-reorganization. At no stage was it considered successful enough to be final, and at every stage – to the justified dismay of the Slovaks – it came nearer to total centralization in Prague. Like every other enterprise, the Bratislava branch of the national export company I worked for was to be gobbled up by the central office. Our department happened to be the first slice on the platter.

It was a depressing task. The Bratislava branch had worked well and with sincere fervour, exporting Slovak timber and related products. Our particular little department exported various brushes and also brooms made of broomcorn, a traditional local product enjoying great popularity in Switzerland and other western states with cleanly housewives and hard currency. I was selling toothbrushes, products of a big old Bratislava factory which had been successfully exporting them long before the war. The old brand name was known throughout the world, so it seemed reasonable to retain it; but as it happened to be 'Koh-i-noor' and thus smacked of queens and colonialism, it became the subject of heated discussions. In the end the more revolutionary members of the management had to capitulate to economic interests. Koh-i-noor toothbrushes were admittedly prosaic things to deal with, but exporting them was a meritorious part of the fight for pounds and francs sorely needed in building socialism. Besides, decorating the map with coloured pins in newly conquered territories could easily be invested with a sense of romance and adventure. Soon I had pins in such far-away places as Malta, Madagascar and Ceylon. I felt appreciated, and altogether good because in our group we were a merry, crazy gang of congenial people.

My first shock came when in December the head of the planning department asked me to make out a table showing exactly how many toothbrushes (what sort of bristles, what colours, etc.) I was planning to deliver to Switzerland, England, Malta, Madagascar and so on during the first half of the coming year. I said that I couldn't possibly know, as our agents in various places were ordinary mortals and as such were subject to illness and death. What's more, as I well knew but refrained from saying, they were also exposed to the temptations of German and Japanese competitors whose emissaries wined and dined them. We could not travel. We met even our Hungarian business partners only seldom, in an abandoned shack on no-man's-land between the borders of our brotherly countries, with police officials in mufti sitting by.

My objections were waved aside and I was told to draw up my

forecast without delay. Next, I was called by telephone to the planning department. When I admitted that I had nothing to show, the man repeated his request with a warning undertone denoting a suspicion of deliberate sabotage. In front of others, he gave me a look that made me feel that my bourgeois descent was sticking out a mile. Fortunately, the planning man caught me that very day on the staircase, and from what he said there I understood that what he wanted was simply some figures, house numbers if need be.

I did not dismiss the possibility that in this initial experimental phase of planned economy any tentative approximate data to work with was better than none. But I felt – and still feel – that he could, even should have told me so in so many words, and should have laced the information with a touch of humour. However, a total lack of humour is – I firmly believe – a basic evil in socialist thought and government beginning with Marx, through Lenin to Stalin (with the possible exception of Khrushchev's crude and boisterously evil jokes that haven't ceased to enchant confident, destalinized Soviet-sympathizers in the West regardless of 1956). Humour is so intimately related to humane tolerance that the absence of one kills the other, and totalitarianism is incompatible with either. Hatred and fear of humour, this unfailing characteristic of totalitarian regimes, is possibly closely related to their blatant inhumanity and their crimes. Why otherwise would the best whispered jokes in history proliferate as means of defence and moral survival where man's spirit suffers worst oppression, no matter whether under Hitler or Stalin? Be that as it may, the little incident with the earnest, insistent planning manager caused the first breach in my confidence in the new economic system. I was far from well versed in its deeper theory, but I did believe that, as it was to result in a better society, it was bound to be more accomplished, efficient and – above all – more honest than the small rackets I had worked with and the big ones I had lived with in America.

When, with a bad conscience, I finally presented my made-up report, the man was satisfied. His staff was then kept busy drawing up a neat chart summarizing similar data received from our other departments. In Prague, the chart was incorporated into an even more artistically drawn-up table which was at last launched on its way to even higher places. On its way up it was mated with similar creations from other economic branches, to give birth in the end to the Plan with a capital P: the ultimate basis of our national economy.

In those days I still harboured the secret hope that such dubious practice applied only to ridiculously unimportant commodities such as toothbrushes and brooms. Surely, plans concerning substantial things such as pipes, engines, building materials, food, clothing and the education of the young must be worked out in a more responsible, reliable manner? However, I learned otherwise.

A few years later I had a job in a firm – an extension of the state administration, of course – which distributed goods within what was called the 'local economy'. One autumn we were told to compile for the coming year a half-yearly plan referring to commodities including sewing thread, lavatory bowls, coffins with their appurtenances and so on. None of us knew, neither was there any person to tell us, whether the numbers to be written in columns on the sheets issued by some higher planning authority were to express metres, quantity of spools or weight in the case of thread, nor could any of us guess the weight of a lavatory bowl, although this was one item with explicit instructions to plan in terms of weight. The head of the planning department was again in dead earnest, as befitted a person in a responsible position, who sat where he sat not because he would know the answers but rather by virtue of his political background. But we, the low-level number-coolies, had wonderful liberating laughs, not only when discussing the weight of toilet bowls but also while guessing at the number of local citizens likely to need coffins during a specified time; a particularly juicy subject given the times we lived in.

I don't know how things developed in Prague after I had heard the news of Oscar's arrest and had to say goodbye to my colleagues so suddenly, but I do know that while I was still there we did practically nothing. This was the fall of 1951, and the Prague staff was living in a panicky hell of its own. Working under newly appointed and inexperienced people, most of the old employees were expecting to be 'reorganized' in one way or another – demoted or sacked. Nobody seemed to have any time for us. On the first day our presence was simply ignored.

On the next day we found the office in a chaotic phase of reorganization and were told to join the local staff in moving papers, files and minor pieces of furniture from the first floor up to the second. Forming a chain on the staircase we passed parcels from hand to hand. Having arrived in a bitter mood in any case, but at least as 'instructors' who had a right to feel important, we found this work humiliating and a big bore. However, there was no way out and we slaved in sullen silence. After nearly an hour of this, a man at the bottom had a bright idea. Instead of an envelope he handed the next in line a packet of contraceptives. As the small oblong box was automatically ascending the stairs, people realized only on second thoughts what it was they had passed on, and presently glum depression gave way to general hilarity. The women giggled, making a great show of being shocked, the men roared with laughter. Soon the progress of each parcel was accompanied by comments peppered with four-letter words. This was childish behaviour for grown-ups, but it was welcome relief, and against the panicky atmosphere and what lurked behind it, it was at least something human. After all, not even our worst jokes were more insane or obscene than what was happening or about to happen to most of us. Nor were they nearly as immoral as the speech our cadre official had delivered a few days before.

Since one of the reforms resulting from the present process of renewal in our government is to be the abolition of cadre officials, and as I hope this will be read both by people abroad to whom the concept is an unknown one, and by a generation at home who will never have to stand face to face with a cadre official, I feel the species should be described here and now while still in sharp focus.

On paper, the cadre official is simply head of the personnel department. In fact, he is many other things. He is a combination of politruk, professional recorder of evil gossip on paper in indelible ink, recruiter, organizer and weekly father-confessor of informers; a provocateur and spy himself. He is a direct link to the

Party's own cadre department in relation to which he is the same trembling, totally defenceless insect that we, the employees, are in relation to him. He has a room of his own where he sits in an atmosphere of ill-boding secrecy, surrounded by well-locked filing cabinets containing our cadre sheets. But here is another word meaning no more to the uninitiated than a piece of paper with personal data. In fact, this too is many other and mainly more sinister things. It is a personal file drawn up about everyone beginning with school, if not with kindergarten. One's cadre sheet follows one from school to school and then to every place of work, constantly replenished on the way, its contents inevitably seeping into the cadre sheets of one's children, sealing their destinies. Your cadre sheet decides everything that matters in life, from your work to your right to a flat, from your position in society all the way to your very right to exist, but you are never, never allowed to have a glimpse of its contents, consequently you are never in a position to control, discuss, disprove or fight them. From time to time you are summoned to the Presence, which in itself in nine cases out of ten bodes no good. You are not asked to sit down but are made to stand at a distance which would be safe even if you had eagle's eyes, and you wait for what the cadre official has to say while he turns over the leaves of your dossier. All you can see are the dramatically timed changes in his facial expression before he pronounces at last his roundabout questions, remarks, advice, admonishment, his opinion on your character from the political angle, one or two indirect threats and quite possibly a verdict that cuts off your future, both professional and personal. All of this is based on evidence you have never been permitted to see. These dossiers are apt to contain such incriminating items as the fact that on a weekend of political schooling held by the firm at some spa, you kept to yourself with a book in the evenings instead of joining the rest in the communal singing of revolutionary songs.

There are probably reports of anecdotes you were heard telling, or possibly only laughing at. There would also be data referring to letters you exchanged with friends or relatives in the West, names and short descriptions of people who visited your homes (furnished by janitors), remarks concerning your habits in private life, your predilections in music, clothes and books, and – if relevant – reports of your having been seen at church.

The cadre official can make you or unmake you. While in making you he acts on directives from his superiors in the inner cadre sanctum attached to the Central Committee, in destroying you he is almost completely free to act on his own. Corrupted by absolute power as he is, he gets more out of scaring and harming his fellow men than out of helping them to a promotion. Like everything else in our public life, the human quality of cadre officials was gradually deteriorating. At first, after rapid overall nationalization, these jobs were given as a sinecure to old comrades who deserved to be rewarded for past merits but had no qualification for any other well-paid position. This initial guard, composed of elderly idealists, reliable, but of questionable class descent themselves, were a harmless enough lot. They did not last long. Soon a new, quick-schooled batch of untainted working-class descent began emerging, clamouring for good jobs. These people were too young to have been tested under conditions when working for the Party implied just about anything else but a career, or to have proved themselves in the political or any other field. Suddenly, still wet behind their ears, their brains full of rapidly pumped-in Marxist dogma, their hearts artificially saturated with class-hate and suspicion against the supposedly ubiquitous enemies of the state, encouraged to take revenge for suffering they personally had never endured, endowed with unlimited power over their elders and betters, understandably enough they lost their heads and turned into a scourge.

In justice it has to be added that much of the nonsense they talked and many of their evil deeds were not of their own invention or doing. They were privileged and therefore unquestioning tools in the hands of the Party. Not all were necessarily fools or power-drunk sadists. However, the one we had at the time I am speaking of was at the least the former. While more intelligent or crafty functionaries managed to cope with the sudden acrobatic contortions of the party line and convey them smoothly, without losing too much face, our man got rattled. Given his education, his talents and his congenital incapacity to put words together into a sentence, he must have suffered a lot when called upon to deliver a speech, while we giggled. We didn't giggle for long.

In quick succession, the policy of the party went from one stage to another, the latest one not only contradicting the one before but sometimes overlapping with it. This gave rise to much confusion. One could never be quite sure which was the only correct and infallible line to follow, which was the slogan to shout, making all preceding slogans into heresies.

In the beginning, cadre officials were told to make everyone in their respective domains join what was to become a mass party, the more the better. They conveyed this message in speeches full of convincing arguments, urgent recommendations and veiled threats. Desks were flooded with application forms, and people signed without much ado, some because it was easier than to explain their reasons for hesitation, some automatically as one signs anything the boss wants signed, almost none out of conviction (the convinced ones were already members anyway), and most in a spirit of 'Why not?'

From one day to the next these forms disappeared. It was decided that the party was to be a vanguard group restricted to a working-class élite. Overnight, joining became a hard-to-come-by privilege instead of the duty it had been the day before. The cadre official had to convey this new message with new arguments contradicting the ones he had just been using, and this time his threats, if he made them, applied not to laggards but to busy enemies who infiltrated the party for evil purposes but who would soon be unmasked. It was not an easy job even for an articulate man.

A bend in the party line so abrupt that it gave out an ominous creak was that concerning standing shoulder to shoulder with the workers in the mines and on the factory floor. For many months we white-collared people were made to feel small and pitiful for being denied this privilege; then suddenly, while still a privilege, it became a punishment as well. It became a threat, used against citizens whose dossiers indicated a lack of political zeal; and also a punishment against those whose desk jobs were needed for the new cadres. This new and frequently applied punishment was called 'placing into production'. What it meant was getting the sack and being forced to work as a totally unqualified factory hand.

In our little brush department nobody could boast a proletarian background. There were some who came from peasant stock, but there was always at least one generation of clerks, teachers or small shopkeepers in between, spoiling everything. I had felt safe to start with because I was the wife of an old party member who had been quite recently promoted to a leading function in the Slovak Ministry for Food Production and Distribution, and I was not seriously anxious even by the time we were called to Prague, but my colleagues had left Bratislava with the threat hanging over them that on returning they would be 'placed into production'.

I hated the idea of parting from these colleagues, about whom I worried, but apart from that I would not have minded leaving this particular job. The management was full of new people, hastily appointed to replace those who were already under arrest, and – for all we knew – awaiting trial. The new manager-general, a young bricklayer fresh from party college, was hiding his initial timidity and his ignorance behind a mask of aloofness. His predecessor used to hold short matter-of-fact consultations with each department twice a week. This one could be seen and heard only rarely and always in the presence of the entire staff. On these occasions no business matters were discussed. He would read out a typewritten speech bearing the marks of our cadre official's style. After a review of the world situation, he would turn to the sins of the former management. He would speak in vague terms because at that point not even the police knew what they were going to be accused of. He always closed with fervent wishes for world peace and an urgent appeal for revolutionary vigilance and for heightened efforts in our work to fill the plan. Some were sure to applaud, upon which we all joined in. Those who were known to have been on friendly terms with one of the recently vanished applauded longest and hardest.

In this latest phase our work itself had become tainted with unpalatable tasks. We were ordered to break off relations with those of our old commission agents abroad who were no longer regarded as suitable to represent us. This applied chiefly to former

Czechoslovak citizens, most of whom had left the country before the war. They worked satisfactorily, and partly for the sake of continuity, but certainly also for sentimental reasons they would have liked to go on selling our products even though the rapid increase of red tape and the sluggishness of newly nationalized factories made business transactions increasingly cumbersome.

Translated into plain language, what our conventionally worded but clearly final letters told them was something like this: 'Did you take your family to Turkey instead of waiting to be deported by the Germans? You did. After having established yourself in a strange country, friendless and against all odds, did you give up everything to come home to build socialism? No, you didn't. So, no more Koh-i-noor toothbrushes for you!'

Or else, this one to my agent who had landed in Belgium some time in the twenties: 'Did you come home with your Belgian wife and Belgian children after a quarter of a century? No. Instead, you chose to go on working for and with the capitalists. True, we take it from your recent letter that you would like to continue representing us in spite of our having announced that we cannot supply toothbrushes with yellow handles (as requested by your customers for inexplicable reasons) any sooner than in the third quarter of the coming year. And in spite of hardening Japanese competition. Rubbish! We shall do business through Belgian, Turkish or if need be Hottentot representatives, rather than through a class enemy . . .'

We had difficulties finding new agents, didn't know the people we found, and lost customers. Under the new travel restrictions we could not even improve things by way of personal contact – though in this matter occasional exceptions were made. Those who were sent abroad to keep foreign trade going were not, of course, businessmen who had years of experience and a thorough knowledge of the merchandise; they were the lucky few who were found reliable enough to be given a passport. Funny as it may sound today, in 1949 I was one of these. More precisely, what made me acceptable was that I was my husband's wife, had two children at home and also knew some languages, which at that early stage was still an asset. On the other hand, while I knew something about brushes, I knew absolutely nothing about timber, prefabricated houses, wooden toys, musical instruments and packing crates except for what I was taught in a great hurry in Prague before embarking on a long business trip to Turkey, where among other things I was to play hostess at the Czechoslovak pavilion at the Izmir world fair.

In spite of my ignorance I managed not to make any grave mistakes for the simple reason that, like all those on similar missions from nationalized firms, I was never in a position to speak or act on my own. I could never say yes or no about prices, time of delivery or the client's specific requirements without first sending wires to Prague and then waiting for answers that came too late or not at all. So I dutifully negotiated with everybody on my list, always in a preliminary, noncommital manner and, of course, without making sales. At first I honestly regretted the needless loss of much-needed orders. Very soon I began to understand and share my more experienced colleagues' attitude of resigned cynicism. Not given the necessary minimum of responsibility, we felt entitled to be irresponsible. Our pavilion at the fair, unanimously acknowledged as being the most attractive one, was called by businessmen 'Potemkin's Pavilion' because none of the exhibits could be delivered in the same quality or within reasonable times. Here we gave parties where Czech export sausages, excellent export beer and Prague ham were served, all delicacies not tasted at home since before the war. Invited to other pavilions and by local businessmen we consumed huge quantities of caviar and French cognac. Eating and drinking were more or less restricted to official receptions, with an occasional piece of cheese and olives on the side, because our daily allowance of hard currency had to be invested in things that couldn't be bought at home: coffee, tea, rice, nuts, raisins, nylon stockings and knitwear and shoes in all sizes for wives and children. As the only woman in the group I could buy most because I needed less food than the men and was taken out to dinner more often.

Upon my return I made out my official travel report, cautiously phrased, rosy and dull, completed by my husband with obligatory references to the misery I had seen and the seething revolutionary spirit of the masses I had sensed. Then, still guided by the feeling that the cause in itself was good and that truth was more likely to serve it than its repression, I sent a private report to Prague, to our old pre-war friend Mr Eugen (Jantchi) Loebl, who was then deputy minister of foreign trade. This report, written in Hungarian, was more critical, and where it referred to the table manners, alcohol consumption, IQ and sexual behaviour of our new commercial and diplomatic representatives, it was ribald. It also quoted foreign businessmen calling us 'pillarboxes', meaning that we were directed or left undirected by wires coming, not coming, or coming too late from Prague.

Soon after this, Mr Loebl was arrested and naturally his papers were seized by the police. Many years later, the woman who was then entrusted with translating into Czech the German, English and Hungarian letters found in arrested persons' correspondence told me that coming across my report, she decided to discard it as a harmless family letter. She knew my husband well from before the war and she knew that this paper would ruin him.

***

It was Mr Loebl's arrest that started the wave of terror in our own sphere. Soon one could not meet anyone without hearing whispers of new arrests. All of the victims were old party members, several of them friends we had known long before the war. Many had fought in Spain, some had spent years in German prisons and con-centration camps.

There had, of course, been a good many arrests and trials before this wave of terror. Like everywhere else in Europe after the war, we had war criminals, collaborators and known fascists who had to be tried; and, after the victorious February of 1948, it was taken for granted that big landowners and capitalists who tried to turn back the wheels of history had to be punished. And black market profiteers as well, naturally. And religious reactionaries who were scheming to undermine the new order before it could prove that man could achieve on earth what the Church slyly promises him only in the hereafter. The better to subdue him to his worldly oppressors. And saboteurs and spies in the service of foreign, reactionary powers. Once the unpleasant but inevitable task of ridding the victorious revolution of such enemies was over and done with, constructive work in a secure, creative atmosphere could begin. This had been the accepted picture in our circles, easily understood if not examined too closely.

When even communists began to find it depressing and strange that a State serving the best interests of the hitherto unjustly treated majority should have so many dangerous enemies coming from this very majority, from the masses of peasants and workers, they reassured themselves by saying that they did not know the arrested people personally and had no reason or right to doubt the authorities who were giving them fair trials. It was less easy to argue like this when it began to happen to well-known old party members. So discussions had to be avoided; but vague hints were made as to what time and circumstances can do to a person's integrity. After all, who knew what had happened to so-and-so during the war, what contact with foreigners, what hardships and possibly temptations his emigration had entailed? Under certain pressures even a good man is liable to change . . .

When the wave finally engulfed our own immediate circle, the subject could no longer be ignored. One had to take a stand, at least in private. By now every one of us knew at least one, if not more, of the victims closely, well enough to be sure of his integrity. By sheer logical induction this cast doubt on other hitherto seem-ingly justified cases. At least, it would have done so by generally accepted human standards, but in those years such standards had no validity for good party members. I watched them fighting against their moral feelings, their logical judgement, their personal loyalties and common sense. I served innumerable cups of strong black coffee (with a grudging heart, because coffee was scarce and expensive) to trusted friends and former companions-in-arms of recently arrested comrades. They came night after night for inter-minable debates full of conjectures. They expounded their theories allegedly to dispel our doubts, but in fact to allay their own fears. The number of Jews among recent victims was alarm-ingly high. The question arose: could this possibly be a sign of anti-Semitic tendencies on the part of our local security organs? (Not even pessimists would have dreamt of mentioning the Party itself in this connection.) Nonsense! There are simply too many Jews in leading positions. Everybody knows that. Also, Jews have always been most exposed to western influence . . . and they are also known to be specially ambitious, let anybody here, Jew or non-Jew, try to say that this is not true! And anyhow, non-Jews are in jail as well. The high proportion of imprisoned Jews having been thus explained, a retrospective analysis of characters ensued. Long-forgotten utterances, even facial expressions as observed in the course of conversations many years ago, were evoked from the past. By the time we were through with this or that arrested comrade, our faith in the infallibility of the Party was duly reinstated.

Listening to all this, I wavered between disgust and distress, hope and fear, but there was also a tickling awareness of the comical aspect of these efforts.

'Now, let's look at things without sentimental inhibition for once. True, we all liked him, and – undoubtedly – we admired his brains.' (Unwittingly they began using the past tense.) 'On the other hand, which of us would deny that he never did rid himself of certain bourgeois airs and tastes? His immaculate white shirts, for one – a real mania with him. Or when he returned from his first visit to the Soviet Union – his remarks about the work women were doing there, about their looks. All that sort of thing . . .'

'Certainly we need brains. But in this decisive phase of revolutionary development it is the whole man that counts. It's absolute reliability that matters. Now, in all conscience, could you say that he has real respect for the working class? I personally doubt it. He may not be a deliberate traitor, of course, but the ultimate effect of his overbearing behaviour may very well be equal to that of the actions of a real saboteur. So there you are.'

'The Party has no time to make subtle distinctions between damage caused knowingly or damage resulting from a man's personal defects or errors. Much better if a dozen people are arrested, investigated and released if found innocent than if a single enemy goes free.'

'Yes, we know. Dreadful, of course. However, as you may

remember, he always had a weakness for women. Women cost money. And besides, I don't want to quote him but I happen to recall certain references he made to Trotsky . . .'

One evening, when we finally got to bed, I asked Oscar what he really thought. I waited in the darkness and had just decided not to repeat my question when he came up with this carefully worded answer: 'Try to look at it this way. These men are perhaps not guilty in the everyday sense of the word. But just now the fate and interests of individuals are of secondary importance. Our whole future, maybe the future of mankind, is at stake. These men may have committed grave errors, and if so, whether we like it or not, they must be regarded as dangerous. If they prove their innocence, they will be released. If they have made mistakes, they simply do not belong in the functions they were in. They can do other work. Of that there is more than enough . . .' His voice carried no real conviction. I pretended to sleep.

Soon after that Oscar began to approach his friends in the inner circles. Without pleading the innocence of imprisoned persons, he only demanded a speedy and fair investigation. He called attention to the danger that the current police practice was apt to spread undue alarm among the backward sectors of the population and thus damage work morale. This was not so much a question of the fate of possibly innocent men but a matter of national interest. He even hinted at the possibility that the class enemy himself found a field of activity in the very heart of the organization created as a shield. In that case the real saboteurs were those who were arresting good men in key positions to wreck the economy and thereby undermine the confidence of the masses.

However roundabout and carefully worded these interventions may seem, in those days they represented a unique act of moral courage. Needless to say, they never helped anybody and did much harm to my husband when his turn came. But these acts had their own sense, significance and purpose, if only in the microcosm of our own relationship – perhaps the same can be said of all one's actions. For a short, unforgettable time I got back the man I had loved. He was behaving like we once thought every man would learn to behave in the better future: humanely.

The time was short because very soon the avalanche buried us as well. But what he had tried to do gave me force to endure the coming decade and to teach my children to love and respect their father whom my younger daughter learned to know and remember only as she saw him behind a double wire mesh at our first visit to the jail, almost two years after they had taken him away.

But on the day of my husband's arrest, there I was in Prague, supposedly teaching my successor all about selling brushes abroad but actually doing nothing, forgetting our worries and having a good time.

When we clocked in on the fourth morning we found that heavy pieces of furniture were now being moved by professionals from the first to the fourth floor and vice versa. Since nobody seemed to need us, we decided to go for a swim in the Vltava. The sun, the cold shower and then the caress of the river on which one could float with the most magnificent city panorama of the world gently drifting by brought exhilarating relief from the past weeks' tensions. To me it felt like a sort of armistice. Deliciously tired after swimming back against the stream, stretched out on the sun-baked planks, I told myself that although by then we knew that Oscar was being shadowed, the very fact that nothing more happened was a proof that at least in his case they must have come to the conclusion that they were on the wrong track.

In the afternoon we wandered about Prague, then pooled some money and returned to our hotel with a big bottle of brandy. After dinner a few girls gathered in my room, which was the only one with a bathroom, for a shower. After a few drinks one of them delivered a political speech, halting at places where the chorus could join in with the right cliché, such as 'everlasting friendship', 'glorious', 'the great . . .', and in places with whole sentences. The unison was perfect, not a single hitch. After a while we turned sentimental and began to recall old love affairs. When the bottle was empty we became gay again.

Fantastic, daring evening gowns were draped out of towels, scarves and table cloths. As an ex-American and therefore supposedly the most sophisticated of the lot, I was asked to initiate the girls into the art of striptease, known in our part of the world only from hearsay. In front of a tall, old-fashioned mirror, with a dotted scarf and a checkered table cloth already cast off, I was just preparing for the grand gesture of ridding myself of the last towel when the room telephone rang. Somebody lifted it.

– It's for you. She says Bratislava is coming on the line.

It was almost midnight and I had talked with my husband the day before. My heart beat in my throat. This could not be a normal call.

The children! . . . I should not have left them! I had to, of course, but I had been enjoying being away and that was unpardonable! Like others who had abandoned the faith of their fathers in the firm conviction that people needed a decent social order rather than a religion to make them good and happy, I had unwittingly developed rites of my own. Between the intellect and the soul there is a space that refuses to be filled in with rational thought. When this space suddenly turns into a frightening abyss, one feels no less defenceless than those who thought up God or perhaps were lucky enough to see Him. At that moment this abyss was gaping at me darkly and I quickly remembered the bridging-over charms I had worked out. The charm to stave off all dangers threatening my children was to think of them constantly. But on that day I had neglected to do so. Another of my beliefs was that denial of pleasure to myself would in some mysterious manner profit those I loved. But just a few minutes earlier, in front of the mirror, I had been thinking only of myself, of my body, of the pleasures I wanted to give and take, of the pleasures I was denied. (For quite some time our pointless, irritated political arguments and the inexorably approaching terror had intruded on our intimate life, reducing our infrequent marital nights to the flight of two terrified creatures into temporary animal-togetherness and the wretched freedom of silence.) With the receiver in my trembling hand I was waiting to hear the price exacted for the evening's light-hearted gaiety, for my frivolity, for having neglected the rites, and mainly for having completely forgotten to worry about my husband.

*

As the fiery streaks from the engine faded into dirty specks against the meagre light of the morning, the young man who sat on the floor said something about a cold shower. Obviously he wanted me to share his mood of pleasant expectation, at least to give him a smile and a nod. I tried my best.

We had about twenty minutes more to go but the passengers began to act as if the journey had ended. Everybody was moving about, gathering things, trying to secure a place near the door. They could hardly wait to arrive, and I was the only one who wished that the train would never stop. Once it did I would have to face the day. Shrinking back in terror from the future, my mind tried to seek refuge in the past, only to be wrenched back. I tried to make my brain hover emptied of thought with no reference to past, present or future. It did not work. Instead, suddenly, all that had led up to what had happened appeared in a new harsh light. To my surprise and shame the perfect clarity of it brought me a moment of intense elation. This was absurdly out of place. But there it was. A sense of liberation. From now on there would be no need to pretend, to lie to myself and to others, to stumble blindly in the labyrinth of loyalty, feeling the enemy's breath on our necks, knowing him but not daring to name him. The vicious circle was broken. Because that's what it was. Naming the enemy implies being his enemy which in turn gives him the right to see and treat you as an enemy. Now at last I could call things by their name. No more false talk and false silence. No longer would I have to see things and say nothing was there, no longer need I invest trusted friends with criminal traits because they were arrested. Everything seemed to have fallen into a pattern and we were at least on the right side of the fence.

This moment of clarity did not mean, however, that I really accepted and understood the truth of what I sensed: I would still have climbed back over the fence if given the chance for the simple reason that I couldn't believe the chance would not be offered. When I tried to review the years since our return from America with the eyes of the enemy who had arrested Oscar and was now about to question and judge him, I found that not even our police could possibly accuse him of anything. They would have to admit, in this case, that in their overzealous hunt they had made a mistake. But what about the others of whose innocence I was equally sure? This was no time to think of others. I forced my mind back into reviewing the past years, my husband's work and his personal life, and I was unable to find a single cause for suspicion. What I saw was a spotless record of absolute loyalty, selfless hard work and honesty both as a communist and as a man. 'They' couldn't fail to grant this. Perhaps, in fact, he was waiting at home for me at this very minute.

The early part of those years since our return to Czechoslovakia had not been easy. In 1946 the housing shortage was so acute that the not yet all-powerful Party could offer us nothing better than the poorly adapted editorial offices of the Slovak daily, which had recently been abolished together with the wartime clerico-fascist Slovak State. The building was old, the rooms felt haunted, the little stove was difficult to handle even for one who knew the art of heating with coal, which I did not. There was no furniture but the little we borrowed from friends. Oscar was working for the Central Committee as an economist. His task was to make the few enterprises the Party owned and operated profitable, and to increase the Party funds by soliciting donations from capitalists. They were probably made to understand that when the Party came into power their helpfulness would be remembered and rewarded with a degree of leniency corresponding to their far-sighted generosity. They gave considerable sums, the enterprises began to function, but Oscar's salary remained low. His work and his political activities took up so much of his time that he was very little at home and I was mostly alone and miserable, standing in queues or struggling with the household or with the Slovak language which I had to learn before I could even contemplate getting a job.

When I first came to live in Bratislava at the start of my marriage, the city bore all the marks of a typical remnant of the Austro-Hungarian monarchy. It was multilingual, inhabited by a jumble of Hungarians, Slovaks, Austrians, Czechs and Germans, each group with its own Jews. Everybody spoke at least three languages, the real natives all of them badly. It was the erstwhile city of Pozsony where once Hungarian kings were crowned, and it was also Pressburg, from where streetcar tracks led to nearby Vienna. Excellent papers appeared in all the languages and knowing Slovak was not an absolute necessity, so during the three years before the war I picked up no more than a few words. But now the city had become Bratislava, the capital of a Slovakia awakened to increased nationalism during its independence under Hitler. In public places I hardly dared to open my mouth. Overheard speaking English with Susie in the street, I was called a bloody German. Hungarians, now a cowed minority, kept silent or spoke the little Slovak they knew. The Jews were dead, gone or going, and of those who survived and remained, the older generation was trying to improve its Slovak while the next one, which already had Slovak schools, was carefully avoiding public use of the language spoken at home. In fact, rabid nationalism was tolerated and even adopted by the Party to such an extent that it put an end to the old illusions which had made me turn to the left in the first place: that dream about tolerant, brotherly internationalism. Soon after our homecoming I went to the nearest district party secretariat to tell them that I wished to join; and eager as they were for members, they told me rudely to go home and learn Slovak first. By the time I knew the language well enough, I had learnt too much about the Party, so I never became a member.

Susie, who was almost ten when she started school in Bratislava, learned Slovak very fast, as children will. I was desperately longing for the second child I could not afford to have in exile. I wanted it while I wasn't too old. I finally decided to cheat to have it, and Tania was born in July 1948. During most of my pregnancy I was earning badly needed money by working as a personal secretary for the provisional American consul who was busy establishing his new office. I was working for him during the Great February events in 1948, and was soon approached by emissaries of the Party who put it to me that it was my duty to watch him and to report on the people who came to see him. Using my advanced pregnancy as an excuse I regretfully quit the job, just in time to avoid going to jail with the three or four local citizens who had been working for the consulate while it was waiting for its own staff to arrive. Very shortly after its official establishment, the consulate ceased to exist.

After February 1948 the Party was no longer in need of donations. Oscar was made manager of a big, newly nationalized business corporation, we were given the keys to a nice apartment abandoned by a fugitive general, and when Tania was old enough to attend a day nursery, I too started to work. In a year or so the flat was furnished, Oscar was promoted to deputy commissioner (to every minister in Prague there was a corresponding commissioner in Slovakia), and we found ourselves in the new upper class.

There were privileges available on this level, but my husband refused to enjoy them. Before Tania was born, I queued up with my big belly for rationed diapers like everybody else. When after three months I could no longer breast-feed her, the doctor prescribed a formula containing fresh milk. There wasn't any fresh milk in the shops, and the powdered milk that replaced it made the baby ill. There were plenty of adults who drank fresh milk because they knew where to get it, but my baby had to do without. With my husband practically in charge of food production and distribution, Tania was not allowed to drink black-market milk or milk that we could easily have obtained by way of 'socialist pull'. This was the tenor of our life.

Who then – except his family – had reason to reproach my husband? Who had the right to suspect him, and of what? Yet he himself had started to be worried some time before his arrest. He had a feeling that for some time he had been kept under special police observation. To me this seemed too preposterous to be true. Possibly they had been checking up on him – it looked as though they might be doing that on everybody who mattered – but while my experiences with the minions of our new leadership made me see them by and large as blundering fools and liars, at that time I was still far from taking them for the ruthless coldblooded criminals they were. Sceptical and disappointed as I had become, I spent my days among party members and was living well by the grace of the Party: I was therefore able to stay fairly blind and go on hoping that once the birth pangs of the new order were over, the ultimate cause would be well served. That a good man could be arrested, accused and then tortured into inventing and confessing never-committed crimes – such an idea was as far from my mind as it was from that of the most devoted comrade. I said to my husband – not without a touch of malice – that listening to too many hysterical calls for vigilance against the invisible but supposedly ubiquitous enemies of the state had started to make him see things.

The early summer of 1951 was a particularly lovely one. The garden suburb on the hill right above our street was just as pleasant, fragrant and peaceful as I had wistfully remembered it when I was a refugee in unlovely, smelly, noisy Chicago. Lilac bushes were blooming on both sides of the narrow street, in some places one could already catch the fragrance of newly opening jasmine, and as we climbed the hill the beautiful landscape surrounding the city and the Danube down below came gradually into view. I had every reason to rejoice in this family outing, and yet I was uneasy and discontented. For the better part of an hour my husband and I hadn't exchanged a single word.

The pram with the sleeping child in it was quite hard to push uphill. Susie was approaching puberty, an age when one does not show much helpfulness or understanding for others, least of all for one's own parents. She was walking at a little distance, making a big show of being bored to death. I didn't blame her. I just wished one of them would help with the pram. My husband was engrossed in his thoughts. His being there and yet absent was in itself nothing new, but this time he was uncommunicative in a sort of sad, crestfallen way. So I hesitated to ask for his help to avoid triggering one of our usual marital squabbles which were usually prompted either by my reproaching him for his indifference and lack of helpfulness in family matters or by his reproaching me for what he called the worm's eye view I took of political life. I found myself feeling sorry for him and kept silent, carrying on with the fight only in my mind.

. . . So you have nothing to say. Why, then, did you insist on coming along in the first place? The child is almost three and this is the first time you have taken a walk with us. I know you never have enough time. But I remember too many Saturdays and Sundays walking or sitting on a park bench alone, with my first and then again with my second child. I remember the sudden painful tightness in my throat at the sight of families passing by together, fathers pushing prams or carrying a small child, probably thinking of simple things and not of the hardships suffered by Chinese coolies, or of what could be done (on that particular Sunday, to be sure) to bring about a better world in a hundred years or so. Yes, you are right, I would never have loved or married such a man. But surely I have shared the coolies with you sincerely and long enough to expect you to share with me both the joys and the hardships of our own common life? At least on weekends? The week is crowded with work, conferences and meetings, I know. But Sundays you spend with comrades you met at those meetings to talk about things that could not be mentioned or questioned there. This I have accepted and by now I have learned not to miss you, almost too well. So this family walk was your idea, not mine. Here we are walking together on a Sunday for once, and you have nothing to say. Not to me and not to the children. I often wonder whether you know that we are not happy together. You don't seem to. Whatever marriage means to you, you seem to be satisfied with what we have. In your distracted and bashful manner you occasionally even assure me of your unchanged feelings for me. I am sure that in your own way you love our children too. In fact, you are the exemplary husband and father people judge you to be. Nobody has ever seen you with another woman, drinking or spending money on yourself. It must be my fault, then, that at a certain point which I can't place exactly, but some time after our return, you began to disappear from our common life. I have earnestly tried to follow you to wherever you are, but I can't any more. To most of my questions you have no answers, or only unsatisfactory, impatient ones. I am left out. Why? There must be something dreadfully wrong either with us or with what is taking you away from us, in other words with your work and what you are working for.

*

As I write this, the lilac is in bloom again. In this early summer of 1968 I know the answers to my questions of seventeen years ago, and I have known them only too well for years. So have others who are pretending to discover them only now. We would probably be having an argument about this with my husband if he were alive. But he is not.

At the time of our Sunday walk he must have been painfully absorbed in explaining the unexplainable and justifying the unjustifiable to himself, while I was plaguing him with questions to which a loyal Party member had no answers to give. I asked how actions morally wrong could be politically right if our politics were to serve what was morally right. I asked why our press had to be full of obvious lies when it was the organ of a party born of the fight for truth. I asked whether our arrested friends were really capable of crimes. I asked what sort of State we had, that could hardly find room in the many jails of the repressive past for all its enemies. I asked why almost entire villages of Hungarian peasants had to be deported way up to the German border into cities left empty by the deportation of Germans. I asked why we were taking notice of the terror only now, when it had begun to touch our own circle. Clichés such as 'When forests are chopped down, the chips will fly' or 'This is a great process of rebirth and the birth of a child is no pretty sight either' only infuriated me. I was ironical, pointing out all that was wrong as though he, personally, were responsible for the Party's inhumanity and its ridiculous blunders. How utterly hateful I must have been in his eyes!

On the other hand, I too had my reasons for despair and estrangement. What had first brought us together had been our common desire to fight for justice and truth. My love for him was born out of gratitude because his teachings came as a revelation to me when I was young and revolted by the inhumanity and injustice of society. In those days I longed to help change things, but could find no one – I lived in Horthy's Hungary – to show me the way, to give me the hope, advice and knowledge I needed. Then, by a curious coincidence, through a common friend, I found the teacher I was in need of, the friend who opened the window and let me see the light. Oscar was working in Prague at the time,

and our first meeting came about only after a full year of correspondence in the course of which we fell in love. (Nobody who
hasn't lived in a socialist country will understand why it is both
tragic and hilarious to think of that now. While I was living in a
reactionary state where revolutionary literature was banned, it was
quite possible for me to take a correspondence course in basic
Marxism over the border without fear of censorship. Our own
secret police confront their victims with photocopies of their most
intimate letters even if they never were meant to cross a border.)

It was the very fact that Oscar had been such a convincing,
assured and truthful teacher which wrecked my love for him now
that events had forced him into giving me answers which were
unconvincing, embarrassed and untrue.

Estranged, angry and neglected as I felt on that Sunday walk,
for once I carried on the argument only in my own mind. He
looked too vulnerable and depressed that day for a good fight.

Suddenly a big black car whizzed by us so close that I felt weak
in the knees after I had wrenched the pram into safety on a narrow
stone ledge by a garden wall. And why, if in such a mad hurry, did
the car stop at the next corner? Without a word, Oscar grabbed me
by the shoulder and made me turn sharply into a narrow steep path
leading downhill. When we reached the lower bend of the main
street another car came zooming by, again missing us by a hair's
breadth. Only a few blocks away it braked sharply and the two men
in it turned round and stared. The car then moved on, but on the
next bend we found ourselves faced by the first one again. I didn't
give all this much thought because the noise and jerking had
frightened my little girl out of her sleep and she was visibly preparing to cry. I stopped to adjust her cover and tried to kiss her back
into sleep. This time Oscar grabbed my arm so that it hurt.

'Don't stop. Go on.'

'But wait, I just want to . . .'

'Don't you understand? Go on, I said, go on!'

I didn't believe my ears. This rudeness was something frighteningly new. It just wasn't like him. I was shocked into hesitation.

'Are you deaf? Move on, quickly!'

Two automobiles with two men in each followed us at a slow

pace all the way home. By then I knew, but neither of us said a word. I gave the children something to eat in the kitchen, but Oscar said he wasn't hungry and retired to his room.

The children were already sleeping when he emerged pale and visibly shaken to tell me that the purpose of the family walk had been to get conclusive proof. Until that day he had hoped that the object of the State security men's suspicion was somebody else at his place of work, or certain people he had been meeting elsewhere. Whatever his hopes had been, now there was no longer any doubt as to whom they were after.

When I got up in the morning, my husband was already gone, but on my desk lay the copy of a letter he must have prepared quite some time ago. Otherwise I would have heard the sound of his typewriter during my restless night. I still have that copy. It came back fourteen years later with other papers the police took when our house was searched at his arrest. It came back when he was rehabilitated, a little more than a year before his death.

The letter was addressed to the District Commander of the State Security police, and here is its translation:

'What had been but a gnawing suspicion has become a certainty which I can no longer ignore. I know that several of your people have been shadowing me for quite some time. I deem it necessary to announce to you my point of view in this matter.

'Try as I may to scrutinize my present activities and my whole conscious past, I cannot find anything that would give you grounds for, let alone justify, your action. I fully agree with our President, Comrade Zápotocký, in that no loyal citizen, not even dedicated Party members, should object to being controlled. To exert such control is therefore not only the right but the duty of our security organs. This is in the common interest of all who wish to guard our country against the internal enemy, and of all whose supreme aim is the preservation of peace. However, considering the number of officers, vehicles and working hours employed in shadowing me for several months, I regard it as my duty to call your attention to the fact that – at least in this instance – you are squandering State funds and possibly distracting attention from real saboteurs.

'My friends and comrades know me for a man who would not hurt a fly. But they also know that, if need be, I would execute with my own hands any and all who would wrong our socialist republic. Should I be – for reasons unknown to me – under some kind of suspicion, I demand to be questioned and investigated without delay; in an open, fair and efficient manner.

'In the present dramatic phase of our development the principle holds more than ever that only those who do nothing are safe from occasional blunders. I am engaged in responsible work exacting often difficult decisions. Even so I am not aware of having committed any grave mistake.

'Not only do I refuse to believe that our Party would suffer the deliberate, unwarranted persecution of comrades in responsible positions who need to concentrate on their work, but I am firmly convinced that our leadership will call to book anyone who is leading it on the wrong track on grounds of malicious and false denunciations.

'Rumour has it that this sort of activity on the part of our police (and I know that I am not the first and only one to undergo similar or worse treatment) is somehow connected with the recent spy-trial in Prague and that it is directed chiefly against comrades who have returned from the West after the war. If so, it only exposes its spiritual author who is unable to conceive of someone returning to his native land with honest intentions. The narrowminded, dogmatic attitude of the initiators of such campaigns reveals their own overestimation of the capitalist world and their own dubious attitude to the Czechoslovak People's Democracy. In their unclean hearts and brains these informers and investigators evidently cannot imagine that a man might prefer to live in the CSR rather than in America without necessarily being a spy . . .'

The letter was posted in June, but I know of no reply to it. Oscar was arrested in August 1951, while giving a lecture at one of the many places where people were being politically schooled.

***

When on that hot August morning the train finally stopped in Bratislava and I got out, I took it for granted that there would be nobody waiting for me. The night had been long enough to allow me to pass from panic and pain to sober thought. On this level, freed from self-delusion, what had happened seemed no more than a logical link in the chain of only too familiar events. In the taxi I didn't need to make myself any special promise to be strong. Others had faced this, and so would I. On the way home I thought of the children more than of anything else.

But they were not there to meet me, which was perhaps good. The girl who lodged with us and did occasional babysitting opened the door and told me she had sent Susie off to school and Tania with her to be left on the way at the nursery. This girl had been alone in the flat when they came to search it, and she was in hysterics telling me about it. She knew nothing about my husband, only that he hadn't come home and what she had deduced from the search. She was very sympathetic but in a hurry to announce that she had already found herself a room elsewhere.

The flat was in a state which was to characterize our whole existence in the coming years. Everything upside down, thrown into senseless confusion by callous, hostile hands. My first impulse was to turn around and go 'home'. This was not home. The air itself seemed infected with the venomous breath of the men who had done their work here the day before. The whole jumble of inanimate objects seemed to be marked with the repulsive traces of their touch. And yet, just like so many of the monstrosities to come, this horror too was mingled with an element of the comical. The ludicrous is an intrinsic component of stupidity.

As I got it from the girl's excited, incoherent account, the two men had made a great fuss about – of all things – an old tin of

American talcum powder they found when rummaging among my husband's underwear. While studying the incomprehensible text on the tin, they exchanged furious, ironical remarks – turning to her for consent – to the effect that this object in itself was sufficient evidence of the fact that the man in the house was a person with decadent bourgeois tastes and illicit western connections, in other words, a dangerous man. In addition to great heaps of old periodicals, newspaper clippings, letters and other papers, photographs, bank book, some cash, a fountain pen and my late father-in-law's old gold watch (there were no other valuables in the house) the evidence they carted away in a small truck thus included the yellow tin of talcum powder.

I was to encounter this sort of funny stupidity in many of my future dealings with our authorities. Not that these encounters were otherwise amusing in any way.

When a few weeks later I was summoned to appear at the nearest police station at six in the morning and was subjected by two civilians to a perfectly senseless interrogation lasting till half-past eight in the evening, the questions they put referred only to my person, except that they asked where my husband was working, pretending and expecting me to believe that they did not know about his arrest. Otherwise, the interrogation was conducted in an almost civil tone with intermittent threats thrown in that if I would not come out with the truth, I could expect to be detained until I did. Leafing through a fat dossier full of data about me, they kept asking pointless questions about my last place of work and my relationship to the former manager, why I had been to Prague so often (they had the exact dates and the names of the hotels where I slept), whether I had a lover there, and if so, who he was. And of course they offered me nothing when they drank coffee or ate sandwiches, nor was I allowed to light a cigarette although they asked me repeatedly whether I was a smoker, and smoked under my nose. Nor could I use the telephone to call the children. In the evening they let me go with the enigmatic warning that I had better watch my step. To this day I haven't the slightest idea what 'truth' they wanted to hear from me or what the purpose of the session was. If it was to intimidate me they did well, because when

I came home I was hysterical enough to scare the children out of their wits.

I thanked the girl for her help and told her she could move to her new place right away if she wanted to. She did.

I decided to do what I could to make the place look as normal as possible when the children came home. The cupboards and drawers were wide open, the couches turned upside down, the floor littered with clothes. Judging from the state of the children's room they must have looked for secret radio transmitters even there. Our humble, innocent, laboriously acquired things looked at me as if they had feelings that were now badly hurt.

We have never been much attached to things as such. When we came home from America it was an easy decision to leave behind most of what we had. Just enough dollars were left to pay for our fare and for the transport of 'what was really important'. Where every kilo counted, this turned out to be a wide and problematic definition. Oscar made giant bundles out of old newspapers, bound volumes of the pre-war *Rundschau* and scrapbooks with his articles and other clippings. I won a little space for my favourite books by persuading him that Lenin's and Stalin's works could probably be easily replaced at home. But no arguments held in the matter of food. 'We shall eat the same as others.'

I had also to capitulate in the matter of the English chinaware and table linen from my trousseau. However, in one matter I remained adamant: I refused to part with my old diaries and photo albums. I was called sentimental, perhaps rightly. Only, who is to tell what is 'important' to another person and why? We all think we can tell – and how many human relations have been wrecked by this misconception?

Now all my own 'important' things lay scattered on the floor, with pages torn where 'suspect' photographs had been ripped out.

The floor was littered with my childhood, my youth, with the world that had shaped me. It was true that I had once felt suffo- cated by that world's narrowness, ashamed of its selfishness; I had turned my back on it when I fled into my husband's world, which seemed open, generous, full of promise of a useful life that made

45

sense. Still, it had been my world, and after years of exile and disappointment I had begun to see it in a new nostalgic light and to
appreciate its values.

My father whom I adored, but lost when I was just over fifteen,
had been a passionate amateur photographer, an unusual hobby
for those times. I knelt down and started collecting what was left
of the albums. There were his attempts at artistic photography: a
cherry tree in full bloom, myself as a child with my little dog on
my lap, other dogs and horses, a shaft of sunlight slanting through
a window, earnest-faced Jews standing in little groups in front of
the old synagogue, on a holiday. A foggy, underexposed picture
showed my father playing the viola with his amateur string quar-
tet. And, of course, masses of family pictures: naked babies lying
on their bellies on fluffy white rugs, my brother as a solemn
bespectacled graduate, wedding pictures, my mother dressed as a
Spanish dancer for one of the twenties' many fancy-dress balls. My
own snapshots from week-ends spent swimming, hiking and
skiing. Ordinary snapshots of youngsters laughing and making
faces at the camera.

It was, in fact, a smiling gallery of the dead. Because most of
them, even the baby on the fluffy rug, had been shot, gassed,
burnt, shoved into the icy Danube to drown, or otherwise murdered.

Some of the pictures had been taken on our annual holiday in
the Austrian mountains where Father took us for long, difficult
hikes all the way up to a height from which the lake looked tiny.
Remembering him brings back the highlights of my childhood.
Perhaps because he had a way of leaving the unrewarding part of
having children to Mother. When he came from work, we were
through with our homework, washed, combed, properly admon-
ished in matters of general behaviour and at least seemingly at
peace with each other. As a result of Mother's endless devotion to
him and her perfect timing, Daddy was never there to witness our
quarrels or the more dramatic aspects of our education. He was
never there to hear Mother's well-meant but monotonously delivered sermons which I learned to endure without paying attention

because what was the use of listening if one didn't have the right to answer? Of course I ought not to have left my room in a dreadful mess and I ought not to have been rude to boring aunts; but why did short socks become legitimate only in May regardless of how warm it was in April? Why coarse ribbed stockings at fourteen? Why was I forced to eat up everything put on my plate when Mother must have known that I was getting fat and was unhappy about it? (Inside I was fragile, slender, almost transparent like Elizabeth Bergner!) Why the tight bra to conceal what was so impatiently awaited and now gratefully accepted from nature? Why were books I loved and had read long ago forbidden? Passive resistance was my way out. Out came the food in the bathroom, off came the bra in the dark doorway. I should have died of mortification had a partner at dancing school discovered the buttons on this degrading prosthesis.

Father had nothing to do with all this. When he came home I was usually standing in the staircase, waiting for the shadow of the elevator to rise behind the frosted glass of the shaft. I didn't really mind if it didn't stop at our floor because this prolonged the sweet mood of expectation. He had a funny new pet name for me every day. He also knew how to make gifts doubly enjoyable. I was about six when he brought me a bag of what he said were the first cherries of the season. In the kitchen I discovered that the bag contained a tiny puppy, a real live fox terrier. This was a moment of unadulterated happiness I shall never forget.

The wounds life inflicted on me later left me with two alternatives. The easier one, to let the blood flow, I could not afford. I had to stick it out and wait for them to heal over. They did. But the tissue on the scars is coarse, and the protection it gives works both ways. Nothing hurts as badly as of old, but nothing is so good as it used to be, either. Only childhood memories have retained their intensity. More poignant than all subsequent real sorrows remains the memory of the shock when Mother gave away my puppy and the bitter disappointment Father caused me by his passive consent. His treason hurt more than Mother's act which – considering her fussiness and sober practicality – was no surprise.

In his diaries which I read years after his death my father

confessed to having done and left undone much for the sake of peace and comfort. With bitter self-irony he described himself as having been only half alive in the tragicomical manner of Oblomov. While I cannot tell whether he had it in him to be a good photographer, writer or musician, I know that he would have been more fully alive if he had seriously tried to be one of these. But in his time and circle it was so much simpler and more comfortable to comply with his parents' wishes, study law, become a white-collar worker, found a family and make a career.

As we grew older, our upbringing began to involve issues which made it inevitable for Father to take sides. This placed him, for me, in the 'enemy camp'. Strangely enough, just when I began to regard him with more critical eyes, I discovered that I loved him 'extra', not because he was my father but in spite of it; and that my 'extra' love was always tinged with a measure of compassion. Though there was no visible reason for feeling sorry for him: he was successful, respected, popular and happily married.

According to family legend, his father, son of a poor village tailor, ran away from home to study on his own in Budapest. By the time he married he was professor of mathematics and natural history at the Jewish divinity college. He died young, before I was born. Under what circumstances he left his village, and which village it was, I never knew. Jewish families know less about their forebears than Christians. The past, if less than a few thousand years old, holds little interest for them. They are more likely to bother about the unpaid rent of a third cousin than about the life and merits of a late grandfather.

A glass cabinet in the 'salon' held a violin, a viola, a cello and a double bass. Father played them all, but he called himself wistfully a would-be amateur. Perhaps I unwittingly shared his frustration. My pity for him also had its roots in another, otherwise trifling episode which – for some reason – left an indelible mark on my mind. I was ten or younger when an aunt invited me to the theatre. I must have misbehaved on that day because I was told that I didn't deserve to go. Since the aunt was coming to pick me up, Mother relented, but first – as a symbolic punishment – I was ordered to sew a missing button on to my white glove. Father looked into my room and seeing me in tears, struggling with my unusual task, he tried to help me. He pricked his finger and – probably to cheer me up – he made a great show of having hurt himself badly. I wasn't amused. Upset as I was, the sight of blood on his finger made me sick at heart. I was also terrified at the thought that Mother might catch him cheating so that he would have to feel ashamed because of me.

Years later, when he died suddenly and I was on my way home to the funeral from a summer boarding school abroad, all through the long journey I was obsessed with the vision of the little white glove stained with his blood. As if he had died for me.

When I was thirteen and had the chicken pox, Father read me a scene out of Goethe's *Faust* every evening. Then he answered my questions and listened to me until Mother came in and put out the light. Except for these evenings, I was alone with him only twice. Unaccustomed to being only the two of us, we were embarrassed on both occasions. Once we went to a dog show and once to the circus. It was understood that he was going only for my sake and I pretended that I was grateful to him for taking me after the rest of the family had declared that these were ridiculous things to want to see, but I knew all along that he loved dogs and horses and the circus as much as I, and that he was glad to have me as an excuse. He never suspected how much I knew about him. For instance that for several months he had been secretly taking zither lessons from an old man in the outskirts of the city. When he was found out and shamed into stopping this nonsense, the whole adventure became a grand family joke, only among the adults of course. But I knew about it, and my instinct told me that he had done it partly to help that old man, partly out of frustration and also because he needed to have a secret. Neither did he suspect that sitting behind him in our opera box I had seen his shoulders shaking with silent sobs. Nor could he guess how many forbidden books I had read and how much I would have liked to discuss them with him.

But I felt that the time wasn't as yet ripe for that. We walked home from our excursions in silence, but if he had given a sign I would have said something like this: 'I don't blame you for not talking. After all, you don't know me and you think that I am still a child. But I am not, and soon I shall dare to speak up and then you will have found a friend who understands you better than all the others, and you will be able to talk to me about things you don't even tell yourself any more. I also know that you don't pray, not even when you go to the synagogue on the holidays. Just now it might still hurt you if I told you that I stopped saying my old children's evening prayer long ago. I know your dreams and your frustrations, I am the only one who understands that your visits to the old zither teacher were not nonsense but a little half-hearted escape into the real life you have missed.'

I was like a mother craving for her child's confidence but putting off the first serious talk. It might be too early, he isn't quite old enough . . .

Then it was too late.

At school my best friends and I formed a close, rebellious little circle which we named 'The Spinach Club' because our parents kept telling us we were much too 'green' for the books we read and the subjects we discussed. We preferred the girls' tea parties we gave at home to the occasions when we met boys at dances, on the tennis courts and so on. I doubt whether my daughters could understand why adolescents of both sexes accepted and enjoyed these segregated parties. Probably it was because they were unchaperoned, we could invite whoever we liked rather than the children of our parents' friends, and men were much more interesting as a subject of discussion than when actually present in the form of pimply boys.

We talked about them, and we talked a great deal about God, in such negative terms that we sometimes scared ourselves – suppose he did exist after all, and was listening? We recited poetry and listened to music, and above all we discussed our elders and the state of the world, for which we suspected they were responsible. We decided that we must change the world. We read more than we were taught, and looked a little further than most of the other girls, and we were impatient to be grown-up.

In our family there was a legend about a giant pretzel: when they were our age our father and his brothers had felt richly rewarded for a whole week's good behaviour if on a Sunday walk their father bought them a giant pretzel. This pretzel became a symbol, a dire warning of how empty we would find life later if we insisted on gobbling it up so fast, so soon, with our movie-going, with our ice creams eaten just like that out of cones instead of solemnly and rarely out of silver dishes, and especially with our premature voicing of doubts and opinions.

That the age-old cleavage between the generations was to be deeper than ever before was apparent in the first coherent sentence of my life. Not that I remember it, but it must have been considered amusing enough to be often repeated. I barricaded myself behind a chair and said: 'I am a Russian soldier, I shoot – boom boom!' I was a child of the First World War.

In our infancy our parents' world lay around them, shattered into fragments, but as we learned to think, they learnt to forget. They put the broken pieces together and passed them on to us as though they were whole. They would not acknowledge that the peaceful city in which they had lived before the war, with its outlook, its way of life, its laws of conduct, had ceased to exist. Nor that it had collapsed through its own fault, not by accident.

'War' in my childhood was a word used as a definition of time in conjunction with 'before', 'during' and 'after', carrying no more weight than 'breakfast' or 'bedtime'. For us children it was void of meaning, smell or taste, until we came across and secretly read Remarque's *All Quiet on the Western Front*. Nobody discussed the war. Not at home and not at school. It was an indecent subject, very much like sex, to which our mothers referred only in terms of marriage, trousseaux, recipes and how to manage servants.

We had to find the truth for ourselves, and one way or another we did so. By the time I was fifteen I understood that my generation – all our thoughts and feelings, our whole destiny – was marked and determined by the fact that we had been born during a war.

After an hour's work, everything the security men had disturbed was more or less back in its place. My brother-in-law telephoned to hear whether I had arrived and said he would come over after work. Then a woman from our wage department called to tell me that they would be sending my salary on the first and that the official announcement of my dismissal was probably already in the mail. There was no need for me to come personally, she added. She also said that she was sorry and hung up.

I still had a few hours to myself before the children were due. I took a shower and lay down, hoping to sleep. But exhausted as I was, I dozed off only for a while to awake in a cold sweat, struck by the thought that I would have to explain things to Susie. She was almost fifteen and a founding member of the first young pioneer's organization in Bratislava. When her group took the oath, she was rewarded for her exceptionally active participation in the movement by being allowed to tie the red scarf around the neck of Comrade Bacílek who represented the Central Committee on this solemn occasion. This was one of her most cherished memories. She identified her father with everything that inspired her. Busy as he was, they did not see very much of each other, but she was proud of him because she knew him to be something quite important in the Party, and the Party was all. What in the world could I tell her without shattering her ideals or turning her against her father?

Back in America, she had grown surprisingly early into a friend who could – or rather who had it in her to – share my tastes and thoughts. We went to museums and galleries, for walks in parks and zoological gardens, and on holidays to the mountains. In Wisconsin there was a chipmunk, 'our' chipmunk, which we crept out to watch as it appeared on the same stump every evening. With bated breath, signalling our enchantment only by pressing each other's hands, we experienced the same oneness with nature. I managed to keep her away from the garish comic books, at that time a cultural menace confined to the States, and she read good books and poetry which we discussed. In other words, or so it seems today, I was on the way to turning her into an intellectual snob with a potentially dangerous dependence on her mother.

But by now she was on her own, or rather she had been taken over by the State. Estranged from me. Or had it started with the arrival of the new baby? Hardly. She had never shown any signs of jealousy. When the baby was born three years earlier she had been like a little mother to her.

I kept asking myself: is it her age or has this new environment degraded me in her eyes? She had a rude way of showing her embarrassment over my faulty Slovak, but if I addressed her in English, practically her native tongue, she invariably answered in Slovak. At the dinner table I was the subject of kindly but unmistakably contemptuous criticism, much like a necessarily tolerated retarded child. It was not only my language which was despised but also my prosaic remarks about having had to queue up for hours for what they were eating, and my failure to join in their enthusiasm over current events. How was I now to win her back? How could I explain her father's arrest to a girl who had telephoned Moscow to congratulate Stalin on his seventieth birthday? This she had done, I was sure, less from sincere devotion than to spite me. The evening before I had made fun of what I called the infantile, idiotic prelude to these celebrations, and this had brought on a joint ideological attack from Susie and her father. She also identified herself with her father in matters she could not possibly understand. Slogans, youth-movement songs, marches, brigades and meetings were what she lived with, to the exclusion of everything else.

Once even her father disappointed her. When *Pravda* suddenly came out with shocking and totally unexpected news about the arrest and 'unmasking' of a band of traitors, all leading Party members, headed by the wife of a dead national hero, they also printed on their first page a long, passionately accusatory poem by the youth organization's official poet. Whether he had enjoyed incredibly fast and fecund intercourse with his muse during the night or whether he had privileged access to his inspirational material, which had given him sufficient time to prepare his diatribe, was an open question only to people with closed minds. In any case, the poem was a solemn pledge to Gottwald to help him crush the viper together with her venomous nestlings, and an appeal to youth for unrelenting revolutionary vigilance. It was a miserable piece of verse, dreadful and malignant in its implications, almost calling for the hangman.

Susie read it out with great enthusiasm at the dinner table. She was expecting her father's praise, like when she had telephoned Moscow. He was visibly disgusted, shocked and embarrassed.

'That's just fine,' he said. 'But I wish you would leave the business of crushing vipers to others.'

She gave him an amazed look of disappointment and after that she withdrew herself altogether. She was hardly ever at home, and behaved as though she were absent even when she was there.

What could I now tell a child who spent all of her free time in an organization whose chief hero was Pavel Morozov, the Russian peasant boy who, during forced collectivization, denounced his father for not having denounced some kulak neighbour? The father was duly shot and 'Pavlik' was subsequently killed by his father's brother, which made him into a martyr. He was held up as a model to our children for not having hesitated to do what had to be done in the interest of the State.

Speaking to her openly would place me immediately in the enemy camp. She was being taught daily to take for a dangerous sympathizer with reactionary forces anybody who did not believe that Stalin was the infallible Great Father, that Tito was a bloodhound and a lackey of imperialism, and that the working people in the West were on the very verge of pauperization, which implied an immediate threat of revolution. Their imperialist masters were therefore resolved to destroy our peaceful socialist country eventually by war, and until then with any and every means at their disposal. It was easy to make children believe that governments which oppressed their own people could not tolerate the existence of free, democratic and flourishing countries towards which the eyes of their starving and terrorized populations would turn with longing and envy. If I wished to retain at least the tolerance of my child I had to keep a straight face when she went for school-organized trips to the country to collect Colorado bugs dropped on our potato fields from American balloons, or when she marched in the streets shouting slogans calling for the rope for traitors before their sins were named and before they had been given a chance to make even false confessions.

*

54

Before Susie was born, my husband and I kept scrapbooks of clippings from the bourgeois press, proving its ludicrous and disgusting dishonesty. The truth about social conditions, about the fascist threat, about colonialism and about dreadful human conditions all over the world appeared only in *our* papers, in *our* books. Ours was the only humane literature, and it was also the only one that contained the truth about the Soviet Union and thus showed the right way to follow.

But what does our press and literature look like today? If we made a scrapbook now, from our own papers, what would it contain? Contempt for the readers' common sense, empty phrases, incitement to hate and fear, stupid contradictions, and lies, lies, lies.

As a matter of fact, I did keep clippings out of *Pravda* from the time just before Oscar's arrest. A few random quotations are not out of place here if the atmosphere is to be revived and my dilemma understood and forgiven even by readers who may, on the grounds of the foregoing, begin to see me as an incorrigibly querulous sceptic.

18th July, 1951: 'Tito's clique, the henchmen of imperialism! Tito's gang, after having joined the imperialist camp and pulled off their counter-revolutionary coup, are now setting off on their march to the fascization of Yugoslavia. But the profound hatred of Yugoslavia's nations against Tito's clique is stronger than Titoist terror and the mendacious machinations of the bandits in Belgrade. Night after night inscriptions appear on the walls: "Away with the fascist Tito! Long live Comrade Stalin!" In the streets one sees cowed, hungry, ragged people, made to work from dawn to late in the night for starvation wages. Tito has changed the country into a fearful picture of ruins, misery and hunger such as history has never known.' (*The author of the above is now fighting for the rebirth of journalism under Dubček.*)

'Josef Vissarionovits Stalin. We owe him endless gratitude, unlimited love and respect for all eternity!' (*Author: an otherwise literate man, former professor, then Vice Chairman of the City Council.*)

'Citizens, do not give credit to the malignant rumours contending that there is again no bread to be had in the city. Saturday

55

was an unfortunate exception. Due measures are being taken . . .'

In the middle of April of 1951, Rudolph Slánský gave a speech at the IXth Party Congress. Here I quote only a part of it. 'The repulsive faces of the corrupt traitors have been unmasked at last! It is a characteristic of this treasonable gang of spies and conspirators that in it Czech and Slovak bourgeois nationalists are united. The Czech nationalists Šling and Švermová and the Slovak nationalists Clementis, Husák and Novomeský are working hand in hand. They wanted to inflict on the Czech and Slovak nations the same fate as the Titoist band of imperialistic agents has inflicted on Yugoslavia, which it has changed into a fascist slave state. But the gang has failed miserably, thanks to the Communist Party, thanks to its bolshevik steersman, Comrade Gottwald! (Prolonged applause and shouts: "Long live Comrade Siroký! Long live the Soviet Union.") We were not sufficiently vigilant. Now we must increase our wakefulness and vigilance! Let us learn from the way Comrade Stalin led his bolshevist, principled fight against all kinds of Trotskyist, Zinovievist and Bucharinist traitors. Sooner or later, our Party will unmask, crush and mercilessly punish every traitor!' (*Three months later Slánský, who was then Central Secretary of the Czechslovak Communist Party and Deputy Prime Minister, had his fiftieth birthday celebrated on a national scale and was awarded the Order of Socialism. His picture was still in every shop window when he 'became' the leader of a treacherous conspiracy in which my jailed husband was supposed to have been 'one of the dirty Jews'. Slánský himself was arrested at the end of November, to be hanged with eleven others a year later.*)

Pravda, August, 1951: 'Soviet literature is our great example and support. No writer who thinks that Soviet literature is a model only in its high ideological level and fighting spirit, while he continues to admire the decadent, cosmopolitan authors of the West in matters of form, will create socialist literary works. The more thoroughly our writers get acquainted with Soviet literature, the better they can learn the methods of socialist realism, the sooner our Slovak socialist literature can come into being. Comrade Zhdanov has enriched Soviet literature with great thoughts to which we shall continuously turn for strength and enthusiasm in our fight for a culture with a high ideological and artistic level. Zhdanov is a bright beacon in Slovak culture as well.' (*1968: The author is now very active, particularly as concerns the rebirth of culture and journalism in a socialism with a human face.*)

Pravda, October, 1951: 'The Stalin Constitution is not satisfied with merely laying down the formal rights of the citizens. It places the main emphasis on the guarantee of these rights and on the means of their realization. The Stalin Constitution gives the Soviet working people an unprecedented degree of freedom and democracy, impossible and unthinkable in any bourgeois republic . . .'

How was I to tell Susie? Whatever way I chose, one of the two pillars on which her life rested had to collapse: her father or the Party.

From her point of view it would have been easiest if I told her that her father was probably getting what he deserved. Quite a few women in the same situation did just that – one of them so successfully that her young son wrote an open and widely disseminated letter asking for the death sentence for his father, whom he called his worst enemy. (A similar letter was published by the wife of one of the chief accused in the big trial which came later.) But these mothers were too high up in the hierarchy for me to know them personally. They were also disciplined Party members in whose eyes the Party could do no wrong. They may have allowed themselves to feel that the Party was perhaps making a first, single dreadful mistake in the special case of their own husbands, but not even that could be said openly by a disciplined member before, years later, permission came from above. If this was discipline, to my mind it was the discipline of spiritual and intellectual corpses. However, utterly unable as I am to enter into the spirit of the zealous at that time, I do feel myself bound to give these wives and sons the benefit of the doubt.

As for myself, I never had a single moment of uncertainty as to my husband's complete loyalty and innocence. Not when he was arrested, not when I heard his confession and not when he was sentenced to twenty-two years. My conviction came less from the confidence of a wife blinded by love, than from the simple fact that I had lived with him for a sufficient number of years to know him, and happened not to be blinded in other ways. This is not to say that I was some sort of an exception, an especially wise or clearsighted person. On the contrary, it means that I belonged to the overwhelming majority of the population, including the workers with whose life and attitudes I became closely acquainted when I was eventually 'successfully transferred into production'. In my doubts and in my disgust I was one of the great majority who usually do not write books about how a certain time in history affects their existence and feelings. Most books are written by men and women who in one way or another were responsible for the time they lived in. The feelings and lives of the non-writing majority of a period are then expressed in the reconstructions of historians, who again must depend on accounts written by history makers, whether in power or in sharp opposition. Hardly ever do they depend on accounts written by people who just tried to live in the time in question. And the silent majority is nowhere as silent as it is in a totalitarian state. Moreover, it was far less silent under a Franco or any other junta than it was under Stalin. At least in writing.

I decided to withhold nothing from Susie, even at the risk of losing her altogether now, when I needed her most.

Before she was born there was so much else to occupy my mind that I was not aware of any overwhelming desire to have a child. Once she was there, she became the centre of my life; and when she was not yet two, the imminent threat of war and disaster turned my love for her into a painfully deep emotion.

On a sunny autumn day of 1937 I was sitting on a bench by the Danube, waiting for the baby to awake. I pushed the pram into the shade of a tree. It was close to noon and all the mothers nurses and children were leaving for home. I was in no hurry because my husband was out of town. The sudden stillness struck me like an unexpected sound. Everything around me – the trees, the dusty shrubs – seemed to have fallen asleep. Even the great river had stopped, hardened into a hot metal plate. On the pavement by my feet a pigeon's feather lay stiff, perfectly motionless, behaving not at all like such a fluffy little thing should. I too felt charmed into complete immobility.

Surely others must also know this exceptional state of mind. Afterwards one doesn't really know how long it lasted; perhaps a moment only, perhaps an hour or more. My best friend Ju and I used to call it 'settling accounts', but only because we could find no better description. In fact it is more, or something else. These rare moments come without warning, sometimes in the middle of a perfectly commonplace activity or prompted by an insignificant thing: a summer storm or a little newspaper item. They can be called forth just as well by the fragrance of a flower or the smell of a new cake of soap, the touch of a silk scarf or the sound of an unknown foreign language. This time it was the sudden stillness in the noontime heat. I should like to string these moments – all equally precious, regardless of what brought them about – on a thread like so many pearls, hang them around my neck and tell someone I love: 'Look, everything else was only accidental, not of my own doing. My essence is on this string . . .'

When it happens, the camera of my mind (or is there a soul?) is set on the infinite. When, as a child, I asked my father to explain to me the mysterious cyphers on his Kodak, he showed me the little horizontal 'S' that meant 'infinite'. In those days I imagined that if the dial was set on it, the lens could see to where we can't. Later, of course, I knew that this was nonsense, but I continued to harbour a secret love for this cypher. It remained a symbol which opened occult perspectives offering escape from the here and now. When my camera is focused on this magical sign, life is suspended. The sharp outlines of nearby things become blurred and everything assumes a meaning only in relation to what is far in space and time. I exist only as part of the past and the future and am one with the whole world and all that's alive in it. My mind expands at a vertiginous rate far beyond its usual range of practical thinking. When it happens, I am either terrified and quickly start washing dishes or doing something very normal to make it pass, or else I stiffen wherever I am, and half happy, half resigned, I surrender to it.

59

Had the baby started to cry or had another mother with a pram sat down by me to talk about first teeth, prices on the market or fall fashions, it would have let me go, and I would have never noticed the dead leaf. But there was nobody around, only an old man who stopped to ask for a light from my cigarette. He behaved so quaintly that instead of breaking the spell, he became part of it. He was walking up and down in front of my bench and talked without caring whether I heard him or not. About misery, loneliness, the last war and the wickedness of the world. He took at least fifteen steps in each direction before turning on his heels in a sort of sharp military fashion, so I overheard only some of what he was saying. Every now and then he stopped to address me directly.

'There is another war coming, missus, take my word for it. It's just around the corner, and I am glad. It's what's coming to us. Lady,' he added politely.

When he stopped next, he said: 'And what can you do about it? I am asking you, little lady. I will tell you: nothing. Absolutely nothing, if you want to know. That's that. So let it come!' he exclaimed triumphantly.

He was a poor old man, obviously asking for sympathy and reassurance. I had none to give. I found him frightening and repulsive, and when he stopped to bend over the pram, I only had enough compassion to check myself from telling him to take his stubbly face and greasy hat away from my baby.

Presently he came up to me and stuck a photograph under my nose. It showed a little boy against a background of artificial rosebushes and snow-covered mountain peaks. He had on a sailor hat with a long ribbon and his trousers were too long to be short and too short to be long.

'What can you do about it? Nothing,' he repeated, this time softly. Then he grabbed the picture as if afraid that I might want to keep it, lifted his greasy hat and left before I had a chance to say something kind.

Only when he had gone did I realize that he had not needed to search for the photograph in his wallet among old bills and tickets, but that he had taken it out of his pocket like a smoker his lighter or a tailor his ever-handy stub of blue chalk.

Suddenly I was looking at hundreds of pictures of dead children on walls, on mantelpieces, in wallets and handbags. I thought of the old man's wedding night when the boy with the sailor hat was conceived, when his wife was as young as I was now, and his cracked voice echoed in my ears: 'What can you do about it . . .?'

People dying in Madrid and in China, political prisoners being beaten to death in German prisons, they all looked straight at me with their eyes glazing over, from under the rubble of their homes, from behind iron bars, and asked me the same question. Women in the throes of childbirth raised themselves on their elbows between spasms and asked me, as if it were my duty to know. Young boys, learning to march and shoot, used a moment when the officer wasn't looking to step out of line and to call to me across the field . . . I wished desperately that my husband were there to help me answer. He would have surely known.

I got to my feet and pulled the pram from under the tree. The child was sleeping naked on top of the white quilt. The sun had coloured the skin of her perfectly shaped little body like the petal of a tea rose. She was breathing deeply, peacefully, a faint smile lighting up her features. Beneath the silky curls, her high curved forehead ended in the dark semicircles of the eyelashes. Her eyebrows were hardly visible yet. Her relaxed arms stretched out above her head looked fragile as if they would break at the slightest touch. The round milk-filled belly, ending in the soft triangle, was rising and falling rhythmically. Her cushioned feet twitched slightly as she was dreaming. On her chest there lay the wilted, prematurely fallen plane tree leaf. It was large, dirty-yellow, veiny, malignant, like the wrinkled hand of a witch threatening to crush the fragile body. Innocent, defenceless nakedness weighted down by this banal symbol of death . . . When I carefully lifted the leaf, my eyes filled with tears. I let myself cry. Crying was good. It broke the spell and dissolved tormenting fear into a mysterious feeling of elation and hope. Suddenly I was filled with the certitude that on my palm the dead leaf had lost its ominous message, that in it, there was hidden the radiant green of a million new buds.

The baby awoke and stretched her limbs with a blissful purr. It was not so long ago that I had felt these movements inside my own body. And like a child in the womb, the thought was conceived, ripened and expanded in me that life could be good and that man was not powerless. Of course we can do something about it all, you old bitter man! The very love for my child is stronger than evil, and at least her father and mother believe that she will grow up into a better world. Leaves will continue to wither and fall, and people will have to die when their time comes. But it will be a world without hunger and fear. There will be work and a decent living for all, a good harvest will be a blessing instead of an economic catastrophe, wheat will not have to be denatured with coal dust to make the rich richer, milk will not be spilled into the sea, justice and freedom will reign, men will be brothers and nations and races will live in peace.

It was a beautiful vision, and we earnestly believed that we held the key to this world.

At last Susie arrived together with Tania, whom she had picked up at the kindergarten as usual on her way home from school. She welcomed me as if nothing had happened and retired immediately to her room. Tania, who was used to her father's frequent absences, asked only about the lodger, and wasn't upset when I told her that she had gone to live somewhere else. She was too young to notice any other change, she played with her dolls as usual, and returned my excessive tearful demonstrations of tenderness gladly, ascribing them probably to the fact that I had been away for a few days. In return she went nicely to bed.

Then I had a long, very open talk with Susie. It was a very one-sided talk. She listened, less shocked than I feared she would be. But she did not say much, nor did she cry. When I finally kissed her good night and left her room I had no idea what was going on inside her. For many weeks, even months she continued to avoid the subject, and as far as possible me. When the police evicted us she took it in her stride. Again, she didn't cry, she only kept to herself. Often when I came home from my factory work, dead tired, on the brink of despair and hungry for affection, I found her sprawling on the bed with her papers. When she was sure I was there to hear, she started singing her young pioneer's songs at the top of her voice. These songs were mostly about the glory of hard work, but she never gave me a hand in the kitchen and just looked on when I was lugging coal up a steep ladder from the cellar. We quarrelled daily, I wept and screamed at her until she took her coat and went out. She never cried, and yet I was full of pity for her, knowing that she was good at heart, and that it was her inner battle that had hardened her against me. Here I was delivering hysterical sermons about unwashed dishes, screaming at her that she was driving me out of my mind with her songs instead of helping her. But the only thing she wanted to hear from me I could not say.

She continued to be gentle and good to her little sister, but between the two of us things got so that we didn't even kiss good night any more. I had no strength left in me to fight for her love. In a short time I had lost my husband, most of my friends, my job, my home, my right to make a decent living, my vitality and self-assurance, my faith in reason and decency, and I felt my health going too. It seemed only logical that I should lose her as well.

That this wasn't so after all I was to discover some time after our first eviction. All three of us had to sleep in the same room in this new place. I still don't know when and how the gradual change, about which she never said a word, took place in her. At first I didn't know what had awakened me out of my restless sleep. When I switched on the lamp and saw that her bed was empty, my first thought was that she had run away from home. I jumped out of bed, and then I saw her lying in the small cot, pressed with her whole body against her peacefully sleeping little sister, her shoulders shaking with convulsive sobs.

I sat down on the edge of the cot and put my arms around both children. When I felt that Susie did not withdraw from my embrace but rather nestled closer to me, a feeling of such happiness took possession of me the like of which only very unhappy people can know. All of a sudden I was so strong that I felt that now I could stand up to whatever else fate had in store for me.

On the third day after my return from Prague I got my dismissal notice, and attached to it, a short communication signed by the cadre official telling me that I was 'placed into production' and at which factory and when I was to report for work. Against such orders there was no appeal even for people in less desperate situations. Besides, I needed a job. The bank book with our little savings was in the hands of the police, and when I telephoned to the Commissariat, I was told that they had orders to hold back my husband's salary until further notice. I had ten days at my disposal, and I tried to reason out what I could do.

Of all the highly placed persons I knew, I decided on Comrade M as easiest for me to approach and most likely to help or at least to give advice. Before February 1948, Oscar and he shared a room at party headquarters, they had been on friendly terms, and I felt sure that he had no personal doubts about Oscar's loyalty. We had even met a few times at the dinner table when he lived as a lodger at my brother-in-law's for some time after his return from exile. Besides, I was on regular visiting terms with his wife Lena, with whom I shared the fate of being a sort of disgrace in our husbands' circles by not knowing Slovak. Talking German and English brought us together. She was a German Jewess who had married M in London after another Czech communist in exile had divorced her. At the time I speak of M had already risen to be 'the grey eminence' in the Slovak Executive Committee, and although his name was not shouted by marching masses, it was generally known that important decisions made on the Slovak Party level by the man whose name was being shouted were in great part made by M.

Lena, a smallish plump woman, was said to have been a professional dancer as a girl, but when I met her this was quite hard to imagine. She was not especially bright, but a good soul and a devoted communist, one of the few who refused to take advantage of her husband's high position. She was incredibly naive in worldly matters, and like so many women with a very active political past, a terrible housewife. She phoned me often for advice on the mistaken assumption that I was an expert. I was nothing of the sort, but on the other hand it was impossible to know less than she did. I must confess that some of her phone calls, and Lena as a whole, provided me with good material for the light entertainment of friends I acquired later in circles where my political leprosy did not matter.

One of the best was when she called me in a panic telling me that somebody had unexpectedly sent them a rabbit. In those days of meat shortage this was a princely gift. Her description of how she had cut the animal up, and then, not knowing what to throw away and what to keep, decided to cook the whole lot, was a real pearl. Unable to learn the language, she had no steady job, but she was writing reports from Slovakia for Radio Prague's English propaganda broadcasts which I sometimes helped to type out. I shall never forget the one about the Bratislava vegetable market. She described in glowing colours how, thanks to the Party, now at last even workers' wives could afford to buy the vitamin-rich fresh vegetables once bought only by privileged bourgeois ladies with maids at their heels to carry their heavy shopping bags. This was in the summer of 1949 when there wasn't a single wilted carrot to be had in the whole of Bratislava. To her mind, this was not lying. Reporting otherwise would have helped the enemies of socialism, and anyway it was only a question of time before all that she wrote would be true.

There was also the story of the books. Like other important people, after February, Lena and her husband were allotted the apartment of somebody who had voluntarily or involuntarily disappeared. It was completely furnished and in one of the two rooms there was a library witnessing to the former owner's curious and well-defined taste as a collector. As usual, Lena was left to cope with the move single-handed, and she asked me to come over and help. When I arrived I found her cleaning the shelves of the large bookcase, its contents in sacks ready to be thrown out. After my years of apprenticeship and catalogue-writing in Chicago a cursory glance at some of the volumes told me that this was a collection of great value. It was not ordinary pornography but consisted of examples of the occasional excursions into the erotic most great writers and poets of the past have made. The few volumes she gave me a chance to look at had exquisite bindings and were illustrated with fine reproductions of etchings and paintings by great artists. It was dreadful to see them doomed to the garbage can. However,

Lena tore the books out of my hand very resolutely, called them 'Popobuecher' and dismissed them with so much contempt that I was ashamed to ask whether I couldn't possibly rescue and take along at least some.

All the same, I didn't dislike Lena. I even felt respect for her unwavering optimism and her devotion to the cause which – among other things – involved sleeping with a sickly, ugly, repulsively ill-groomed husband, a totally humourless apparatchik who was growing greyer, dryer and uglier in direct proportion to his rapid rise in the hierarchy. But in our circles he was admired as an exceptionally well-versed Marxist theoretician, almost a genius in the field of political economy, a good man and an indispensable pillar of the Party.

Poor Lena. She was over forty when she bore a probably accidentally conceived dead baby to M. Her adolescent son by her first marriage was living in Prague with his father, and she hardly ever saw him. Very soon after Comrade M's arrest she was deported to a remote village where she was put to work in a brick factory and continued to act as a propagandist among the local population. Just about then, they hanged her first husband in Prague after her son had achieved ugly world fame with his widely published open letter demanding the death penalty for his father. His letter tells more about 'pre-January' Czechoslovakia than all current retrospective pseudo-scientific analyses of 'temporary deformations caused by the personality cult' and by President Novotný's personal shortcomings so much referred to in this our spring of political rebirth. At the time I speak of, Novotný was nothing but a little cog in the big wheel. If the boy wrote the letter of his own free will, it is a frightful portrait of him and his stepmother; if not, it's the portrait of a frightful system.

Poor Lena remained a good communist throughout. When, more than a decade later, about four years ago, her hanged first husband was posthumously rehabilitated, Lena was busy nursing M, who had a heart attack after his release from jail. Then she fell suddenly ill, and after a few months of dreadful suffering she succumbed to cancer. M survived her long enough to be rehabilitated while still alive.

My attempts to get an interview with Comrade M proved futile. I never got farther than his secretary. He was much too powerful and busy. So I went to see Lena. I assured her that I wanted only five minutes of his time and that I didn't dream of asking him to plead my husband's innocence. But surely, I said, she knew as well as I that he had the connections and the power to make the police speed up his interrogation. That's all I wanted, and possibly some advice. Lena wept with me, but she could only promise to try. Next day she called to tell me that M was really quite unable to see me. Not that he didn't want to, he simply had absolutely no time.

I went straight over to her place, trembling with indignation. 'Listen,' I said, 'you know Oscar well. Your husband knows him even better. I want you to tell me here and now whether you can believe that he is an enemy of this State, or whether you can conceive of M possibly believing such a thing?'

She made a big fuss of adjusting things on the table, which in itself was an unnatural thing to do since the room was otherwise, as usual, a mess.

'Answer me, please!'

'I don't know . . . As a matter of fact, we haven't known him for quite so long. And not quite so well as you say . . .'

I jumped to my feet, but before going I left a message for M. What I said was merely vengeful wishful thinking, not prophecy.

'Tell him that if he is too busy to take notice of what's going on and too busy to give me five minutes of his time, he might easily find himself soon in a place where he will have too much time on his hands!'

She must have recalled this phrase when M was arrested not so long after. She must have interpreted it as a good Party member should, and must have expressed her thoughts to somebody at some time; because soon it was whispered widely enough to reach my ears that my husband and M were obviously members of the same conspiracy, and that I knew all about it and was trying to see M to warn him.

After my failure with M I immediately made new plans. I simply had to contact somebody high up. With just a bit of good will anyone could do what I was going to ask for without endangering himself, or so I thought. The police must get orders to question Oscar without delay. Given a fair chance, he must go free. The important thing was to have someone intervene before they took him away to use him in some other 'case' they were working on. I was convinced that he was still only a few blocks away at police headquarters, and I even hoped to be allowed to see him.

In fact, by then he was already in Ruzyně. It may surprise tourists but Ruzyně is not only the name of the Prague airport as it appears in the 'Čedok' prospectus inviting progressive-minded western holidaymakers to the Golden City, the capital of our democratic people's republic. Right behind the elegant airport there is Ruzyně prison, the hell-hole where uncounted numbers of innocent people were detained for years and subjected to the treatment our police had learnt so perfectly from Soviet experts; to that unique combination of terror, deceit, provocation, blackmail and alternate physical and mental torture that goes into the mass production of faultlessly performing witnesses against themselves and others in political show trials.

This is where Oscar spent his first two years of imprisonment. The first news we got was a short note from there seven months after his disappearance. As for seeing him, the children and I got our first visiting permit exactly three years later. By then he was already working in the prison camp at the uranium mines in Northern Bohemia. After having played his part as a witness against the Slánský 'gang', he was tried separately and secretly and sentenced to twenty-two years by the Supreme Court as a Zionist spy, for sabotage and high treason.

But, in 1951 I still believed that there were communists who would help another communist. The thing was to find the right person, act quickly, not give up. I decided to call on Julo B. Before the war he used to be one of our good friends and, involved as we all were in all sorts of leftist cultural activities, we used to meet often. He was now a top Party government official in Prague. I had not met him since he reached this eminence, but as both Oscar and he were dealing chiefly with matters of national economy, the two of them had been seeing a lot of each other lately at

68

the Ministry in Prague. I felt sure he would try to be helpful if I could only reach him. I remembered him as he was during the hectic pre-Munich days: an exceptionally brilliant boy, an excellent, convincing public speaker, and surprisingly enough, while a staunch communist, also an amusing companion, handsome and cultured. What was most important just now, he knew Oscar well and was known to hold him in high esteem both professionally and politically.

Today I find it difficult to reconstruct the reasoning that made me call on these people. Did I make myself believe that the other victims I knew of were imprisoned for good reasons? Or that I was the first one to call the Party's attention to the transgressions of the state police? A probable explanation is that if I had acted rationally, it would have led me into utter despair and immobility, which, for the children's sake, I could not afford. I did what I did prompted by the instinct for self-preservation rather than by critical thought.

Top officials were difficult to approach in those times. Fortunately, somebody revealed to me that Julo B was just then vacationing in a villa in the High Tatra Mountains. What a stroke of luck, I thought, this gave me the chance to see him without the formalities a visit to his office would involve. I left little Tania in Susie's care and took the first express train. As soon as it was in motion, I felt better. I was *doing* something.

It was a superb summer day, and the majestic mountains were at the peak of their beauty. As I mounted the steep, narrow path leading between fragrant pine trees to the little isolated villa, I was full of hope. On the way I stopped to pick a few ripe blackberries and to prepare myself for the meeting. I took a little mirror out of my handbag, adjusted my hair and put on fresh lipstick. When I reached the garden gate of the pretty Swiss-style wooden house, my excitement was more pleasant than anguished.

At the entrance, a man in civilian clothes gave me the communist greeting: 'Čest' práci!' The nearest translation would be 'Homage to work!' It was the obligatory form of greeting not only at work but also in shops, at school and everywhere else. Children could come home and say out of sheer habit: 'Čest' práci, Mummy, can I get something to eat?' One gets used to anything, I suppose. To have said 'hello' or 'good morning' by mistake could easily have been interpreted as 'bourgeois baggage' by somebody with a critical eye on you.

The man did not act like an ordinary house-servant.

'What do you want?' he asked. He was unusually tall and very fat, and he barricaded the whole door.

'*Čest pràci*,' I replied dutifully. 'Is Comrade B in, please?'

'He isn't seeing anybody here.'

He eyed me with such hostility that I felt guilty and at a loss what to say.

'We are old friends,' I stammered. 'I am here on holiday down at the hotel, and I happened to hear that he is here. Could I see him? Will you please announce me?'

I spelled out my name very distinctly and with as much self-assurance as I could muster under his annihilating gaze.

'You heard me, Comrade. Or are you deaf? *Čest!*'

He disappeared and slammed the door on me.

I was trembling all over, and the absurd thought struck me that this man already knew. That from now on it would be enough to say our name, and all doors would slam. I was overwhelmed with the urge to flee. To run down the hill as fast as possible, to drink three or four glasses of brandy in quick succession at the hotel bar and to go to bed with the first halfway attractive man who approached me . . . let things happen as they would, I thought angrily, none of this was my making.

But I didn't let myself run. I ordered my knees to stop shaking, my heart to stop thumping. I forced myself to think of the children, of my husband, of the long, expensive trip I had made on borrowed money, and last but not least, of Julo's smiling eyes as I remembered them, his sharply carved, intelligent, handsome face which had always reminded me of illustrations in a little children's Old Testament. If I only could get through to him somehow, everything would be all right.

I walked round the garden, and under cover of a hedge I reached a neglected backyard. Through a half-open back door I slipped into the house and tiptoed up a flight of carefully polished wooden stairs. From behind a white door I could hear the shower running; another open door led into a sunny room with a large balcony. I went in. Presently Julo came in from the hall, wearing a dark bathrobe. Encouraged by his almost unchanged appearance, I said in a light, conversational tone: 'Hello, Julo. I am staying down at the hotel and I happened to hear that you were here. I supposed you would remember me . . . Sorry to barge in like this, but that gorilla of yours just wouldn't . . .'

'Oh, him! Forget it. *Čest práci,*' he said. He put his arm around my shoulder, shook hands cordially and made me sit down.

'Let's look at you! How many years has it been? And what years! But you haven't changed, no . . . So, what's news, tell me.'

He looked well, perhaps a little too well. It was rumoured that he had serious lung trouble during the war. Perhaps they were overfeeding him now. While exchanging small talk about our children I was admiring his teeth, perfect as ever, and trying to decide how to begin. Obviously, he did not know yet. But he must have had his own second thoughts about my visit while chatting because suddenly he asked me in a somewhat unnatural tone: 'And how is Oscar? Busy as always?'

Now I had to come out with the real purpose of my visit. I don't remember what I said or for how long I had been talking before I became aware of speaking into the air. He was standing with his back turned to me at the open balcony door. I inserted pauses, hoping to get some sort of reaction out of him. I could not see his face.

'You know him, you have known both of us for years, Julo. Why don't you say something for God's sake?'

He turned around and took a few steps towards me, but his eyes were fixed on an empty corner of the room. He hit the table between us with his clenched fists several times as he spoke in a high-pitched voice unlike his own.

'Listen! I want you to know that I have full confidence in our state security organs. Is that clear? If he is innocent, as you say, he does not need any help.'

As he stood there in the dark brown bathrobe, his glittering

71

black eyes staring into a void somewhere above my head, he reminded me of a medieval monk.

We exchanged only short, embarrassed words while he was showing me out.

***

I still had a few days left before I was supposed to report at my new place of work. I was frantically running around seeing people, hoping to snatch some 'inside information' or a word of advice.

My husband's last boss received me immediately. He was a former social democrat, turned communist in 1948 in the eleventh hour. This made him rather civil, but especially careful. No, unfortunately, he had no suggestions about where to turn, nor could he find out under what sort of absurd suspicion Oscar could have fallen. Nor was there anything he could do about the month's salary they were ordered to hold back. He gave me a few minutes of sympathetic silence and a warm handshake, which in his position was in itself an act of courage. Then he hurried away to a meeting.

The reactions I met with elsewhere ranged from inane attempts at explanation and tentative insinuations, to sad silence and shrugging of shoulders, accompanied by not very encouraging practical words of advice, all according to where the person I saw stood at the moment.

'You must understand, the Party is in a very special phase of development right now . . .'

'If you were one of us, you would bring more understanding to the matter. You say you know him. Very well. But how much do you know of his work, of the people he was meeting, of what he was doing away from home? What do you know of the temptations a man in political and public life is exposed to? . . .'

'Are you really trying to say that somebody against whom there is no evidence gets arrested just like that? . . .'

'Did you say he was being shadowed? For how long? How did he notice? What? Cars? Oh, my God! . . .'

'Take my advice! Let it be. There is nothing you can do. Keep

72

quiet, think of the children. If you have valuables, don't keep them at home. The inventory, you know . . .'

'Try to recollect. Think carefully. Whom has he been seeing lately? Any relations abroad? . . .'

'I told him over and over not to stick his nose into other people's troubles. He wouldn't be warned . . .'

'Of course we have difficulties, and mistakes are being made. But we will overcome all this. I? No, I can't. Sorry. All we can do is wait . . .'

Wait! For what? For how long? How??

I decided to go to the Executive Committee in Prague. The man at the Control Commission received me with great courtesy. Encouraged by his manner I spoke not only about our own problem, but also about the whole disquieting wave of arrests in Slovakia. He made notes, shaking his head in surprise and disapproval. In the end he assured me that this was valuable information which he would discuss with his superiors. Prague would look carefully into the matter, and I could expect to hear from them very soon.

Like the idiot I was, I believed him. Walking along the long, silent, shiny corridors of the modern building I was filled with pride and relief. Who said one had to take things lying down? I should have come here in the first place!

When things are worst, one is prone to the most foolish variants of gullible optimism.

As a reward for my cleverness and courage, I bought myself a sleeping-car ticket and spent the first peaceful night since it had happened.

When Susie opened the door, she was ashen in the face. She said that early in the morning three policemen had come to announce that we were to be evicted. The one of them who was to be the new tenant had looked over the apartment very carefully. The written decree arrived in the mail half an hour later. We were to wait for further information as to where and when we were to move. Our bureaucracy, known for its sluggish work, was incredibly fast and efficient in such matters.

73

Decree in hand, I hurried to police headquarters. The Czech Party official's encouraging words still ringing in my ears, I asked energetically to be shown to the department in charge.

When I entered the room, the youngish man behind the desk did not lift his head and did not answer my greeting. Without offering me a seat he just reached out for the paper. I started to explain that this was probably a misunderstanding. My husband was likely to be back any day now. I had two children, one of them quite small. Should the flat be regarded as too large during my husband's absence, I was willing to take in lodgers, and use only one of the three rooms. Couldn't they wait at least until the case was cleared up one way or another . . .? The man shook his head with an ironical smirk on his face. It was the look of a man listening to the gabble of a thief caught red-handed.

To get up my courage, I even referred to my recent visit to the Control Commission in Prague and to the promise I had been given. I should not have done that. The man burst into a sudden rage. The mention of Prague triggered a bull's reaction to a red rag. He jumped up.

I should be glad, he said, that they were finding us a place to live in Bratislava. For the time being at least. Soon the Party would find a way to clean the capital of Slovakia of all dirt, of elements like me and the likes of me! By now he was shouting at the top of his voice, and I left the room followed by a shower of humiliating abuse.

What I did not know then was that the ominous hints he let fall in his rage referred to something that was then only a plan under strictly secret preparation. Less than two years later it became public and was carried out under the name of 'Operation B'. Nobody ever knew why it was called 'B', and nobody asked because mentioning it even in whispers could bring the curse on oneself. 'Operation B' was the forced eviction and deportation at a few days' notice of 'unreliable elements' from Bratislava to some place in the country where they had to live in rooms, sometimes sheds, seized from peasants by the police for this purpose. The police needed apartments for their rapidly multiplying new cadres so badly that the 'dangerous elements' of which the city had to be cleansed soon included, in addition to 'dirt' like myself, helpless pensioners or anybody whom a janitor did not like. But when I stood trembling in front of the police station, 'Operation B' was still a strictly kept secret.

It was pouring, and I remembered that I had left my umbrella upstairs. But I couldn't possibly face that man once more, not for anything in the world! Unable to move, like in a nightmare, I stood on the sidewalk. The rain and the cold wind seemed more bearable than the presence of that man. They would cleanse me of the dirt he had flung at me. I wanted to stand there until the rain washed me away, the wind blew me off, the cold froze me lifeless. I simply could not go on any longer.

Of course I could, and I did. So did others. These had been only the first few days of a worse decade to come.

The factory was way out of town, in a little community on the other side of the Danube. To clock on on time I had to get up at half past four, fix breakfast and prepare things for the children, catch a streetcar and then the five-thirty bus at the bridge. Since my pay was the lowest possible and I was doing copytyping almost every night, this was not easy. However, it wasn't so much the getting up and the work itself that made me hate the job. It was its smell. It was a synthetic rubber factory, and it stank.

I am bad at remembering names and numbers, I can't recall melodies and sometimes I don't recognize people in old snapshots, but I do remember and relive smells because I register them more intensely than anything else. In fact, smells stand as shorthand signs for everything of any importance in my past. Childhood days spent in bed with a comfortable cold, that's the faint stench of the spent cigar stub our old family doctor kept between his lips while bending over my chest. A certain after-shave lotion blended with the smoke of gold-tipped Egyptian cigarettes, that's Father's good-night kiss. The scent of eau de Cologne, the original 1147 really made in Köln, that's Mother who in her puritanical way never used any stronger perfume. My first kiss is the smell of rain-drenched mackintosh with an admixture of gasoline. School is the smell of moist chalk and sponge when called up to the blackboard, and the pungent odour of poorly washed young bodies in the gym. Baby oil and powder, wet diapers, that's the bitter-sweet compound of the joys and sleepless nights of young motherhood. The coat of my little white dog of long ago, the men I had, the places I worked at, the countries I visited – all seem to be stored in my brain in concentrated distillations of nostalgic fragrances, repulsive odours and exciting, pungent exhalations.

In my new place of work not only the workshop itself, but also the cloakroom, the toilet and my immediate superior stank; each in its own way, but all offensively. What's more, when I came home I felt myself stinking.

Worst of all was the workshop where I started a hopeless struggle with the adjustment of a single little component of a giant mixing machine. Every time I had to touch it I expected it to explode and therefore I always touched it at the wrong moment, in the wrong way and with disastrous results. I hate machines. I know very well that modern civilization and progress and so on are unthinkable without them, that there are going to be more and more of them; and I am told that although they are now enslaving man, eventually they will liberate him. But they terrify me and I can't even handle a sewing machine.

Since they could not fire me, after a month or so I was transferred to the raw-material testing laboratory and taught a few simple chemical and stress-testing procedures. This work I mastered, but here again the fumes were suffocating and that's where the old engineer with the bad breath came into the picture. He was a Hungarian born into the gentry, and therefore doubly afraid of losing his job. There wasn't always enough material to test and the laboratory, in which he was the only professional, was heavily overstaffed with all sorts of bottle-washers and other unskilled helpers like myself. He must have thought that the more people were working under him the safer the position was, and although half of the time there wasn't enough work to go around, he was constantly running from table to table making himself important and admonishing everybody to keep busy. In eight endless hours I did what I could easily have done in two. I couldn't breathe, my feet hurt and I was bored stiff. Once I tried to hide a book under a slab of rubber behind the analytical scales and read as I stood with a bottle and weights in my hand. He soon discovered my ruse and, bending very close to my ear, begged me in a malodorous whisper to stop it for his sake. I whispered back that I was dying of boredom. After that we had a few whispered conversations under the loudly hissing exhaust while he was ostensibly helping me handle a pipette.

He couldn't understand how we could have been foolish enough to come back from the States. And why did it surprise me that things were now going as they did? Where was I, for God's sake, when the purges were on in Moscow?

I shrugged my shoulders.

Where were we then? A justified question. Naturally we were on the side which was against Franco, against injustice, against Hitler, against racism and war. We were on the side where in that phase of history every decent, thinking person belonged. We were on the side of the Soviet Union. There was nothing in between. Where else could we possibly belong, when every word of doubt or criticism concerning Russia brought grist to Goebbel's poisonous mill? Once having taken a firm stand on the side one has chosen, one becomes voluntarily blinded to what it stands *for*. And so we were also on the side of Stalin.

Under the hissing exhaust I also wondered, but without even whispering the question, on which side he himself had been during the war. While I gave him the benefit of the doubt that he was no very active fascist, I despised him. But, bad breath and the odour of Szálasi and Hitler notwithstanding, I began looking forward to our few minutes of whispered conversation, because to start with, the workers froze me out. As I was soon to learn, this was not because of their political convictions but out of fear that I might be planted on them as a provocateur.

The only occasion on which I had experienced an ecstatic feeling of solidarity and oneness with the masses was in the summer of 1938 in Paris, when I listened to old Cachin and La Pasionaria speaking to a crowd of forty-thousand people in the Vélodrôme d'Hiver. I joined in the thundering shouts of '*No passeran!*' and '*Ouvrez les frontières!*' I was young, several of our friends had gone to fight in the International Brigade, and it was the first time in my life that I had seen so many of my fellow men inspired by the same just cause, united in one great outcry of indignation and in the will to fight. It was like the books my husband gave me come to life. Otherwise, except for the few professional activists I met in the pre-war movement, my earlier contacts with working-class people had been slight, with no political thoughts attached on either side. But it was against the background of the Vélodrôme that I after-wards thought of the working class, the decisive factor in history, the class whose political consciousness we could hope to achieve and share only after having rid ourselves of the encumbrances of our descent and the environmental conditioning of our childhood.

My first task every morning was to fetch several bottles of water from the boiler, to be tested for sediment and other impurities. Walking across the badly lit, littered factory courtyard and then climbing, torchlight in hand, a steep spiral iron staircase dripping with rusty water, I recalled scenes from Soviet films that used to warm our hearts before the war. I tried to evoke suitable emotions. The nobility of physical work, the unimportance of boredom or discomfort so long as you were working for the common good, shoulder to shoulder with the working classes who had now finally begun to play their role in the shaping of our country's future. Perhaps, I told myself, they will stop staring at me after a while. If they see me clock in on time and work as honestly and well as they do, they will come to accept me. I shall become one of them, and since all that is happening is for their good, as one of them I shall learn to see things from their perspective and accept them. I am prepared to renounce my old bourgeois values and adopt theirs. From this new point of view everything will make sense and will thus become honourable – even, perhaps, our individual tragedy which I will learn to see as an unimportant sacrifice for the important common good.

Gradually, my co-workers began to thaw. In the cloakroom the women started drawing me casually into their conversations, and when I passed the men in the adjoining workshops they began to shout the same dirty jokes after me as they did after the other women. During the ten-o'clock break I had to run with the others to the canteen, and I did so although I could not bring myself to eat the greasy tripe soup, the past, present and future quality of which was the main subject of discussion every morning. After a month or so the 'class barrier' was down. The girls told me why they were afraid of me in the beginning. They also taught me the art of looking busy when not working and how to get sudden cramps, attacks of migraine or a sprained ankle – all complaints entitling one to a couple of working hours away from the boss and the stench, resting one's aching feet in the doctor's waiting room.

By the time we became really friendly I learnt that almost every one of them had a close friend or somebody in the family who had been victimized in some way by our régime long before we ourselves had even noticed that there was a police and authorities to be afraid of. After a few months in the factory the last shreds of theoretical notions about the mythical 'working class' that might still have clung to my well-drilled leftist mind were gone. These people were neither better nor worse than anybody else and on the whole not even very different. As long as they were not exposed to too much obligatory free-time political schooling (which incidentally workers shirked much more frequently and cleverly than any 'bourgeois' dared to), it never occurred to them to think of themselves as living in the box to which political thinkers had assigned them more than a century ago and to which political dogma continued to relegate them. Older men and women certainly remembered having hated the factory owner who used to exploit them. But this was no mythical class hate leading to the great liberating explosion. They hated their present exploiters just as badly, or worse. Only now that they 'owned the factory', since they could not hate themselves they hated 'Them'. The more bitterly because they could not even strike.

In our workers' state, however, they did have some advantages. They could afford to gripe a little more freely than clerks and similar rabble, and often they had potatoes and a bit of fruit while we did not, because most had an old relative in the country near enough to the fields and the trees to steal such things before they went rotten or were exported. Everyday conversation on the factory floor centred around the same things as in any other place

79

where I had worked: the weather, the boss, wages, sex and family, illness, food, drink and gossip. The only new additions were bitter whisperings about 'Them', occasional scare-news and the incessant discussion of shopping difficulties and shortages of meat and other basic necessities. However, these shortages were so acute that they had become just as boringly prominent in the conversation of high intellectual circles.

On the occasions when an exchange of thoughts transcended these categories and someone expressed her or his dreams and wishes, these were totally bourgeois. To my surprise, but also with a certain relief, I found that these people had no more urgent desire than to become what we had been taught to despise in ourselves: owners of things, holders of better jobs, have-mores, exhibitors of property to be coveted by others. In other words, more than anything they wanted to be middle-class men and women. It was among workers that I learned that in moral outlook nobody could be more 'bourgeois' than the worker, least of all a young bourgeois with a thinking heart who already knows what 'the lower class' has had no chance to learn: that small material comforts, once possessed, do not necessarily offer the contentment they seem to promise to the one dreaming of them. Real petty-bourgeois mentality, as referred to with disdain by Marxists, has survived in its classical form only among the workers of our industrial age.

The few who did care enough about public life to have a superficial knowledge of what was going on were less discontented because they had hopes that 'They' would eventually give their sons – as a reward for their descent – a chance to make some sort of quick career and thus to lead a middle-class life, which would, in fact, be more than that. Because in our day what satisfaction did we get from living in a decent flat, crossing the border into a neighbouring country, wearing a raincoat that was watertight or a sweater that washed well? It was all right, but it never made us feel special. Whereas nowadays such simple things have not only acquired a new and disproportionate value in themselves, but have also become symbols of privilege and status.

All in all, during that year at the factory I got rid of my

lingering malaise about having been middle-class, but at the same time I also lost the little hope I had that among workers I might perhaps find some ultimate higher justification for what was happening to us and to the country.

The girls were kind and helpful. They taught me how to spin the work out so that it could be spread over eight hours and the norm wouldn't be raised, and how to get out of the building unseen when word got around that there were soup-greens at the nearby shop. I also learned how to simulate – at well-spaced intervals – menstrual fainting spells or sudden backaches so that I could spend some time at the dispensary. There I could rest my feet and read in the waiting-room, and then spend an hour or so stretched out on a couch in a quiet little white cubicle with a prickly electrical appliance on my leg, my belly or back – a gadget which our doctor used for an infinite variety of complaints. This was a blessed place of retreat, the perfect nowhere. There was just enough of a not quite unpleasant medical smell to suggest the idea of sickness, implying possibilities of escape, release by death or hope of healing. Lying there, I had a chance to commune with myself.

How did I get into this? Was it out of my own free will? Did fate bring me here? But what was fate? God? I could not make myself believe in him, much as I needed him just then. At any rate, I felt responsible for my own life. On the other hand, how could the result be so bad when I had always meant so well?

There I was, married to an estranged husband whom I had loved but perhaps loved no longer but to whom I was now tied closer than ever by pity and loyalty. Nobody knew where he was. He was probably being beaten at that very moment because how else could they make him sound guilty enough to keep him there for so long? . . . Mother of two children whom I had to support and bring up without a father, in a society where we were outcasts. With the police at my heels, never knowing when the next summons would come and whether they would let me go again. Wages hardly enough for food . . . The constant fear of worse to come.

Trying to work out how I had got into this mess, but too tired and sleepy for systematic thought, I would sometimes recall the first simplified lessons in Marxism my husband gave me when I was nineteen. His little stories were so convincing that I was ready to embrace the theory behind them before I had the chance to study it.

– Imagine that you see two men sitting next to each other on a park bench. One is well-dressed, well-fed, visibly satisfied with life. The other one is in rags, hungry, grey in the face, despondent. If you had to change places with one of them, naturally you would pick the first man. Wrong! Your decision was based on static instead of dynamic perception. To make the correct choice you would have to consider the two men within the framework of their past, their development and their potential future. In other words, historically. That would lead you to the discovery that the well-dressed, contented gentleman has an incurable disease, and while he is puffing on his fat cigar and making plans how best to enjoy his fortune, the shares he owns are just about to become worthless in a crash. While his seemingly pitiful neighbour is healthy, only hungry and tired, and that can be helped. He has nothing to lose, everything to gain . . .

Or:

– The workers can't afford to buy oranges or real coffee. Why? Because between the plantations and the consumer there is a whole chain of profiteers: the plantation owner, the packing company, the shipper, the wholesaler, the shop-owner, and the State which needs money to pay the police and the army and the bureaucrats (all to be done away with, because superfluous in the future). The people who work with the goods at every stage and who ultimately cannot buy them, are the oppressed, the proletariat. Under communism, oranges, coffee and everything else will come directly through the State to the consumer without enriching parasites and profiteers on the way. That will affect their price so that everybody will be able to afford them.

So logical and promising, it had sounded. But something had gone wrong. If before Christmas (or rather, before the arrival of 'Grandfather Frost' as it was called now) a shipment of oranges arrived, and you were lucky and patient enough to get some, you would have to pay three or more hours' wages for a kilo. (There was no shortage of coffee and a kilo cost only a week's salary.) Of course, one did not necessarily have to eat oranges. But it so happened that apples were non-existent or rotten, and their price was sky high as well.

The State paid no more for oranges and coffee than any capitalist importer; the life of the poor pickers was not being improved.

Who, then, was the profiteer?

Trading with the Soviet Union, administering terror, constant bungling and employing ten people to do the work of one cost a great deal and the money had to come from somewhere.

A few days before Christmas 1951 two policemen came to tell me that our eviction would take place next morning. It was snowing. The carelessly stacked furniture in the open van, topped by a naked little Christmas tree, made a pathetic sight. The driver had two helpers so that in less than an hour everything was in our new home.

The entrance was a door with cracked glass panes in a long courtyard, leading through a small windowless kitchen to two dark rooms. The kitchen was bare of any equipment, and although there was a little iron stove in the first room, I had nothing to heat it with. Coal and wood were rationed, and coming from a centrally heated flat we didn't have a card. Before it got dark, with the help of a neighbour, an old man who gladly accepted a little money for beer, part of the furniture was stacked in a shed in the far corner of the yard. Susie sat stunned on a suitcase, holding little Tania, who cried herself to sleep. I undressed the child and tucked her in under whatever warm things I could find. For Susie I fixed a couch, hoping she would forget that we had eaten nothing that day and had no food in the house. She acted as if I had deliberately chosen to move and had shown poor taste in my choice. I was too tired to argue.

Once left to myself, strange as it may sound, I felt better than I had for months. I found it easier to be evicted than to fight eviction, as I had tried to do, or to wait for it. I knew people who had gone through worse during the war. After all, what was a cold dark flat compared to a concentration camp, the Warsaw ghetto and prison? Nothing. Now that the line was clearly drawn between the enemy and ourselves, there were no more soul-searchings, no more illusions about a 'mistake', no more running for advice to comrades. They could keep their idiotic explanations to themselves and go on crawling to the Party while the rats climbed over their bent backs up to the heights from which they were bound to shit onto their comrades' heads sooner or later. Healthy anger and spite gave me new strength.

But I was exhausted and couldn't make myself get up from where I was sitting to prepare some sort of a bed. Almost asleep in the chair, I heard steps approaching the door. I didn't want to see anybody, and besides, who else could it be but one more official person with one more bit of bad news? I didn't even turn around. There was no lock on the door, and Bronia walked in.

She was the last person I expected to see. We were not even friends at the time, just acquaintances through our husbands. Her husband was a party member, an editor, a Jew whom she had married during the war in London – in other words, a man logically predestined for trouble . . . so what on earth was she doing here at a time when everyone was avoiding me and I was probably more closely watched than ever?

She put a loaf of bread, some butter and some cheese on a suitcase.

'Here, I thought you had probably no chance to shop or cook today,' she said.

We embraced and kissed for the first time since we had met, and then we sat in the cold kitchen in the light of a single bulb among messy bundles of books and pots and pans, and had a good cry.

Trying to find a clean spot for the bread, I was holding it in my arms, hugging it like something alive. It gave me warmth. It wasn't a loaf of bread, it was a precious piece of what I had feared was lost for ever. It was a piece of human decency, a beautiful little flag of civil courage unfurled under the nose of all-pervading cowardice.

Next day I had another unexpected visitor. It was my sister-in-law's neighbour's husband, a man I hardly knew except by sight. In the street he had often lifted his hat to me with an especially friendly smile, but I had always found him rather repulsive, so I hardly ever stopped, and we never passed the 'how is everything' stage of conversation.

Susie was at school, and Tania at the kindergarten. Thanks to the kind factory doctor I was on the sick-list, and thanks to my brother-in-law a small load of firewood had arrived that morning. I was struggling with an axe borrowed from the next-door neighbour. Never having held an axe in my hand before, it seemed pretty hopeless, so I was quite glad when this gentleman appeared and offered his help. He made a neat stack of kindling in front of the stove, then looked around with an expression of infinite sadness on his heavy face and extended his hand in a ceremonial gesture of condolence.

'If there is anything else I can do for you, please feel free to ask,' he said. 'Here, take this.'

It was a small paper bag of freshly ground coffee. It smelled wonderful, and considering its price, it was an impressive gift. I thanked him and asked him to sit down. I was waiting for the water to boil on the hot plate when he grabbed me from behind, pushed me into the other room and onto the couch and landed with all his weight on top of me. While he tried to reach my mouth and I was struggling to avoid his, he babbled something about how sorry he felt for me, a woman all alone, with no one to stand by her, and why was I so stubborn when he meant so well. Revolting as the whole incident was, and illogical as this may sound, the fact that it took me only a few minutes and not too much effort to get him off me frightened me more than if he had persisted in pretending to non-existent feelings. In that case I could have said in a civil tone that I did not lay any claim to such feelings and could not reciprocate them, which would have saved our faces. As it was, he left with an angry mumble, and I felt a dreadful need to take a shower, but there was only a trickle of ice-cold water coming from the rusty tap. But there was at least the cracked yellowish bowl under it into which I could be sick.

As far as my fellow men were concerned, the following years

brought me a few precious crumbs of Bronia's bread, many bags of coffee and even more reasons to retch.

Our dank, low-ceilinged rooms were in one of those ancient one-floor houses formerly owned by wine-growers. People used to drink the young wine at long tables set up in the narrow yard, and our rooms must have served as store-rooms and kitchen where they used to prepare the slices of toasted bread rubbed with garlic which were served with the wine. Someone was still using the cellar for its original purpose and the sour smell of fermenting wine came up through the wide cracks in our floor. To fetch wood for our stove I had to uncover a hole in the kitchen floor and climb down a steep little ladder into the cellar, and the thought that anyone could get into my flat through this hole took some getting used to.

You entered the yard from the street through a heavy wooden gate, and our door was the first you came to. Next came a row of small windowless rooms which must once have housed seasonal labourers or have been used as store-rooms. Each of these holes was now inhabited by a family of two or more, living without daylight except that which came through a glass panel in the door. They must have envied us our windowed rooms, but they were glad to be rid of the small policeman who had moved into the flat of the big policeman who had moved into the flat from which we had been ejected; and it may have been this gratitude which moved them to warn us against using the common privy in the far corner of the yard. The family living next to it consisted of two adults and four children, all in various but very evident stages of lunacy and decay. So we soon learnt to use a lidded pail containing water and disinfectant, and in time we even learnt to laugh about it. The few people who came to see me – some new friends eventually, and one or two brave old ones – were always warned to go to the toilet before their visit.

Partly because of real illness, partly thanks to a sympathetic doctor, but mainly thanks to the fact that the whole process of 'placing into production' was administered, like so much else, by blockheads too incompetent to keep track of what they were doing, after a year I was able to leave the factory. It was absolutely necessary to find employment as otherwise we were not entitled to ration cards. While job-hunting, I lived on copy-typing and translating.

Since it was impossible to get rid of the Hungarian population, it was decided that this minority – in actual fact a majority in our part of Slovakia – had to be accorded its rights, above all the right to political education, so a Hungarian publishing house had been established. One of the editors was a youngish woman coming from one of those villages in Eastern Slovakia where everybody was Hungarian and everybody, including the numerous Jews, was poor. She had fought with the partisans in the Slovak uprising during the war, and was one of the few survivors. On the grounds of merit and as an ardent Party member, she was now enjoying a good position; or rather, being the exceptionally bright and honest person she was, she was not enjoying it any longer. But she was there, as an editor, and simultaneously getting the high-school education she had missed as a girl. Having known my husband well, she now found a way and the courage to give me indirect help. I was given a regular supply of Party propaganda brochures to translate from Slovak into Hungarian; disgusting work that brought me good money through the third person allegedly doing it. In addition, a good man with an awakening conscience who worked in the theatre would sometimes let me type out roles on stencils.

Eventually I landed a badly paid, dull office job, but this employment came to a dramatic end very soon. I was thrown out of this job on the 21st of November, 1952, half an hour after an extra edition of *Pravda* with the fat headline 'Before the Court of the People' appeared in the streets of Bratislava. It reported the beginning of the trial of the 'anti-State spy group headed by Rudolf Slánský', and my husband was among the first witnesses heard.

The evidence Oscar gave in court, which incriminated him no less heavily than Slánský and a few others, was the first intimation I received of what he had been arrested for. Until that moment I still had hopes, based on other cases, that he would eventually be charged in connection with his work, perhaps with economic sabotage or possibly with insufficient vigilance and lack of class-consciousness in picking people for jobs in his office. His testimony, which amounted to confession, put a definite end to these 'hopes'. It was a dreadful story consisting of such evident, easily proved untruths that my first reaction was that he must have gone mad. This was immediately followed by the horrible thought that a man who had been forced to lie like this, in a trial which was obviously meant to determine the whole policy of the State and the Party, could never never be allowed out alive.

He said that he was an American, having accepted citizenship shortly before leaving the States so that he would not be subject to Czechoslovak law and could thus go back to the United States if his anti-State activities should be unmasked.

At home I had all our papers showing how we had renounced American citizenship three years earlier.

He said that he had returned to Czechoslovakia on the orders of American Zionists with the aim of promoting their interests by undermining our people's democracy.

At home I had the Party's letter bearing Bacílek's signature, which had called him back; and my own scrapbook, overlooked in the search, with clippings of a series of articles he wrote in 1948, fiery denunciations of Zionism on the grounds of the Jewish debt to socialism and of the promises socialism held for Jews in their native country. They were written in answer to a speech made by President Benes in which the President had expressed sympathy with the Jews and had urged them to emigrate to the safety of Israel.

He said that a leading local Zionist had referred him to Slánský, who was to give him concrete directives on how to make use of the law of restitution of Aryanized Jewish property in Slovakia. By manipulating into Zionist hands the property of even those Jews who never came back from the concentration camps he was to expand their economic power, thus putting them into positions which would enable them to overthrow the new democratic regime of Czechoslovakia.

No one who knew anything about Oscar's job could have supposed that it was connected with property restitution, and even less did he have the power for such manipulations. If ever a decision concerning some little village grocery or textile shop and its former owner was made on his initiative, the paper needed a number of signatures from higher-ups in Bratislava and Prague.

Then followed his story about a series of conspiratorial meetings held at our home, naming a number of people.

I knew, of course, only too well who had been frequenting our home and consuming my expensive coffee, and I recalled only too well their loyal rantings. Politeness and my husband had forced me to partake in these evenings against my will.

He said that he went to Prague in August 1947 to see Slánský and work out a plan for putting Zionists and bourgeois nationalists into crucial positions in the economy regardless of class descent. Between the two of them it was decided to brand as anti-Semites all who might raise objections to this line.

If my husband had ever met Slánský I would have known about it particularly in 1947 when – considering their respective positions at that time Oscar would certainly have told me about an event so exciting as meeting the First Secretary. It never happened, of course.

He said further that he had received a letter from Slánský with directives on granting permits to emigrating Jews to take with them expensive machinery in order to undermine the country's economy. 'I also got an answer to my letter concerning anti-Semitism,' my husband added.

Presiding Judge: 'What did you do with these letters?'

Langer: 'I destroyed them.'

Presiding Judge: 'Why?'

Langer: 'Because it was dangerous to keep documents that could unmask the hostile activities of Slánský and his associates.'

This was the only part of the transcript that contained a grain of truth, although the destroyed letters never existed. Oscar *did* write a letter to the Prague Central Committee, addressed to the first Secretary, in which he called the Party's attention to the fact that anti-Semitism, so widely propagated and still virulent in Slovakia after its years as Hitler's show-window republic, was not being sufficiently counteracted by Party propaganda. He raised the question whether 'the Party should not do more about this in its work of enlightenment before anti-Semitism could infiltrate, by way of the rapidly growing membership, the Party itself.'

There was no need to destroy Slánský's answer because he never sent one. Far from being a Zionist agent, he was one of those communists who hate being Jews so much that they would destroy another Jew rather than hand him a crumb.

Subsequently, both Slánský and my husband were accused of and confessed to a number of other heinous crimes. But at this point it was the Zionist element in their well-planned mosaic which the Party was concentrating on, and they needed Oscar as a stone to fit in to the pattern. His own secret trial was to come more than a year later, when eleven of the Slánský 'gang' had already been hanged.

A few minutes after lunch our cadre official, Comrade Kafana, appeared in the room where I was sitting with several others. He had the special edition of *Pravda* in his hand. After reading out the headlines he pointed to my husband's name over the confession which was printed in full as a dialogue between the Presiding Judge and the accused. I must have been in a state of shock because I am quite unable to recall my first reaction or that of my colleagues. I remember only the burning sense of humiliation when Kafana made me get up and stand at a distance from my desk while he rummaged through my drawers one by one before telling me that I could take my things and go. Nobody dared to say good-bye.

In the evening a girl and two young men from the office came to see me and we listened together to what was transmitted about the first day of the trial over the radio. My husband's voice sounded normal, like in a telephone conversation, and he was saying exactly what was in the paper. What could we say? My friends found no words of comfort and I had no explanation to give. So we drank the coffee they had brought and they vented their indignation at Kafana and his unspeakable behaviour. He seemed to represent in miniature the evil forces behind the dreadful thing we all knew was going on.

On the second day, the trial began to sound even more absurd. On a sudden impulse, I went to see a young woman who had been Oscar's secretary when he was working at the Party Headquarters in 1947. I was no longer seeking help. All I wanted was to talk to somebody who was 'inside' and who would be able to offer some sort of explanation. Or perhaps I only felt the need to sit with somebody who would rave and cry with me. I knew her to be Oscar's unconditional admirer, his pupil in political science and his ideological confidante where I had failed. In a political sort of way I think she was in love with him.

She was surprised to see me but asked me to sit down. Like a fool, I was expecting her to share my horror and indignation when I started to point out the absurdities in his testimony. She answered in a mild, compassionate tone, but very firmly.

'You know quite well that Oscar and I didn't only work together but also used to discuss everything we thought and did. Also, as his personal secretary I naturally knew of every move he made. However difficult you may find it now to agree with me, you must learn to face facts. If he did not tell me of such an important matter as a personal call on the First Secretary in Prague, he must have had his reasons to keep it a secret. Believe me, it's a dreadful blow to me, too. You know what he has meant to me all this time, but . . .'

At first I was petrified. Then it came to me that I was talking to a creature from another planet with whom I had no common language. Still, I asked her: 'Do you mean to say that it has not even occurred to you that he might not have told you about his trip to Prague for the simple reason that it never took place? Do the others in the trial sound credible to you?'

Perhaps this thought had occurred to her, but if so she was not going to admit it. My husband's confession was published in *Pravda*, and *Pravda* – as its very name implies – prints nothing but the truth.

As the trial continued the press and the radio smothered the nation in poisonous avalanches of lies, lashing up an artificial storm of hatred. Letters collectively signed by all the workers in a factory or all the employees in a firm were printed daily, expressing horror and anger and calling for the death penalty. Leading publicists and many of our foremost writers competed with each other in barbarous rhetoric. One had to read it in order to believe that centuries after the invention of the printing press such bloody – in the real sense of the word bloody – nonsense could be put on paper.

'The head of the most loathsome of all gangs of imperialist agents was answering in court like a trampled snake unable to wriggle free . . .'

'Under Comrade Gottwald's leadership the people will thrust irresistibly forward like a true Stalinist shock brigade, resolved, shoulder to shoulder with the great Soviet Union and the whole peace camp, together with Comrade Stalin, to crown with victory the age-old struggle for peace and socialism . . .'

'No, these fourteen accused creatures – these are not people! . . .'

'The Tito clique has been unmasked. They are a repulsive gang of imperialist lackeys and spies, a band of treacherous cosmopolitans, who serve for dollar pay with equal willingness the British Intelligence Service, the Gestapo and the CIA.'

'The destruction of the criminal gang has confirmed Comrade Gottwald's message pronounced in February 1951: "Trust the Party, comrades!" The Party has not failed us, for it has shown that it deserves the great trust placed in it by our people!'

And as though this demented rhetoric were not enough, the indicted men confessed their crimes in a style that outdid that of the prosecutor, the judge and our literary men.

Of the fourteen in court, eleven were sentenced to death and hanged in early December 1952.

Three were sentenced to life imprisonment. One of them, a good friend, Eugen Loebl, has tried to give an honest account of the trial and his ten years in jail in a book published upon his rehabilitation. The second was Arthur London. Because his wife (who clamoured for his death in a public letter) was the sister of someone high up in the French Communist Party, he was released long before the others and allowed to move to France with his family. What and how much and how he will perhaps one day say or write about the trial is probably up to the Party there. I don't know anything about the third survivor.

***

I think it better to curtail description of the winter months following the trial because these months were so bad that it might easily turn into an orgy of self-pity. I lived by translating the Party's ravings for the edification of Hungarians, and – after having sent an almost coded SOS letter to my husband's American cousin – on what I could sell of the used clothes, coffee, chewing gum and knitting wool which she sent in occasional parcels. Being without a job, I had no ration cards, which meant buying food on the 'free market' at almost double price. At one point an elderly gentleman who had known my husband as a boy started organizing a group of friends who would collect a small monthly contribution for us. I wasn't allowed to know who the others were, and had to collect the money in a very discreet manner late at night at his flat. This only happened once, however, because the good man was a Jew and the police soon warned him to stop what looked to them like a Zionist conspiracy.

I lived in constant fear. While I was desperate for a first sign of life from my husband, I was afraid of the form it would take. I was terrified of the police, afraid to be arrested as an imperialist spy when I went to the post office to pick up an American parcel, afraid to open the newspaper in the morning, afraid to switch on the radio, afraid when Susie came home from school (expecting every day to hear that she was expelled), afraid that the translations would stop coming, afraid of deportation when the first rumours about 'Operation B' started circulating, and afraid beyond words for little Tania who was inevitably affected even though she could not understand by what. She refused to eat the little food we had and was getting thinner and paler from day to day. One winter morning, after a bad cold, she fell unconscious, pale green in the face, mouth open, in convulsions. I had to leave her like this while I ran to phone for a doctor from the nearby pub, and I was convinced that help would come too late. When the doctor came and restored her to consciousness with an injection, she assured me that it was only malnutrition and lack of calcium – plus my influence. After that I realized that from now on I would have to be

93

afraid of myself as well, and cuddling the fragile warm little body to my breast I made a firm decision to stop being afraid once and for all.

Thinking back, I can't tell how much this decision taken for my children's sake helped me to steel myself, or how much should be ascribed to the mysterious quality in humans that enables them to get used to almost anything. But the fact remains that after this shock I began to take everything more or less in my stride.

So I kept my composure when two uncommunicative persons appeared to make a detailed inventory of our belongings in case my husband should be sentenced to loss of property. When I tried to object, arguing that he hadn't yet come up for trial, they pretended not to hear. The paper I had to sign stated that none of the listed items could be sold or given away. Since the list included everything from underwear and spoons to the furniture stacked at the back of the yard, when our turn in 'Operation B' came, we had to lug along stuff for which we had no use nor place, and our bookcases and books continued to rot in a shed behind the pigsty. The men assured me that when confiscation came, we would be allowed to keep whatever minimum of furniture and household equipment the children and I would need for one room. I thanked them.

A couple of weeks later I was summoned to the National Committee where they handed me the decree. We were to move out on the 5th of March, and I was allowed to choose between two villages. The man in charge took great pains to stress how lucky I could consider myself, seeing that I had three weeks' notice and could choose, while others often had to leave the city on shorter notice and go to whatever place they were assigned to. The names of the villages were new to me, but since they let me take a glance at a map I chose the one that was nearer. I thanked the man for this privilege.

My husband's first letter reached us two days after this. It was written in capital letters on a small sheet of lined paper, giving a coded address to which I could send my answer in a limited number of words. It did not reveal his whereabouts, and its contents seemed to confirm the impression I got when I heard him on the radio, that they must have driven him mad. After having publicly incriminated himself no less than the men who had been hanged, he now wrote that he was very well and hoped to join us soon at home. What else could I answer than that we were happy to hear that he was well, that we too were very well and that we hoped to see him soon. I gave the new address without explanation.

And yet, inexplicable and frightening as the letter was, it still lit a spark of hope and mobilized me into action. It was more than a sign of life, it was proof that he was still being held in custody on remand, without having been tried and sentenced. I wrote to Prague asking to be received by Bacílek, the Minister of National Security, and a positive answer arrived within three days. Only, by then I'd had time to think and to see that this was not only an utterly hopeless but also a humiliating undertaking. Not long ago, shortly after the mass executions, this same Bacílek had publicly praised the personnel of the State Security forces for having worked tirelessly day and night to unmask the conspiracy, for having proved their loyalty to the Party, to Comrade Gottwald and the Soviet Union. I did not believe a single word of the trial. Why was I then going to see this arch-murderer, what did I expect from him? Was it a perverse wish to go into the lion's den to get a sniff of its stink? Was it out of a sense of duty that I wrote, or was it simply a piece of bravado? I didn't want to go. But now it was too late and too dangerous to stay away.

On the night express I found a place in an empty compartment by the window, hung up my coat, huddled up behind it, and putting my feet on the opposite seat I went to sleep. It must have been towards dawn when I half awoke to a sound which did not startle me but woke me gently, and I remained motionless for fear that it might stop. Something inside of me, that shock, fear, overwork and compassionate loyalty to my husband had paralysed, frozen and repressed, began now to move, melt and flow all over my body in a tide of painful pleasure. What I heard was the peaceful rhythmical breathing of a sleeping man. I had not heard a sleeping man breathe next to me for years. And at that moment, in that mood, this struck me as the greatest injustice of all, as a loss towering above all the others I had suffered. In the faint light of a single small blue bulb above the door I could discern no more than the sketchy outline of somebody sleeping sitting upright, an ability I always envied men travelling by night. I listened to the breathing, sensing or imagining that I sensed a male emanation from that stranger's body. Deeply ashamed of myself, I crept back behind my coat. But I could not sleep again. Not quite, at least. In a sweet, exciting doze I was reliving every moment of desire and fulfilment I had ever known. I wanted desperately to be touched.

I don't know whether he had seen me watching him or whether my silent intensity in some mysterious way penetrated his sleep. Quite possibly I shifted my feet to touch him. I don't know. Nor did I then care. All I knew was that I felt his fingers lightly encircling my ankles and when I did not budge, smooth, hot hands began to stroke my feet and my legs. Anonymity in the dark was a silent mutual arrangement that enhanced the intoxicating interplay of nothing but senses. All that had been repressed and dead in me for so long now rushed to meet this stranger's hand, and every one of my toes responded with greater intensity and passion to his touch than my whole body had done in long nights of love. I felt myself slipping away, miraculously relieved of the eternal compulsion of rational thinking, in wordless communication with a mysterious presence beyond reason. However, when my feet were firmly pulled into his lap it became evident that what was enough to carry me away into a seventh heaven of my own was only the first step towards what a normal man was entitled to expect from a woman who had gone as far as I had done. When I pulled back my feet and crept out from behind my coat, he was all over me, stroking my hair, trying to kiss me, fumbling with my blouse. I felt like a despicable bitch when I pushed him back, because his approach was sweet and gentle. Fortunately, the train pulled into a station and a new passenger entered the compartment and switched on the light. The boy was back on his seat, with a nice hopeful smile on his face, proposing in a whisper that we should have breakfast together and then meet in the afternoon. Relieved and thankful for the interruption as I was, I returned his smile. He was very young, and his extreme handsomeness was accentuated by what, unfortunately, does so often enhance male beauty: an immaculate, well-cut uniform. He was a young State Security man. For a brief moment I considered meeting him after all, and a few ugly thoughts passed through my mind about what I would have a chance to do to him. However, feelings of tenderness and gratitude prevailed. His eyes reminded me of the eyes of Blackie, the cocker spaniel I had to abandon in New York. When the train stopped in Prague, he joined a couple of colleagues and I disappeared in the crowd.

The audience lasted no more than ten minutes and was as senseless as I expected it to be. After entering an enormous panelled room I had to walk quite a distance before getting anywhere near the desk behind which Bacílek was sitting. He looked even more like a toad than in photographs. Less terrifying than loathsome. Something of an anticlimax. He knew my husband and listened politely, nodding and making notes on a large sheet of paper. Only a year or so earlier I would have interpreted his manner and the whole audience as a huge and promising success. Now I already knew that when he said that he would look into the matter carefully, do what he could and let me know, he was only making use of the civilized mask carefully worn by the top hierarchy. He even shook hands with me when I left, a thing Kafana would never have done. Needless to say, I never heard from him again.

On the way out I passed a group of four or five young officers lining up to enter for a group audience. Perhaps they were going to get medals for exceptionally well done work. As capricious fate would have it, the last in the row was the boy from the train.

Poor Blackie, I thought. Surely, most of the man-eating beasts snarling in the concentration camps and on our borders could have grown up elsewhere into faithful, lovable pets.

I find it difficult to account for the absence of any sort of beauty, natural or man made, that characterizes the typical Hungarian village. After all, Hungarian peasants are known for meticulously hand-embroidered and colourful national costumes, for a unique treasury of folksong and dance and for exquisite objects of age-old peasant art. However, their aesthetic feeling seems to have stopped short and gone blind where the environment begins. The village where we got a room and kitchen vacated by a single man who was doing forced labour in a mine was situated on very fertile land and was known to have been prosperous. With its several thousand inhabitants it wasn't even too small. And yet, while it lacked every advantage of a town it offered nothing one hopes for from life in the country. Rows of low, small-windowed white-washed but no longer white houses gave directly onto the road, with no sidewalk in between. And the road was a river of knee-deep mud or of blinding, high-flying dust according to the season and the weather. Here and there a scrawny, hardly man-high acacia; nowhere the smallest stretch of turf, not a single tree offering shade on hot summer days, not a flower anywhere, with the exception of the churchyard where attempts had been made to plant a few bushes – but the bunches of flowers on the graves proved on closer inspection to be of wax. There were, in fact, gardens at the back, not visible from the road, but there the few flowers were crowded out by potatoes and other prosaic plants, and were drowned like everything else, including entrances and verandahs, in chicken-, goose- and duckshit. When passing through such villages by car I had always made a mental note followed by a question mark: how could anyone live in such a place, and why was it that as soon as one came to Slovak, Moravian or Czech villages, although most of these were considerably poorer, the houses took on colour, strips of green grass and a few tall trees appeared, and tiny flower-gardens separated the houses from the road.

I don't know how far this can be generalized, but for me uncertainty and fear were always worse than the disaster I was anticipating. Behind the easiness of my mind in this seemingly catastrophic situation there must have been also a seed from Buddha's tree. A few years earlier I would have been miserable if a bottle of ink had been spilt on a couch. When I was first thrown out of my job it seemed the end. Only a couple of years back I was trembling and fighting for our flat as if it were the world outside which there was no life for us. Until quite recently I had been still undergoing the painful process of being stripped of certain last reminders of my faith in ideas and people. Now, having so little left of both hopes and things, life was easier. For one thing I had become fairly certain that the police had no special use for me. What's more, I felt inebriatingly superior in freedom to those who still had their husbands, jobs, flats, possessions and false illusions to lose, which made them into trembling silent slaves while I could speak up.

That I left Bratislava behind in such a devil-may-care mood was of course also due to the fact that the news of Stalin's death came just as I finished packing. Partly because there was nothing left to cook with or on, but also because I felt a need to celebrate, I took the children out for lunch. At the restaurant we met an old pre-war comrade who was still holding on to some function in the union leadership. He came up to our table and asked in a whisper whether it was true that we were being deported. He refused to believe it, he said, and now that he saw me sitting contentedly in a restaurant he was reassured that it had been the malevolent non-sense he thought it was, spread by the usual rumour-mongers. I heard him out, then said that it was true, that we were leaving next morning, and that if I looked good it was because the old beast had croaked at last. This was a time when some people were crying sincerely and some were informing on others who did not cry loudly and visibly enough. Having said these words, I felt that I was at that moment the only free person in our part of the world, and this elation lingered on long enough to make deportation bearable, something like an adventure.

Spring came late that year, and when we reached our village the mud was still frozen and there were patches of dirty snow here and there. By the time the truck was unloaded it was dark, and when it left I discovered that two suitcases of clothes and a small orien-tal silk carpet were missing. The carpet was a keepsake from Budapest, the one thing I had from my childhood home, and, in fact, the only piece of any value in the load. In practical terms, of course, the clothes were the real loss. The only thought I gave the matter was that I would have to account for the carpet, which was listed for confiscation.

Our landlord, Mr Kovács, was the only one left in the village of a family which – judging from the location and size of his house –

must have been one of those prosperous peasant clans that used to branch out into business. The low, long building encircled a huge yard containing sheds, stables and all sorts of workshops. The brother into whose place the police had brought us turned out to have been the owner of the now empty and locked butcher's shop in the front. Another brother, with his family, had received the 'white ticket' two years earlier, which meant deportation to Sudetenland to take the place of deported Germans. Mr Kovács himself was blacklisted as a kulak; in fact he was so black that the agricultural co-operative which he had refused to join when pressure was greatest could not accept him now even if he changed his mind, which he hadn't done. After keeping him under arrest for a week or so for his refusal, they let him go, the co-operative took his land and his cattle, and he was allotted a few acres way out at about two hours' distance by horse and waggon. I heard him leaving in the mornings at about half past three. I could never understand how he managed all alone with only two horses, but however much of an exploiting kulak he had been in his time, the man could work. His wife stayed at home with two little girls, expecting a third child, caring for a few chickens, ducks and a cow they were allowed to keep. There was also always a pig, but being an outlaw, it was well hidden.

Having always lived in big cities I knew as much about agriculture as I did about astronomy – or less, because while I could vaguely distinguish the Big Dipper from the Milky Way, I couldn't tell sugar beets from tobacco, wheat from oats or baby ducks from baby geese. This gave rise to great hilarity when, after a time of understandable hostility towards the strangers who had been dumped on them, the local people became friendly. I was then taken along to the fields where in the summer, miraculously enough, things were actually growing.

I helped to single sugar-beet and pick garlic, which was gathered into big baskets after the stem had been cut off with a sharp knife.

Mr Kovács was indestructible. He took the régime and its antics as a temporary joke which he and his kind would outlive. He must have had the money to bribe local functionaries, because he wasn't afraid of persons in whose presence everyone else trembled. When, shortly after our arrival, President Gottwald died, the Kovács family, who lived at the other end of the huge yard, invited us for a festive dinner and served delicacies which we hadn't tasted or even seen for years: home-made spicy sausage, freshly baked bread, goose-liver, fried chicken, cake with real whipped cream, and quantities of delicious wine.

Understandably enough, the joke Mr Kovács enjoyed most of all was the state the local agricultural co-operative was in. His single cow gave more milk in one day than the entire collective stable of miserable skeletons produced in a week – before their tuberculosis was diagnosed and they were all slaughtered. His sly peasant's brain worked like a computer, keeping precise track of the co-operative's financial situation. Interestingly enough, he ascribed its failure not to the system itself but rather to the incompetence and dishonesty of the people in charge. Peasants who knew how to use their heads and hands and didn't shirk hard work, he said, had gradually reached a certain prosperity which qualified them to be treated as kulaks. The luckiest of them, therefore, were now badly paid workers in the co-operative, living and supporting their families mainly on what they managed to steal. On the other hand, people whom the whole village knew to be hopeless boozers, and who were consequently have-nots when the 'revolution' came, were therefore automatically considered proletarians, and thus reliable enough to be entrusted with collectivization (with police help) and with leading the co-operatives. Mr Kovács was convinced that he could make even such a harebrained invention as an agricultural co-operative work if they let him, and for all I know, he may have been right.

I did not need to hear my landlord's financial and political analysis to know that the co-operative was going to the dogs. From our window I could see the main building, the stables and the yard across the street. Rusty machines were standing about, some in pieces, none repaired, none ever in motion. If ever anybody appeared to load or unload a truck, it was done with lazy reluctance and carelessly. Consequently, the place stank of neglect. The members were assigned to work they did not know or care for and were paid very little cash. The rest of their wages they were supposed to get in kind out of what was produced. If the crops failed, they got little or nothing. It was a vicious circle. Earning too little, they worked badly, working badly, they had no earnings; and since they had to live, they were stealing fodder to take home for their geese and a secret pig or two. Everybody knew that, but nobody seemed to be willing to do anything about it. So the cows got sick and gave no milk, and – to our never-to-be-forgotten horror – when Tania and I once crossed the big yard of the co-operative, we saw two horses lying behind the shed with outstretched legs. When I asked the stable boy what was wrong with them, he just shrugged his shoulders. They would get up when they wanted to, he said. Next day the horses were still there in the same position. I told Mr Kovács and he had a big laugh, explaining that the animals were simply suffering from starvation. Nobody felt responsible for them, nor did anybody dare to kill them outright out of compassion. They would just be left lying there until they died of hunger. Which they did, but not until ten days later.

The good soil of the back gardens, the tenacity of the people and the general simplicity of country life made existence here easier and generally more normal than it was in the capital. There were only three shops: a grocery, a generally empty vegetable shop and a shoe shop. While women in Bratislava were constantly run-ning around and standing in queues for hours every day, often going on a wild goose chase when the rumour spread that apples or nylon panties could be bought somewhere, here we knew from day to day what the situation was. If it happened that there was a delivery of cheese or a few kilos of lemons or a barrel of pickled fish, one did or did not get one's share, but there was no running and no standing in line. Nylon panties and such were, of course, not interesting here. Also, since the population formed an uncom-plicated but firmly united bloc against the régime, the oppressive fear of informers was absent. The government was represented by a few implanted foreigners, functionaries who were glad of their well-paid sinecures, and being even more simple and incompetent than their city counterparts, they were sloppy in their work, fairly easy to bribe or to circumvent. Deportations, forced collectiviza-tion, nationalization of the shops, the initial omnipresence of police and political propagandists, the sending away of certain per-sons to the mines – all that lay five years back. Things had settled down, life had become what it was and the people tried to make the best of it.

For us, and especially for Tania, deportation at that point proved more of a blessing than a punishment. The child was drinking fresh milk in the stable directly from the cow, and when she visited her friends she was sure to come home munching a giant slice of bread spread with fat and chopped onions, or chew-ing on a chicken leg. In accordance with the new order, there was a newly established day-nursery. Old-fashioned as the mothers were, the number of children was never more than five or six. I left Tania there for a few hours every day, mainly because of the food. The nursery had extra rations, and the two 'aunts' in charge served meals prepared with the genius and dedication common to Hungarian women when handling food. Tania put on weight and her cheeks became rosy.

This idyllic picture only goes to show the truth of the old adage about everything being relative. The village lay three-quarters of an hour from the nearest railway station, and there was no bus. The men who worked in factories in Bratislava, as many did, had to leave at three o'clock at night to catch the train to the nearest town, where they had to wait for another train to get to Bratislava, where they had to take the streetcar or the bus from the station to wher-ever they had to clock in at 6 o'clock. Susie, who was seventeen and was thus one year before graduation, would have had to walk to the station and travel almost an hour to the nearest high-school. I say 'would have had' because she never got the chance. When we went to inscribe her, the headmaster asked questions about her father, and after having made a few telephone calls from another room, he came back to announce that there was unfortunately no place for her. I had to take the chance to send her 'illegally' to Bratislava where her school was willing to let her continue and graduate, on the understanding that I could not expect them to recommend her for further studies. It is more characteristic of the times than of the persons involved that although my husband's sister and brother were living there, Susie had to be a lodger at a schoolmate's house, for which I had to pay a high monthly sum that did not cover food. She got lunches at my sister-in law's, and in the evenings she raided the kitchen where she lived, discovering that acute hunger could be stilled with a handful of breadcrumbs seasoned with mustard.

The water from the pump in the Kovács' yard could be used only for washing and scrubbing floors. Drinking and cooking water had to be fetched from the communal artesian well. It was only a few hundred metres from us, but this seemed a long way with two full pails hanging from the yoke carried across my shoulders. There was electric light, but the current was regularly cut off for several hours every night, and there was a constant shortage of both paraffin and glass mantles for the lamps. Candles were unobtainable.

Glad as I was when winter at last gave way to spring, I soon discovered that the windows had to be kept shut. Not even that kept out the stink of the dunghill in the yard or the literally millions of flies and noisy bluebottles that invaded our place from there. At first I refused to use the strips of sticky flypaper I saw hanging in every house because I couldn't bear the sight of the insects' seemingly endless death struggle. Very soon I got to hate them so that I could have tortured them to death with relish one by one. Not only did I get used to the horrible flypapers, but as the neighbours taught me, on warm summer days I made a big fire in the stove, until the top was red hot, after which I sprinkled it with DDT. This resulted in a dreadful cloud of poisonous smoke, heaps of dead flies on the floor and a few nights of suffocating but peaceful sleep. Thinking back I shudder at the thought that it never occurred to me to ask what the smoke did to us.

Letters from my husband were now arriving more or less regularly every month. Always only a few printed, meaningless and incomprehensibly optimistic words. Only the coded return address was changed. Of course, he made no comment on our new rural address. But the letters were signs of life, and I answered in about the same vein.

A couple of months after us, another 'wife' was brought to our village. Our husbands were friends, only while mine had been high up in economic life, hers had been higher up in the Party machinery itself, which was better. She was getting similar letters and she knew even less than I what it was all about, because nothing was ever published about her husband's 'crimes'. By that time both of us were pretty hardened, and close as we became, we found it relaxing to say openly to each other what we would have never disclosed to anyone else: that our feelings for our husbands were not pure love, longing and pity. All that, and loyalty, was there of course, but there was also anger, resentment and regret at having married them in the first place. She had a little son, and while our children were playing together, we were lustily exchanging the common experiences of women married to men dedicated to the Party.

We agreed on a theory I had developed long ago and had often, I am sorry to say, elaborated on in marital disputes. My contention was that Party members were like monks who had decided to devote their lives to a faith. So they ought to live like monks in their own monasteries where they could hold their eternal meetings, read and discuss their Bible, and occasionally have each other excommunicated or burned. The main advantage of such an arrangement would be, of course, that they would be absolutely forbidden to take wives and make children.

The firm for which my friend had been working as a bookkeeper was more humane than mine, and so – for better or worse – she had a job while I did not. Somewhere halfway between our village and Bratislava she was allowed to work as a warehouse clerk. I say 'worse' because her job entailed getting up in the dark and walking to the station. She was a pretty little woman who never neglected her perfectly bleached hair and her make-up, even on Sundays when there was nothing better to do than to sit in front of her door in a yard which was, even by local standards, exceptionally thickly infected with noisy, aggressive geese and what came with them. I admired her immensely for sticking it out with her morning tramp to the train, often through deep snow, in her stiletto-heeled shoes and thin stockings which she refused to exchange for anything warmer and more practical. All of us had to construct something to lean on. One 'wife' I knew was said to be whoring around and drinking heavily; another was suspected of working for the police to save her job and apartment; some were catching up on Marx. My friend had her hairdo, her eyelashes and her high heels to keep up her morale.

Never much interested in clothes, I rather enjoyed not having to care. I put on whatever seemed to fit the weather, and as Susie told me on her rare visits, I looked a mess. My friend decided – for practical reasons – to keep it a secret that she was Jewish and to go to church with her little boy on Sundays like everybody else. She advised me to do the same, but it was too late. Having arrived earlier, and since the thought never occurred to me, I was by then already known as 'the Jewish lady'. This never hurt us. Instead, as the only Jews in a population of several thousand, it made us into a sort of rarity. The Jewish families who had lived there before the war were generally remembered with liking and expressions of horror at their ultimate fate. It is also probable that the daily pogrom-like rantings of our press and radio helped to silence any dormant anti-Semitism there was. It is possible that, if our press had extolled the merits of the Jews, the village might have turned against us.

In the beginning, a little money was still coming in from translating the Party brochures, and I also had a book on artificial manures to translate. However, this was not enough to live on and pay Susie's rent and modest expenses. Luckily, only a few people in the village knew enough Slovak to cope with bureaucracy. There were petitions to be written, forms to fill in when dealing with authorities, and the people who used to go to the nearest town for help soon heard that I had a typewriter and knew Slovak. I got my customers through a clerk at the local National Committee, a little old hunchback spinster, who was a real monument to the shifting fortunes of this spot in the heart of Europe. For over forty years she had been sitting behind the same desk. She was now serving the fourth régime, from Franz Joseph through Masaryk and the fascists to ours. I don't think it made any difference to her as long as her files were in good order and people gave her due respect. It was said that nobody ever dared to fire her because she knew too much about everybody in the community and for miles around. For my services I got flour, fresh vegetables and fruit in season, and in the fall when pigs were killed, white pudding, black pudding, lard and crackling. And of course butter and eggs. And more eggs. I never ate so many eggs in my life. Since the shop only rarely had bread, the neighbours taught me how to make it, after which it was taken to the baker's and fetched by the children next morning. Tania got a crown a day from our landlord for taking the cow to the well, and as there were no sweets, she spent her money on yeast, for which she developed a passion. I myself had a thing about cows and would never have dared to drive one, walking behind it with a little stick as she did. I knew cows only as I had met them as a child on summer hikes, and my fear was rooted in those years when I was small and they were so immensely big and strong that I could not understand why they let people use, beat and drive them. There were so many cows in a herd that to my childish mind it seemed a logical proposition for them to launch an attack in which they could easily have destroyed their puny masters. It was only a question of mutual communication and common action. If a cow stopped to contemplate me, I took the proverbial dumbness of her gaze for a sly mask behind which I fancied thoughts moving in the direction of my plans for her and her sisters. But Tania, untouched by such revolutionary dreams, continued undaunted in her chore, and I was careful not to infect her with my fixed idea. The end of her cowherding came when one day she came running home crying, tiny as she was, covered to the top of her head with an unspeakable mixture of mud and what her cow had dropped and stepped back into.

Once in a while I left Tania with the neighbours and went to Bratislava to deliver or hunt for work, see the few friends who would see me and renew my supply of reading matter at the library. In those days the janitor in every house had a book in which persons sleeping over as guests of a tenant had to be registered. My trips were therefore difficult and depressing. Banished as I was, I could not go to a hotel. Relatives and old friends were, or more or less justifiably felt that they were, in much too precarious a situation to have me listed as their overnight guest. Since I could meet people only after work and there was no late train, I spent several nights on a bench at the railway station. But then I met others who offered spontaneously to take me in: a girl from my old toothbrush office, a doctor and his wife who hardly knew me – just ordinary people who had never pretended that they were helping all of mankind but who didn't hesitate to take a risk to give help to one person who needed it.

I avoided reading our papers and never listened to the radio until late at night when I could catch the BBC. I heard that the eight Jewish doctors in Leningrad accused of planning to murder Stalin had been released and that Beria had been shot. But where I was, nothing changed and nobody cared. I was longing for Bratislava less and less and preferred to listen to ghost stories and gossip in the village instead of making political speculations.

In early June, however, political reality struck our remote corner in a manner that could not be ignored. Overnight came the currency devaluation. Suddenly fifty crowns in cash were worth one, and only bank deposits of less than 5,000 in a book retained a value of ten to one. Peasants keep their savings in the mattress or in an old stocking because the nearest bank is likely to be a long way away. Exchange took place at the National Committee. The waiting crowd was silent, and although there was great discipline and no complaints, the officials from the capital shouted rude orders at us as if we were a bunch of criminals. Afterwards, losses were not discussed. Legally, nobody was supposed to have enough of a fortune to suffer much. When all was over we knew that a young couple had committed suicide. They had cash saved up for kitchen furniture and were waiting their turn in a queue to hear when they could buy it in the nearest town. Now they couldn't have paid for a chair. I had less than 200 crowns, so my loss was negligible.

My escape was reading. In the library I discovered an old edition of the complete works of Anatole France in six beautifully bound and illustrated volumes. I read them from beginning to end, including the ones I already knew, looking up every unknown word in a dictionary. I think I was mostly fascinated by the beauty of the language. After that came all of Proust.

Quite unexpectedly, I got a job. There was a little pharmacy run by its former owner and his wife who did the laboratory work. In late summer a new government decree came out to the effect that former owners were no longer allowed to run their own pharmacies. This resulted in a sudden uprooting and migration of chemists and their families. The couple was transferred to somewhere else, and the former owner there was put in charge of our pharmacy. He was a nice elderly Hungarian, understandably unhappy at being obliged to leave the business he had founded and run for almost forty years. Being a bachelor, he also had to find a new laboratory assistant. On the departing couple's recommendation I got the job. Three or four hours a day, no fixed time, according to need. I learned how to mix, weigh out minute portions on a tiny scale and then distribute powders on small paper sheets which had to be folded in a very special way. He taught me how to use a marble pestle to pound and mix various ingredients in a small mortar. I learned to mix ointments, salves and creams and fill them neatly into jars. Soon I was able to read most of the doctor's prescriptions and give out patent medicines on my own. There was also a little old machine in which pills and suppositories were pressed. The place had beautiful old wooden shelves with rows and rows of china jars and dark bottles, never used, but carrying decorative Latin inscriptions suggesting exotic fragrances and poetic associations with classic poetry. I liked it.

My boss came from the old Hungarian gentry. He was a passionate music lover with an immense collection of records, mainly operas. While playing them, he liked to show the albums containing his other collection – letters and autographed photographs of world-famous opera singers. He was also a deeply religious man, and I spent many pleasant evenings after work listening to discussions between him and his new friend, the local priest. This old man had in fact been a professor of theology, sent to this post as a minor punishment when on the occasion of a casual house search the police found a few letters and greetings from an old friend who happened to be Cardinal Mindszenty. The two men and the doctor, who looked in almost daily at closing time, liked my company and the biscuits I baked out of my inexhaustible supply of fresh eggs. I enjoyed the wine, the music and the adventure of entering through these men a world hitherto unknown to me. Here I was sitting with a bunch of arch-enemies who represented everything we had condemned and who were supposed to despise everything I represented: I, a Jewess and the wife of a communist, sitting with three reactionary Goyim, one of them a professional one. Paradoxically enough, they were much more tolerant of the régime than I. While to me it was a dreadful disappointment, to them it was a pleasant surprise compared with what they had once thought bolshevism would bring. The professor had lost his chair, but he was preaching to a full church and had been neither roasted on a spit nor shot or worse, as happened – so they knew – in Spain during the civil war. True, the doctor was getting a very low fixed salary for which he had to see hundreds of people a day, which was pure nonsense. But he was living very well on what he got from patients who wanted serious examination and treatment. On the whole they thought that although the communists were responsible for a lot of injustice and for stupid government and were shamelessly lying their heads off, at least they did not kill en masse like the fascists, and when they did kill it was mostly each other, which was not so bad.

For quite a while they made kind and earnest attempts to convert me to the Catholic faith, and then they compromised and would have been satisfied to convert me at least to what they thought should be my own. Never did I need faith more than then, and I really tried. But I was and remained a hopeless case. I was quite incapable of producing the intellectual absurdities I was asked to produce. I begged their pardon sadly, they forgave and gave up, and we remained friends on a strange basis of mutual curiosity and tolerance.

On a summer Sunday Mr Kovács took us along to his faraway fields. While his wife and I were helping with the garlic, the children caught tiny green frogs to take home. In a tall glass with a little wooden ladder in it they would foretell the weather. We were unpacking the lunch basket when a boy came running from the road shouting my name. A strange 'uncle' had come to see me, and the boy's father, who knew where we were, had offered him a ride.

Looking up towards the road, shading my eyes against the sun, I saw my husband's tall slim silhouette emerging against the light. I jumped to my feet and, catching Tania on the way, I ran up the slope. In that single moment, resignation to the point of indifference gave way to a surge of indescribable joy and love. With no trace of surprise in between. Nothing seemed more natural and logical than that he should have come at last.

A few seconds were enough to see that it wasn't Oscar but his brother who had suddenly decided to visit us. In fact, they didn't look much alike, and under normal circumstances I would have never mistaken one for the other from twice as far. Which goes to show that in spite of all I still loved him and did not seriously believe that they could sentence him.

But they did.

***

The garlic was drying in the shed, ripe plums were bubbling in a big cauldron in the yard, the geese were getting fat and subdued and the BBC was sounding frolicsome about evident signs of de-Stalinization when I signed at the post office for the following registered letter:

Prague, 29th September, 1953

LEGAL ADVICE CENTRE NO I

We inform you herewith that our member Dr Vorel defended your husband at the Supreme Court in Prague today. Your husband was found guilty of high treason and espionage and was condemned to twenty-two years' imprisonment. Secondary punishments are confiscation of property and loss of civil rights for ten years.

Hail to Peace!
Sg. Dr Vorel

In Hungarian and in a few other languages, a certain auxiliary verb is prefixed to the main verb when addressing someone politely in a request or a question. This little prefix can be roughly translated as 'to find pleasing', but a sentence cast in this specific polite form cannot be adequately rendered in English. This makes it impossible for me to convey the excruciating tragi-comedy of the honestly well-meant question Mr Kovács asked me when I met him early next morning in the yard.

'We couldn't help thinking about you all night, my wife and I,' he said. 'I hope you don't mind me saying this, but we just kept asking ourselves how come you don't find it pleasing to commit suicide . . .'

An official letter followed soon, giving my husband's new address and announcing that I could now apply for permission to visit him.

His first letter after this was written almost two months later, in November, and showed that several of my letters had never reached him.

'The last letter I have from you was written in August. That's a long time. I hope you have received the letter I wrote after my trial, if not, I repeat that the essence of the sentence is twenty-two years and loss of property. I ask you not to despair and to hold out. Try to arrange your life so that it is as bearable as possible for both you and the children, *without any regard to me*, including divorce if you should be so advised. I am afraid I shall have to renounce your visit, much as I long for it. I am very far away, the trip would cost too much and visits are very short. Unless you could secure ahead of time a special permission that would allow us to talk longer, and also about my case. Such a visit would be *extremely* important. Up to the day of my trial I knew nothing of what happened during the past two years. I should like to write more, philosophical and emotional considerations, but I lack both space and possibility. I am constantly with you in my thoughts, trying to make a picture for myself of how the children are developing, of your life. Perhaps it is worse, perhaps better than my picture of it. One meets both bad and good people everywhere. Even here. All my love to all of you. Daddy.'

Theoretically we were allowed to write every fortnight, and of course I did. But his next letter was dated 10th December.

'I was deeply moved by your letter of 18th November. This was the first news from you since August, and no photos arrived. I too will put in my application for the visit. Your application was complied with but no date was set. It is of utmost importance to me *to talk* to you. Not only for emotional reasons, much as I long to see you. This is not for my own sake in the first place. What is foremost in my mind is that I want to make you understand that neither you nor our children need to be afraid because of me and my past of looking into the eyes of decent people and mainly into those of every honest communist. Don't worry too much about me. As to where I work and your other questions I can't give you any answers. I am healthy. Don't think I did not worry about you all this time. But I have been constantly reassured – and that is what they tell me here as well – that according to our laws neither you nor the children can be subjected to any discrimination or harassment in employment, school or social life. The court hearing was secret, but the sentence is not. You should try to procure a written sentence stating its grounds. When it was pronounced, I was too dumbfounded to ask for it and my defence attorney forgot to remind me. Write about everything. I don't even know where Susie goes to school. Try to get away from that village. Don't be too modest in your demands in this respect, and I repeat that none of you needs to harbour any feelings of inferiority because of me. Try to send the photos here. But nothing else. I will be with you in my thoughts during the holidays. The new year will be hopefully a happier one for us. I love you and the children above all . . .'

After that we were theoretically allowed to exchange a letter a week. The censor held up so many that we were often without news for months. Most of our letters referred to information never received and to our having been worried. And yet the file I kept of almost ten years of such correspondence would make a book in itself. We wrote most about the children. Our love and longing for each other, expressed and repeated over and over, was perhaps never so real, intense and sincere as in these years. Aside from these feelings, which were true, both of us were of course lying about our respective situations and health. After a while, my husband took courage and started giving me instructions and tasks in connection with his case, which he wanted to have re-opened. Knowing the political situation and the fate of so many others, as he did not, I also knew that everything I undertook on his orders was hopeless. But I did go to see his defence lawyer in Prague who told me disgustedly that if my husband had listened to him he could have got away with ten years. But he had been stubborn and had refused to confess. It also turned out that the two of them had met for the first time ten minutes before the trial. Although this lawyer assured me that absolutely nothing could be done, I came away from this visit immensely relieved. The fact that this despicable tool of our unspeakable juridical system was accusing Oscar of stubbornness was the first definite proof I had of my husband's sanity. I also wrote to the Supreme Court and went to see the judge who had presided at the trial. Thus I got entangled in a network of unbelievably shameless lies. The lawyer said he did not have the relevant papers because they were filed at the district court where Oscar had been tried in the first instance. The district court did not – and could not – have the papers because what the lawyer said about a first instance was a lie. There never had been one: Oscar was tried and sentenced in secret by the Supreme Court, and that was that. The judge kept me waiting for several hours and then took two minutes to tell me with a cynical smile that there had never been such a case in the Court. I wrote to the President, as bidden, but there was no answer. My husband did not seem to understand why I did not make further attempts, and began to sound reproachful. I could not explain. We lived on two different planets, and although many letters were exchanged, at that point we knew very little about the other's life: how little, was revealed only when we met again after ten years of separation.

Only here and there can I find a smuggled-in meaningful sentence that escaped the censor's attention or was beyond his grasp.

21st October, 1953
'Having had much time to think I have come to consider people's attempts at assimilation a tragic error. Heine failed, and so did Fast.'

What made him turn to thoughts of Jewishness became clear only almost two years later when his first smuggled-out letter reached me with instructions to copy it out and send it to the President, the Central Committee and several other high places. It was a detailed twelve-page description of how our police made him confess by methods which differed from those of the Gestapo in their greater sophistication, but not in ideology. But to this letter I want to revert in the context of events.

Now and then we tried to cheer each other up with sparks of humour. He wrote that as a result of my glowing descriptions of Susie's budding beauty she had acquired several admirers there, although 'many of my colleagues here would admire her even more if she had telephoned to Truman rather than to Stalin.'

I wrote that when the little Kovács baby was born, Tania absolutely wanted us to have one too. When I promised to have one as soon as her father came home, she said: 'No, Mummy, you must get it now, and imagine how glad Daddy will be when he comes and finds a brand new baby!'

In one letter I tell how Tania asked me one evening how to say in Hungarian 'Kiss my arse', a proposition quite often made in Slovak. She explained that she needed to learn the phrase for next day, when she expected to meet again the 'ugly boys' who had hollered at her 'We know that your father is in jail, boo!'

Susie was alone in Bratislava and in love up to her ears for the first time in her life. He was a schoolmate, and one Sunday she brought him along. They were both seventeen and made a handsome couple, but I thought that he was rather dumb, and was worried to death about what would happen on the socialist harvest brigade they were being sent on together. In 1954 such brigades were already considered a necessary evil, to be shirked if possible, but these two were very much looking forward to it. All I could do was to give my daughter a quick, concentrated course in physiology with less emphasis on what not to do than on how not to do it. The days of the Pill were far away, abortions were unobtainable, and if done and discovered, punished with three to five years. She listened patiently and I did not ask what was new to her. When the two of them left hand in hand, I felt weighed down with responsibility, helpless, abandoned, worried and a little envious.

It was about then that a university student dance band discovered Susie as a singer. It was her hobby to listen late into the night, patiently, over and over, to the same songs transmitted by foreign radio stations, until she had learnt them and could write down the English texts. Ella Fitzgerald was her God; and she got down a lot of Gershwin, Cole Porter and some of the latest hits. As this sort of music was unobtainable on records or otherwise, it was all the more loved by the young. Once she sang into a microphone at a dance and had a terrific success. The band asked her to continue with them and offered her money, but her school warned her not to do it, at least not before she had got her high school diploma. They were taking a risk anyhow, they said, letting her take the examination.

The brochures for translation stopped coming, and by the time the manure book finally came out, the currency devaluation had reduced to a pittance the sum in the contract on which I had expected to live for several months. I was unable to pay Susie's rent and she was sleeping on a couch where a friendly family was giving her temporary refuge. She finished high school with excellent marks but further study was out of the question. I wasn't there, I couldn't help her, I couldn't even support myself and Tania. It became imperative to give her a home, to help her make plans for her future, to find work for her and myself. All of this was impossible so long as I stayed where I was.

Slowly but surely the rumour spread, and then it was confirmed by a few cases: the return to the city of people deported in 'Operation B' was tolerated if they were able to stay with relatives or could find themselves living quarters. They could not claim their own flats back but by now, two years after it had been put into practice, it was beginning to be whispered that the 'Operation' had been an illegal excess. My friend, whose husband had been sentenced in the meantime to fifteen years, was given a room and a kitchen in the little town where she was working. I started answering ads in the papers, trying to land a job somewhere, anywhere, so long as the firm would give us a room.

Nothing. Until at long last, with the help of friends of friends of a lady I didn't even know, I got an address in Bratislava.

It was that of an elderly widow of a lawyer and her spinster daughter, who lived in the city's outer suburbs in what might have been a villa before the war, but was now so neglected that it hardly resembled a house. There were two rooms, but they lived, cooked and slept in only one of them because the roof had collapsed over the other. In the little backyard some steep wooden steps led down to the door of two rooms in the basement, one narrow, the other larger. The windows were fitted with thick iron bars and were high enough to give a view of a passer-by about up to the knees. There was electricity and a sink with running water. To reach the privy one would have to climb up the steps and then up a little hill, but the wooden structure was falling apart and my future landlady remarked that it could not be used. A notice was stuck on the door of the bigger room announcing that the premises had been inspected and found to be uninhabitable by the National Committee and that the owner was forbidden to rent them out. The landlady assured me that this inspection was such an old story that nobody would ask, and named a rather high monthly rent. I didn't care; indeed, I was delighted. At last we had a home in Bratislava where we would be together with Susie and where we had at least a chance to find some sort of work

In early June we moved in. Hardly a week later two men from the National Committee arrived with a paper declaring not that we had no right to live in Bratislava, since it was true that we had never been legally deprived of such a right; nor that the rooms were certified uninhabitable; but they had been officially assigned to somebody else. We were to move within a week. Where to? That wasn't their business, they said, and on the way out one of them turned round to drop a hint that I might well end up living in prison if we did not get out.

I don't want to go into detailed description of the following days. I was in a frenzy and firmly decided not to give in. I wrote to the President, to the Central Committee, to the National Committee and to the governor of the prison camp. I went to see a lawyer, a judge, an old friend of my husband's who was still working at party headquarters, journalists, writers and everybody whom I believed to have some sort of connections. The officials promised nothing, the letters remained unanswered, but in the party members whom I hadn't seen for years I noticed a great change. None of them said so in so many words, but it was evident beyond any doubt that all of them knew as well as I did that the Slánský trial had been a gigantic fake, the hangings murders, and that we were living in a cesspool. I was at the bottom and they were in yachts on the top, but the stink was beginning to reach them. It would take them over ten years to begin saying what they already thought in 1954, but their consciences were already sufficiently bad to make them try to help. I don't know what did it in the end. Probably the telephone call a woman writer made to one of her old comrades at the National Committee whom she hysterically called all sorts of names in my presence. In the books that had made her famous years before she had written more enthusiastically and with more emotion than the men writing about the same things at the same time. Now, she was again reacting with unmasculine emotion, and was mad enough to act on her feelings into the bargain.

However, when we finally went for our first visit to my husband in early July we still did not know whether we had a home to come back to or not. The permit and the last decree according to which we were to move out set the same date. But gradually the thing sort of petered out, we were left alone, at least as far as staying put in the basement was concerned, and it became our home for the next six years.

We were to report at the prison camp at nine o'clock in the morning. The summer that year was very hot. We took the night express to Prague and changed trains at dawn to travel several hours more to Northern Bohemia, where the uranium mines are. I was awake all night with Tania on my lap. Susie, finding no other place, had resolutely climbed up into the baggage net above the seats where she could stretch out and sleep a bit. At first, we were too excited and deeply moved to feel exhaustion. We almost ran the whole distance from the station to be there on time. In a few minutes we would be seeing Daddy again after three years. When we arrived we were surprised to see a motley crowd of well over a hundred people already standing in line before the gate. Old peasants, many-skirted women, whole families with children in city clothes, young women alone and groups of gypsies of all ages – the only ones not on their feet, because they didn't mind sitting on the dusty ground. The gate was closed and remained so for three hours. The sun was scorching and there was no shade and no drinking water anywhere in sight. Children began to cry, some ran around and were shouted at by parents who were afraid to move from their place in the queue. Some families began to unpack sandwiches and thermos bottles. The people right in front of us were chatting in a normal tone as if they were in one of the usual queues, for apples or potatoes. They were habitués. But we were new, we had no sandwiches, no water and their behaviour seemed incredibly cynical to us. Of course, after a few years' visiting we became just like them. But this time we had come in a very solemn mood, both sad and elated, expecting to be let in at nine o'clock as the paper said, tidied up as well as we could be after the night's trip, with smiles and first words prepared.

After three hours' standing in the scorching sun with a thirsty, tired child, in an impatient but otherwise seemingly indifferent crowd, our mood faded into anger and exhaustion. When the gate opened at last, at about noon, everybody's thoughts, including my own, centred more on trying not to be pushed back, on aching feet, on thirst and on whether there would be a toilet inside than on the purpose and the emotional implications of our being where we were. Perhaps this was a well-thought-out part of the whole arrangement.

A uniformed man let in only a small group at first. Exclamations of dismay and impatience were heard and the crowd surged ahead. The man planted himself before the entrance with feet wide apart and shouted at us that if we acted like a herd of cattle we could get back on the train and learn to behave better next time. Silence. My heart stopped. But nothing happened; silent group after group was let in, and at about one o'clock it was our turn.

We were led along a corridor to a badly lit room with a few wooden cubicles in a row, like stalls in a stable. Told to step into one of these cubicles, we faced a small window covered with a double layer of fine-meshed wire screen. In a few minutes my husband appeared behind this window with a guard standing close by. We could see him only from the shoulders up. The guard took out a watch and said: 'Ten minutes, no foreign language, only family matters permitted.' What could I say? We looked at each other with tears in our eyes, and smiled. He was very thin, very pale, and looked much older, but when he smiled he was himself. I said that he looked well and he said that I looked well. He tried to say something about his trial but the guard interrupted him. I stepped back to let him see the children. Susie lifted up Tania because the window was too high for her. The holes on the wire mesh were just big enough to let through her little finger and he kissed it. The ten minutes were over and he was led away

After that we didn't receive a single letter for five weeks. Only years later did we know that for having kissed Tania's little finger he was punished with a week's isolation in a dark cell and prohibition of correspondence for a month. There was a regulation forbidding bodily contact between prisoners and their visitors.

***

After all this time it is difficult for me to find the right words for our landlady and her daughter. Were they evil, quaint, peculiar or outright mad? As both of them are dead by now, I prefer to describe rather than to judge.

At first they were all smiles, sympathy and helpfulness. Once it became apparent to them that we were still being persecuted and they saw me stiffen with fear every time a truck happened to climb the little-used road, they doubled the rent. During the first months of total insecurity the daughter, who otherwise hardly ever left the house, would make mysterious trips to town and come back dropping dark hints at bad news for us, refusing to say more. This would be followed by a further raise in rent. My proposal to pay half of their telephone bill against occasional use of the instrument was at first accepted, then refused – for security reasons, so they said.

As my position became more secure, depriving them of opportunities for emotional and financial blackmail, they had to limit themselves to minor harassments. I became a partly irritated, partly amused observer of the life they led; and to this day I can't tell if it was a tragedy or a joke. They were living on a small pension the mother was getting after her husband's death, a sum hardly more than what I paid in rent. Pension and rent together would just have covered the very modest basic monthly needs of two normal persons, but they lived way below this level. The girl, somewhere between twenty-five and thirty, was allegedly preparing for her entrance examination to the university although we never saw her with a book. Both of them refused to seek employment. Both of them spent the day in old tracksuits, never washed, and slept in them as well. On the few occasions when I was invited upstairs, talk centred around the mother's revolutionary youth and her interrupted medical studies. I never saw them eat anything but bread, thin garlic soup and potatoes. Their little iron stove was used only when they cooked potatoes, never for heating. Against the cold they crawled into bed under a pile of quilts without covers. They owned a huge orchard about half an hour's tiring walk away. It was as neglected as the house, but a few apple trees still bore fruit, and in late summer the mother (never the fat, lazy daughter) would plod up and down the hill, lugging home heavy sacks of tiny unripe apples. If she didn't pick them now, she said, somebody would steal them. The apples were then dumped and left to rot in the tub of the former, now roofless, bathroom.

In moments of exceptional communicativeness the mother would call me in and show me a box with things she was keeping for her daughter. There was fine jewellery with precious stones, heavy old gold watches with chains, cigarette cases, rings and coins of gold. Any one of these items would have brought a price big enough to repair the house, the privy and the entrance gate. The orchard alone, if divided into building lots, could easily have been sold for enough money to enable them to spend the rest of their lives in a decent house, under silk-covered quilts. However, she never considered selling or repairing anything. They went on living on potatoes in their unheated room, the laboriously harvested apples rotted in the tub, their stink surpassed only by that of the messes left by the three black cats, by the perpetually reheated garlic soup and by the ever-present, rarely emptied and never disinfected pail used instead of a toilet.

The entrance gate, too, deserves to be remembered. It was of heavy planks and very large. It hung on rusty hinges and lacked a latch. At first there was a hook, but when this broke the landlady started to use a string threaded through the holes left where a lock had once been. After climbing the slippery hill on winter evenings, carrying shopping bags full of whatever I happened to be lucky enough to get in town that day, I had to struggle with ever more intricate knots. After futile discussions about a latch I took to using scissors. This resulted in a further deterioration of our relations. Tania had just started school, and when I complained that the gate was too hard for her to open even if she succeeded in undoing the string, I was told that she was too weak because I did not feed her properly. This answer was accompanied by a hearty laugh. I forgot to say that both of them were constantly laughing, and in fact, in their own way, they were the happiest people I had met in years.

A few years later the girl moved to Prague where she got a job with the state travel agency. Alone, the mother became even more quaint, or odd, or mad. The door to her place was divided into four squares of glass. One day she couldn't find her key on getting home, so she kicked in one of the panes and climbed through the hole. It didn't occur to her to get a new key, she came and went through that hole for months before she found the 'lost' one in her handbag. Years later we heard that the girl died long before her mother. She drowned in the Volga. It was said that having at last found a lover on one of her trips as a tourist guide, she went to bathe with him although she had never learnt how to swim.

In spite of everything, I now thank fate for what these two women were. In 1954 our world was so mad and evil that no really sane person, however good, would have dared to take us in as they did.

Nor, for that matter, would anybody in his right mind have

moved into that place under normal conditions. The floors were rotten, the ceiling was mouldy, with great threatening cracks in it. In the kitchen – I call it that only because there was a sink in it – clusters of slimy mushrooms grew along the wall. There was no stove, and when somebody gave us one in the fall it turned out that the smoke had no place to go. It was two years before I could afford to have a new chimney built, and to this day I don't know why we did not die of smoke poisoning or freeze to death. Yet, Tania remembers the basement as the funny place where she spent a happy childhood, Susie as the impossible but real home she liked to come back to from her hotel rooms between two engagements, and I can laugh with them nostalgically. I was young, and I had found new friends who did not mind the long streetcar ride or climbing our hill. They came to spend evenings with us, filled with serious talk or silly games at our big round table with food and drink on it. This table filled almost the whole room, leaving space only for the one big couch where Tania and I slept together, a cupboard with books and kitchenware and a narrow couch for Susie if she happened to be at home. Years later it took Tania a very long time to learn how to fall asleep in a room where no one was talking and no typewriter was hammering till dawn.

Soon after Susie finished school, when the question of her future had become acute and seemed to be insoluble, the leader of a local dance band entered the picture as a *deus ex machina*. Having heard her sing with a student band he approached me to ask if I would let her work for him. An excellent popular pianist, he was very sure of her talent and her voice, and knowing our situation he advised me to consent. This was certainly not one of the many careers Oscar and I had once planned for our daughter, with her interest in literature, her exceptional talent for languages and her good school record. Wandering Jews that we were, we had never acquired a piano. I knew that Susie could sing dozens of Slovak folksongs learned from the maid when she was hardly three years old, and that she had been much admired in Chicago at the age of five for her rendering of 'God Bless America' and 'Old Black Joe', but I thought of these achievements as part of my child's charm and left it at that. Probably because I always was and still am a musical illiterate. At that time, however, I would probably have consented if someone had offered her work as a professional jockey, after assuring me that she had a great talent for it – and a bandstand was less likely than a horse to throw her.

Susie herself, although she loved to sing, was shy and reluctant at first, but then accepted. A name had to be thought up that would not identify her with her father, she needed an evening gown, and she had two weeks in which to prepare herself for an examination, including theory, which she had to take before an official committee. As she hardly knew the notes, the theory part was a bit of a problem. Fortunately, my new circle of friends included Maria, who played the harp at the opera and was also teaching at the conservatoire. For two weeks she devoted all of her free time and one whole night to hammering into Susie the basics of musical theory, and thanks to her, all went well. This was celebrated with two or three other friends from the theatre and a bottle of gin at home. Only Susie did not drink. From her father she has inherited a distaste for drink which was to prove a real blessing considering her future work environment. Soon posters with her new name appeared in town, a daringly strapless long black dress was made almost overnight by a friend from the contents of an American parcel, and her career began.

At that time singers – with the exception of a few already big names – moved from band to band, from place to place, on engagements lasting from a few weeks to a month or two. All this was arranged between bandleaders, musicians and singers, but contracts were formally procured and officially confirmed against a fee by a state agency led by 'cadres' who knew and cared more about bureaucracy, intrigue and politics than about music. However, the class origins and the political attitudes of artists were scrutinized somewhat less closely than those of citizens in other fields (few, if any, dance bands, would have been left had it been otherwise). Susie met with some initial harrassment, such as objections to her American accent, her decadent intonation and vibrato, and her western repertoire, which had to be counterbalanced with a few Russian numbers every night. But she was quickly appreciated by bands, composers, the public and soon also by the radio, and she was allowed to go on working under her new name. A professor who heard her in a café offered to give her lessons, and while teaching her the basic technique discovered that she had a voice worth developing for opera. He insisted that she leave the bars, but financial necessity as well as her love for jazz soon put an end to these lessons. To make a living, she had to travel. This was just as well, because in her hotel rooms she had the heat and comfort our home could not offer, after a few months in Bratislava she sang through the summer at several holiday resorts, first in Slovakia, then in Bohemia, and in the fall she was already singing as a steady member of a big band in Prague.

Meanwhile I was applying for job after job with no result. I was told that getting a divorce would help.

In the past we had talked about divorce more than once: thoughtlessly in moments of anger and mutual irritation; seriously and calmly in periods of sad estrangement; and often in analytical discussions of our incompatibility which usually ended in tearful promises, reconciliation and renewed love. In retrospect I knew exactly when we should have given up the attempt to live together. I should have divorced him three weeks after our wedding when he made a scene about my having bought a ceramic water pitcher for our new home. There I was waiting for him with my surprise. The pitcher stood in the middle of the white tablecloth, its beautifully curved lacquered belly sparkling in all the colours of the rainbow, a gay spot of beauty in the centre of our common home, which would laugh for us every time we sat down to dinner. True, a pitcher was a necessary thing, he said, but a simple one made out of glass costing less than half would have served the same purpose. It wasn't the money, it was a matter of principle. There were millions who didn't even have clean drinking water. A utilitarian object had no business to be beautiful. I was wasting money, and if I didn't accept his objections it meant I was unable to share his view of life.

I should have divorced him when one night I switched on the light and he quickly switched it off as if making love were something shameful. In fact, for him it was shameful, not out of modesty but because it was good and we had no right to pleasure in a world so full of suffering and poverty. In the very years he taught me to be most enthusiastic about the Soviet Union, people in the Ukraine were eating earthworms or each other and perishing by the millions, but the currently accepted symbol of oppression and poverty was the Chinese coolie. I should have divorced him when I discovered the omnipresence of this coolie. He had a place in our bed and at our table, his emaciated yellow hands covered the pages of the poetry that had been my music – poetry that was just beautiful, not committed. He seemed to fade away only if things were very bad for us.

My husband should have divorced me when I was hard and competitive instead of soft and understanding and patient; when I ridiculed his faith; when in my flight from the coolie I had affairs with other men who did not switch off the light . . .

But divorce him now? Now, when he was innocently suffering, when he needed me, when we were full of longing and saw each other not as what we were but as what we had once loved in each other? Divorce him because the despised enemy would have it so? Never! Not for a stinking job, not for anything!

I was giving a few English lessons and lived mainly on translation and copy-typing jobs nobody else would take, not because they were especially difficult but because as a result of the prevailing sloppiness they were given out too late and had to be done in an impossibly short time. This entailed killing work for several days and nights without sleep. No wonder I find here a postscript on a letter by Tania when she was six years old: 'Dear Daddy, I hope you are all right, we are all right, only Mummy is always typing and at home it's always cold. That's why I am writing this at the Savoy.'

The 'Savoy' was an old café near our streetcar stop for getting home from town. Being only a few steps away from the National Theatre, it was also a hangout for members of the orchestra and the corps de ballet between rehearsals. Through Maria I got to know this crowd of gay, refreshingly apolitical people, some of whom were to become regular guests at our big round table; friends and artistic advisers to Susie when she was at home, and aunts, uncles, playmates and collective parents to little Tania.

Whenever I had to go to the city to fetch or deliver work or take a bath at somebody's house, I took the child along, and before returning to the loneliness of our icy dungeon we used to stop there for a bit of warmth and company. Sometimes we got free tickets to opera or ballet matinées, and the ballet girls were customers for exotic rags from American parcels which nobody else would have dared to wear.

But what I am about to relate took place during our first winter back in Bratislava, when I had met Maria privately only when she prepared Susie for her test. It was a particularly cold December evening, close to Christmas, without snow so far. But when we said goodnight and left to wait for our streetcar, we found ourselves in the middle of a raging blizzard. It was difficult to cross the street, and as we stood waiting at the unsheltered stop the wind battered our eyes and faces with sharp particles of icy snow. The tracks soon vanished under the snow, and no streetcar appeared. Even warm boots and furs would have been inadequate against this sort of weather. As I was dressed, I soon became numb and stiff and the only feeling I had left was unendurable pain in the toes and finger-tips. When I tried to pick Tania up I found myself too weak. She was crying. At first silently, then loudly like a baby in distress. The streets were empty. Rows and rows of lighted windows with people sitting in warm rooms behind them only heightened my despair and rage at the world. Even if a streetcar finally turned up it would take us only to the foot of our dark, by now unclimbable hill, and our unheatable cave.

'Mummy, please, please let's not stand here, please let's not go home!' Tania sobbed.

It was too much. Half carrying her I struggled back to the café. I was offered and drank two glasses of brandy in quick succession, Tania got hot tea and biscuits. Somebody removed her shoes and rubbed her feet. I was trying to think of a place where we could sleep the night. There was my husband's family, there were friends from way back before the war. Making a quick mental review I came to the conclusion that we had to go back into the cold. This was 1954. Most of our old acquaintances were at least nominally communists and thus either unwilling or unable to see us. Others were in jail or soon would be. It was a miracle that my husband's brother, who had been recalled from his post as military attaché in London and whose chief had been hanged in Prague, had escaped so far with nothing worse than exclusion from the party, much fear and a little job. Others I could think of were already crowded into half the living space they needed. I sat silently, at a loss. Tania was falling asleep in someone's lap.

Maria, who was unmarried and had a room of her own near the theatre where she shared only the kitchen with a family, got up and said in her usual boisterous manner: 'OK. It's getting late, what are you waiting for? If it's one more brandy, you can have it at my place!'

I feel frustrated at my utter inability to convey what this matter-of-fact invitation meant to me. How can anyone who wasn't in that place at that time understand its tremendous import? Bombastic and improbable as it sounds, I may perhaps get near the truth if I say that for one moment the café disappeared, the heavens opened and I glimpsed the God I had never believed in.

There had of course been others who were kind to us – I classify as 'kind' even those who did not hurt us more than was absolutely necessary for their own survival. But behind most acts of kindness there had been a special reason. There were my friendships with other 'wives' based on shared suffering, no more. Some men were kind to me because I was a woman. A few party members helped secretly because they loved and respected my husband, and some to ease their consciences. In the village I had met with compassion and helpful friendliness mixed with naive curiosity. But people who gave me work made me understand and appreciate the risk they took, and most of the help and friendliness I received was offered in a condescending, humiliating manner, like the famous dime given to the bum with the tacit understanding that he himself is responsible for his state of need. Perhaps I was not easy to befriend and other people's experience was different; but that was how it had been for me.

Maria and her friends did not know my husband and owed me no respect because of him. Neither did they have reason to feel guilty. They were relatively safe and well off, so they were not fellow-sufferers. Nor were they under an obligation to be kind, as relations are. Maria's invitation was thus a freely made and spontaneous act of human sympathy and kindness, and that made it an event that changed my view of life and of what it was all about.

Her room was cold, but a good iron stove in which kindling and coal were prepared was soon crackling and spreading heat. By the time Tania was undressed and snug under a quilt, she was wide awake and asking to be read to as usual. Maria tucked me in beside her, went to bed herself and offered to read to both of us. Her book club had just sent her a volume of a new Czech translation of Andersen's tales, and she read us the one about the ugly duckling. I had the most liberating good cry of my life, and by the time the duckling was happily flying with its swan brothers, both of us were fast asleep.

***

In 1955 I had still no job, but I was earning enough just to survive, and Susie was contributing out of her beginner's earnings for little luxuries for Tania or in transitory emergencies. Quite often I felt very ill. Not daring to refuse any work, I often typed three days and nights in a row, only to start a difficult technical translation with perhaps a day in between. Most evenings I was alone, completely isolated without a telephone. The doctor found my blood pressure too low. Next time it was too high. He said I needed a rest, a healthy place to live in, distraction and better food. None of this could be had at the pharmacy. Reassured that there was no serious illness behind my misery I went on working nights, freezing, being much alone, eating badly.

For all that, I considered our situation very much improved. I was no longer afraid of the police. To start with, especially during the mysterious, senseless questionings, I was constantly aware of dozens of reasons why they might arrest me. I could recall many occasions on which I had made fun of Stalin and other, smaller gods, and had said things in the presence of possible informers that must surely qualify me for a hundred years considering that so many perfectly loyal people were getting ten and fifteen. But nothing of that sort ever came up, and by now it was pretty clear that whether one did or did not land in jail had nothing to do with facts. They could have made me look like a foreign agent without the slightest effort since they knew that I had worked for the American consul, but they preferred to put years of hard work into manufacturing spies out of their most devoted slaves.

My friend Fritzi Loebl, whose husband was in for life and who had spent a year in Ruzyně prison herself, did much to help me shed my fear of the police. She had been arrested when our police were still learning the intricacies of how to prepare a show trial, so she was questioned by Russian experts in the presence of whom she had to perform knee-bends completely naked while being called a stinking Jewish whore. She was seriously ill when, after dreadful imprisonment, she was released without being tried or sentenced, but she was forced to work in a factory somewhere in Bohemia under police supervision for another year. Now she was back in Bratislava, lodging in one room with her son, who was not permitted to continue high-school. Fritzi had well-to-do parents in Vienna who were supporting her through the devious channel of our hard-currency shop, the so-called Tuzex. Foreign tourists and people who were lucky enough to receive Tuzex vouchers from relatives in the West could buy things at this shop that were unobtainable otherwise: cocoa, good chocolate, tea, edible biscuits, imported textiles, immediately available cars, building materials, knitting wool, Nescafé – I remember a time when Tuzex was featuring apples. A lively, though strictly illegal, business was done in vouchers, and Fritzi, like many others, was living on their sale. In time she even managed to assemble enough for a bribe which enabled her son to go back to school and get his diploma.

Although her parents' support was now saving Fritzi from the struggle I was enduring, it was they who had been the basic cause for her imprisonment. Because she was their daughter, Fritzi, at the time of her husband's arrest, owned jewellery, a couple of good fur coats, good paintings and carpets. After her release she had to borrow stockings and a bra from friends, because everything had disappeared. (None of it was ever recovered, not even years later after her husband's rehabilitation.) Fritzi is a courageous, intelligent woman with much vitality and an excellent sense of humour. She saw clearly, and she convinced me, that the police had never been after her, but only after her things. Therefore, now that she had nothing she need no longer be afraid, and since I had always had nothing I could easily make the same decision. Thanks to her, I did. And it was a fantastic relief when my heart no longer stopped beating every time a truck happened to climb our hill.

In addition, although we had no heat, no water when the pipes froze, no toilet and plenty of mice, we did have a home. Susie loved her work, was well on her way to popularity, and spent as much time as she could with us between engagements. In the summer she crowded us into her hotel room at a spa and shared her meals, which were part of her salary, with Tania. So we even had a holiday. And we had friends. Humiliating contacts with former friends had ceased because now I found my own. They did not know Marx by heart, but they had hearts. They were not busy manufacturing a better life for one and all, but they knew how to make life better for a friend, if only for a few hours at a time. So little was needed to light up an otherwise hopeless day. A hot bath at Jucka's house with something good baked in a real oven and served in a warm room with a warm smile and good talk after- wards—that was enough.

Tania was doing well at school and spent much time with her best friend Renka, whose parents owned a house with a big garden near to us, and always welcomed her. In the winter the two little girls went sleigh-riding together; in the summer they took their dolls for walks or climbed trees and stuffed themselves with fruit that could not be bought. We kept a little cat who had followed us home one day. Soon, instead of mice we had kittens. We loved them all, and Tania was on the whole a happy, healthy child who took our abnormal life for granted.

And yet in spite of all this improvement I felt worse and worse. Now that our immediate problems were partially solved and the initial shock had worn off I became increasingly aware again of the political situation as a whole. Ultimately, it was this, and the con- flict between my perception of it and that of my husband, which broke me up and set the tragic pattern which was to prevail during the few years we were to live together after his release five years later.

As time went on we were able to write more often and our correspondence was less carefully censored. Oscar's letters showed more and more how little he knew or wished to know about reality outside the prison; and I could not free myself of the impression that although he was cut off from much vital information, there was just as much that he knew but deliberately ignored. He kept giving me senseless and impossible tasks and then reproaching me for not having achieved anything although I had done everything according to his instructions. With admirable perseverance, but with what seemed to me irritating naiveté, he enlisted me in his fight for the reopening of his case, as though his arrest had been a dreadful but exceptional mistake in an otherwise normally functioning state with a reliable legal system. He was always telling me to see comrade so-and-so whom he knew to be an honest communist and who was sure to get things started if only I would not persist in my pessimistic cynicism. Needless to say, I approached everybody I was told to see and never got anywhere. Nobody could do anything for us, not even if they had wanted to. The show trials were the house of cards on which the whole power system rested, and if anyone started tampering with even one small part of the structure, the whole thing would collapse.

I could not understand that this was not clear to Oscar. He told me to ask for another audience with Bacílek. I did, but of course I got no answer. He told me to engage a lawyer. I did, and although the lawyer could not refuse to go through the formalities for which I had to pay him, he did not even try to hide his opinion regarding our chances. My husband urged me not to suffer discrimination passively, to demand a healthy flat, the return of our bankbook, an adequate job, all of which I was entitled to on the grounds of his innocence. He reproached me for letting Susie sing in bars instead of making her study to become an opera singer, and for the lipstick he noticed when she visited him. We succeeded in working out a sort of code that allowed us to carry on our old disputes. Rereading our letters I find growing irritation and diminishing understanding on both sides, as well as much evidence that the censors were either idiots or had begun to shirk work like everybody else.

I could write things like: 'The people you told me to see, and whom I saw, know perfectly well what we know, but none can or will do anything. Please understand.' Or: 'I can no longer conceive of the necessary sacrifices you refer to as inevitable concomitants of development, but rather as the *sine qua non* of the whole. I wish you would too.'

My husband enumerated the petitions he was allowed to write to various party and state authorities asking for the reopening of his case. He revealed, too, that at least occasionally, he was reading the papers. He seemed well enough informed about the Rosenbergs' tragedy, to which he devoted a whole letter. He urged me to stop avoiding old friends, insinuating that it was I who started the avoiding. It was exasperating.

In the middle of February a stranger brought me a typewritten letter from Oscar, given him by somebody he would not name. It had been smuggled out by a non-political prisoner recently released from the camp. To the thirteen typewritten pages addressed to the President of the Republic, Antonin Zápotocký, a little note in my husband's handwriting was attached asking me to type out copies, send the original to the President and the copies to First Secretary Antonin Novotný, to various members of the Central Committee, to Karol Bacílek and to the Procurator General. One copy I was to hand over in person to Julius Lörincz, who was a close personal friend of Viliam Široký, Minister for Foreign Affairs, and was (with Novotný) the man in the leadership best known to have been directly involved in the campaign that led to the trials. This Lörincz came from a Hungarian village in Slovakia and was originally a graphic artist and painter. Before the war we had been friends. When he came back from Hungary in 1946 with a wife and child, they had no place to live and nothing to live on. At that time we were in the abandoned editorial office – two and a half rooms – and my husband insisted that we take them in as lodgers and found Lörincz a job with an advertising agency.

As the existence of the Hungarian minority was gradually discovered and acknowledged, he started rising in the party hierarchy and rose so fast that he stopped painting and became editor-in-chief, chairman of the Czechoslovak-Hungarian Cultural Association and a member of the Central Committee. We did not often meet in the street because he was driving his own car long before most people, but if it did happen, neither his wife nor he showed the least sign of recognition. I could not see myself visiting him and asking him to convey the letter to his friend Široký.

But after having read Oscar's letter I was so shattered and so deeply ashamed of having thought myself a victim of suffering that I decided to do everything according to my husband's wishes whatever the risk involved and however futile it might be. Horrified as I was, the letter's contents also kindled a new hope in me that, after all, what he wrote me in his unsmuggled letters was perhaps half meant for the censor, and that the abyss between the two of us really wasn't there. Because how could he possibly be on their side after this?

I give here a digest of the letter, quoting only passages which seem best to reveal the essence of it all.

After referring to the unanswered letter he had written to the Politbureau in October 1954, my husband continues:

'Now that I am no longer under the physical and psychological pressure of the investigating organs, I consider it my human and political duty to help the Party leadership to unmask the heinous crimes perpetrated in Ruzyně prison where unlawful methods were used to extort signatures to untrue statements. These inhuman methods combined with outright fraud have produced false evidence, confessions to criminal acts that were never committed, and have thus led to the arrest and conviction of innocent people and to personal tragedies the like of which it would be difficult to find in history. As a result of these methods, besides actual criminals, people devoted to our people's democracy were also convicted and our jurisdiction was discredited with evident untruths. All this has inevitably caused unprecedented terror and fear in all strata of the population, doing incalculable damage to the building of socialism in our fatherland. While just and convincing sentences serve to reinforce the régime, these now no longer entirely unknown methods undermine it. In the trial against the anti-State centre I gave evidence against Rudolf Slánský and Jozef Frank. The text of this evidence was composed by the State Security organs in Ruzyně and I was made to learn it by heart.'

There follows the essence of his testimony, part of which had been printed in *Pravda* and reproduced on the radio, presented as ten points, each followed by a detailed analysis and proof of its absurdity. For example, according to his confession, he had granted export permits for machinery to emigrating Jews as an act of wilful sabotage, but these Jews were demonstrably non-existent. So were the 'Zionist agents' whom he confessed to having contacted on secret trips to Vienna. One of the 'agents' named was Emma Lazarus, the long-dead author of the poem inscribed on the Statue of Liberty – with whom, according to the statement, he had also had a love affair. When he confessed to taking bribes he again named people who did not exist, as well as a Hungarian minister then in office.

He 'confessed' all this on the advice of 'messages' received after he had been in solitary confinement for many months, refusing to sign anything. The 'messages' came through a cellmate, a certain Kovarik, who said he was a building technician sentenced for some minor financial fraud, and who was often allowed to go out on parole in order to help the man who had taken over his job. This made it plausible that he should have been contacted by me and by a lawyer engaged by me, whose name was given as Dr Loescher (there was, of course, no such lawyer). The advice conveyed by this tool of the police, and purporting to come from me, was that the best thing to do under torture was to sign absurd statements, because their absurdity could easily be proved once he was in court. Whereupon the secret machinations of the clique of fascists running Ruzyně, who were undermining socialism by doing away with its most useful men, would be unmasked and the Party would immediately take whatever steps were necessary.

'Why did I give false evidence against Rudolf Slánský? Why did I confess to crimes I never committed? Why did I sign false statements? Why was I so credulous? All this was the result of the unbearable methods of extortion to which I was subjected, of a sophisticated combination of physical and psychological violence and fraud, of the purposeful misuse of my devotion to the Party, of my love for my family. My credulity was of course increased by long periods of solitary confinement.

'After my arrest I was kept under constant interrogation for twenty-five months, nine of which I spent in solitary confinement. Eleven months I spent with *agents provocateurs*. Thirty-eight days in a dark cell, twenty of them on bread and water. I was threatened with the dark cell every week and kept in one for two days before the Slánský trial. When I was let out on that occasion I declared that everything I had said against Slánský was a lie. My interrogator assured me in a phlegmatic voice that I would be saying much more than that. Interrogation under inhuman conditions continued and was accompanied later by my so-called "lawyer's" demoralizing messages until finally, one year and one day after my arrest, I signed the first statement against Slánský, which was also the first that could harm somebody else, somebody who was – as far as I know – innocent. I was forced into false confessions by unbearable cold and hunger, slaps in the face and beatings, by being made to kneel during interrogation. After my second suicide attempt, I was kept repeatedly in a strait jacket, once for thirteen days and nights in a row. I made confessions after not being allowed to sleep for weeks and by the humiliation of myself, my wife, my brothers, my honest friends, etc. "How many crooked noses did you surround yourself with?" – "In case you didn't know, it's time for you to hear that during the German occupation 50,000 Jews were acting as agents for the Gestapo!" – "You Zionist whore, you bourgeois son of a bitch, rotten through and through with syphilis!" – "Swine, dirt," and worse, I cannot repeat here . . . Day after day, month after month . . . When they wanted me to confess to being of Jewish nationality so that they could classify me as a bourgeois nationalist I refused. I said truthfully that although of Jewish descent, I was born in Slovakia and always thought of myself as a Slovak. I was being interrogated in shifts by two officers, eight hours each. One of them jumped on my foot every time I did not say what he wanted to hear me say. In the end I conceded that I was of Jewish nationality. This statement I was made to repeat a hundred times, with my arms stretched up and then kneeling. From that day on my name appeared in documents with the appendage "prisoner under interrogation, of Jewish nationality". Allow me, Mr President, a question. Every time *Pravda* has occasion to commemorate the concentration camps, where my father, my sister with her children and five more of my close relatives were murdered, why does it state that 150,000 Czechs and Slovaks perished in Auschwitz, Sachsenhausen, etc?

'Repeatedly I was threatened that my wife would undergo similar treatment if I did not sign, and my children would be left without a home. Since I myself was experiencing this treatment, although I was innocent, these threats sounded dangerous and plausible. I am 180 cm tall, my weight at that time was 54 kg. The prison doctor knew that as a former sufferer from tuberculosis I felt hunger more than the average person. He knew that in my weakened state I had to empty my bladder eight to ten times every night. On these occasions I regularly ate part of the toilet paper ration. In spite of this I got my first permission to buy bread with my own money only after the first ten months and after my first untrue confession.

When I revoked it, the permission was revoked. After
seven months of solitary confinement, on 7th March 1952,
a new, higher officer joined my usual two interrogators.
He shook me, threw me against the wall, kicked me in the
shin and shouted at me: "Now we have had enough of
this!" He dictated a statement which they needed in my
own handwriting. "I confess that I am an important link in
the anti-State conspiracy of Zionists and Jewish bourgeois
nationalists. I will make a separate detailed confession of
my actual misdeeds and activities."

'These methods, and many more which I prefer not to
describe brought me into a state of mind that cannot be
considered that of a normally thinking sane man. This also
explains my two attempts at suicide (7th October, 1951
and 9th May, 1952). Beginning on 2nd January, 1953, in
several periods lasting from three to fourteen days, I was
on hunger strike for a total of 54 days. I was artificially fed
through the nose, in a way deliberately more painful than
necessary. After each feeding I bled copiously.'

The first 'news' Kovarik brought him was that I was under constant surveillance and interrogation, and that the security people
had succeeded in saving me and the two children from a collective
suicide attempt at the last minute. Then came the 'lawyer's' advice
to confess, thinking up crimes corresponding to those suggested
by the police and to the false evidence extorted from others against
him. According to the non-existent Dr Loescher, the Procurator
General had been informed and planned to use Oscar's case to
unmask the unlawful activities of the State Security people. By
doing as he was told, my husband would help to purge our system
of such evils, and would thus be helping the Party. His false evidence against other people would hurt them only temporarily
because everyone involved would be tried, about twenty altogether, at the same time. Besides, as he could see from documents
shown to him, others were doing the same under similar conditions. He was to be tried, among others, together with his brother
who was involved in an alleged military conspiracy but who would

also – 'Dr Loescher' had this from the Procurator General himself – be cleared as soon as he came into court. He was assured that the Slánský trial would definitely not be held before the New Year, so that he himself had a chance to correct any false accusations included in his confession at his own trial. The thing was to confess quickly enough so that his trial could be scheduled before Christmas.

Collaboration between the *agent provocateur* and the interrogators was so perfectly timed and arranged that all this seemed credible enough, at least to a man in my husband's condition and with his ideas about the Party. And 'Dr Loescher' pointed out urgently that if he did not adopt this plan and follow it precisely, the consequences would be catastrophic not only for Oscar himself, but also for his brother and for me.

After a time Kovarik disappeared and was replaced by a less sophisticated man who made a great point of criticizing the régime. My husband recognized him immediately for what he was and was struck by the horrible suspicion that this was perhaps not the first *agent provocateur* to share his cell. After a few sleepless nights he discarded the thought, telling himself:

'The very absurdity of the thought that high security officials whose cooperation and consent would have been needed to work out such a complicated plan should debase themselves so in the name of the Party, of the working class, of the noblest ideas humanity has ever brought forth, made me refuse this possibility.'

He decided to follow the 'lawyer's' advice. When it became clear that the Slánský trial was imminent and would thus precede his own, and he was given his text as a witness against Slánský to learn by heart, he refused. He was told that if he would not comply, he would never come out alive. A day or two before the trial he again contemplated suicide, but found no means even for an attempt. On the day of the trial he told his interrogator that he would not give evidence in court because every word of accusation against Slánský and others was a lie. He demanded to be confronted with

Slánský, whom he had never met, and who had most probably never heard of him. This demand was refused. His cellmate described most vividly what he could expect if he refused to appear in court: death, and before it, worse than death. On the other hand, he said, if Oscar gave evidence now, he could hope to live and some day perhaps undertake something in the interest of truth.

When the barber came to give him a shave and a haircut Oscar knew that there was no way out. He was still clinging to the hope that once in court, he would find a way of giving a sign that would make everyone there understand that he was lying. No such possibility arose. Nor did Slánský question him, or say that they had never met.

While waiting for his own trial, Oscar demanded to see the Procurator General, and to this end he started another hunger strike on 2nd January, 1953. The interview never took place, the trial came up in September. He was tried alone, not with twenty others as he had been led to expect, and instead of 'Dr Loescher', his lawyer was a total stranger who appeared ten minutes before the hearing, and then asked that his client should be punished more severely than the prosecution proposed because, he said, Langer had committed the crimes of which he was accused over and over again.

'I preferred to accept Kovarik's word rather than to believe that such stratagems were possible in our State. In retrospect I can't help but experience anew what was only a fleeting impression in Ruzyně, which my mind immediately dismissed as absurd: that the secret police is in fact the highest organ in the State and thus stands above the Party. It is to free myself of this idea that I write. I also wish to repeat what I declared in my letter of 10th October, 1954: that I never was a member of any Zionist organization, nor of any Jewish Society, religious community or other such group. I state this not because I consider this a merit or because I am ashamed of my descent, but simply because it is a fact.

'In conclusion I wish to emphasize that I do not contend, nor have I ever contended, that Rudolf Slánský and his associates were innocent when they were condemned. I cannot contend this because I know nothing about any criminal activities of theirs, not even what it is that they were accused of. What I do know, however, is that they were innocent of what I accused them of in my testimony at their trial. I also know and can prove that people were being forced by means of promises and threats into collaboration with the police and made to act as *agents provocateurs* . . .

'My experience in Ruzyně, which I have described here only superficially and in part, continue to occupy my mind day and night. I am unable to reconcile them with the principles that form the basis on which a society building socialism rests.'

In conclusion my husband expressed his conviction that he was doing his duty and a service to the Party and the Government by revealing these facts to the highest leadership, and his hope that in possession of this information the President would start an investigation and at the same time take immediate steps to have his case reopened.

The family and the few other people I confided in were horrified, even if not too surprised, at the contents of this letter and unanimously dissuaded me from following Oscar's instructions. Everybody knew that it revealed nothing the people it was addressed to did not know, and everyone was sure that while it could not achieve anything positive, it was likely to have catastrophic consequences for both my husband and myself. I was advised to burn it. I agreed with my friends but could not follow their advice. I made the copies and sent them off, partly as an act of duty and partly as a sort of self-punishment for my self-pity and the irritation and estrangement I had started to feel. Lörincz received me and we had ten minutes of idiotic conversation about our children and the weather. Without glancing at the letter, he took it and made an unconvincing promise to give it to his friend Široký: I had an extra copy which I decided to deposit somewhere in case I should be arrested for knowing too much. Nobody, including the family, would take it. In the end it was again Maria who nonchalantly hid it between her clean sheets.

What happened afterwards proved that my having felt heroic was a sign of a naiveté which I ought to have outgrown long ago. The highest leadership was neither shattered nor mobilized into instant remorse or revenge. What happened, in fact, was nothing. The letters undoubtedly reached their almighty addresses, the bomb landed – but there was no explosion. Except that my husband was transferred to a stricter prison in Slovakia from where no further letters could be smuggled out.

On the 10th of April 1955, when the country was celebrating the tenth anniversary of its liberation, *Rudé Právo* came out with a leading article by the Minister of Justice, Dr Bartoška, in which he made oblique references to certain speculations concerning the political trials of recent years and emphatically declared that not even the possibility of an amnesty was thinkable in this connection. At the same time Široký assured foreign journalists in an interview that there were no political prisoners in Czechoslovakia. This statement was dryly reproduced in most of the western press and enthusiastically elaborated on in *l'Humanité*, *Die Volksstimme*, *Unità* and other papers of this sort.

In Czechoslovakia everybody from the very top to the very bottom knew, but nothing happened, nothing changed and not a single word of truth was heard for more than a decade to come. No investigative journalism, nobody arrested for protesting. Quiet, peace, and constant public celebration of our unique successes and progress in every field. Then came Stalin's second death, the risings in Poland and Hungary, and after a period of increased repression of the word, a hesitant rumbling at last was heard from the brains (or in spite of all, perhaps from the finally revolted stomachs) of certain leading intellectuals.

I am writing this more than ten years after I copied out and sent my husband's smuggled letter to our leadership. Quite recently

Novotný had to go (more for economic than for moral reasons) and now we have Dubček.

Dubček is, of course, a relatively decent man. I say 'relatively' because I know he was taken to Russia as a child by his fanatical old-guard father, and made his career as a party official under Stalin and Novotný, all of which sets limits to both his decency and his wits. Possibly he has a sincere wish to be better than his predecessors, but I doubt that he is very far-sighted – nor is his memory too good. All these prophets of 'socialism with a human face' have the elastic memory so characteristic of good communists. They truly seem to forget that it was Imre Nagy, also a communist, who first coined this notion, if not this exact phrase (I believe his was 'socialism that does not forget the human being'): Imre Nagy, whose Soviet-ordained murder they condoned in 1956. And it doesn't seem to occur to them that in proclaiming that *our* socialism has a human face, we are telling Brezhnev that the face of *his* socialism is inhuman. Are they expecting him to say 'How right you are! Go ahead and good luck to you'?

All of which raises questions I want to ask those people in the West who, outraged by the injustices of the capitalist world, see their only hope in a revolution of the working classes and in the socialism to which such a revolution is supposed to lead and has allegedly already led. The main question, hardly ever honestly raised or answered, is 'What is gained, and at what price?'

The Russian working man's living standard has improved. That is true. And I am prepared to concede the general assumption that the way to such progress must lead through revolution and that revolution exacts great sacrifices. I do not consider this proved, but let it be accepted that the millions who perished in the Russian civil war, in the cold-bloodedly induced mass famine and in the prison camps were the necessary price paid in a good cause. Let us even leave open the question how much would the life of the Russian masses have improved in half a century under any, even a deficient, parliamentary régime. Let us accept that all these sacrifices were needed for the creation of the world's first socialist state, and grant that the Soviet Union has truly gone through a miraculously fast development considering its starting point and all the odds it had to fight against.

It has become a highly industrialized country; the moujik has been brought out of his hole in the ground; the living standard has been brought up to the level of the lowest in Europe; the Sputnik has been launched; illiteracy has been eliminated to the point where semi-literates wield unlimited power over the souls, and indeed, the lives of their fellow-men. Hunger has been abolished, and everybody drinks, and as far as the country's status in the world is concerned, it has reached the top. It has become an imperialist exploiter as good as any other superpower – and what's more, instead of having to deal with backward colonies it has colonized a number of formerly civilized and well-developed countries, which must have been a tougher task. It has also become a maker, owner and seller of the most sophisticated murdering machines, and its military power is overwhelming and ubiquitous. Kitchen faucets don't function, tractors are rusting without spare parts, but atomic bombs are in good order. So much for material progress.

At this point we come to the second part of the question: 'At what price?' I put this question not to western party members but to those more dangerous because more intelligent and therefore more influential people, the fellow travellers. Hypnotized as they still are by the mystique of the Great October Revolution, have they ever really looked at what it did to those who did not die in it, and to their children? Those of them who have visited us, and after having been properly wined and dined by our Potemkin brigade have seen the endless queues for fruit or meat and our desperate housing shortage and so on, must have consoled themselves with the saying that after all, man does not live by bread alone. What are such minor hardships compared with a just social order? A negligible, transitory nuisance. They themselves had plenty of meat, fruit, and toilet paper, but all that did not make them happier in their unjust, doomed, immoral, corrupt world. We were living on a higher moral plane, for which they envied and admired us. But have they honestly tried to find out the truth about what the existing socialist régimes have done just to that particular part of man that does *not* live by bread alone?

They have made innumerable young men who were meant to be workers, clerks, scientists, harmless watchers of football games, writers, artists, doctors, bums, petty family tyrants and occasionally criminals, each according to his talents, disposition and the intricacies of fate, into Kafanas on the lower level and Novotnýs on the higher one. They have endowed these men with unlimited power to bungle and bully, a power affecting whole nations and, in certain instances, the world. They have turned a large percentage of their populations into informers, either for self-preservation under threats, or for the sake of things like a few square metres of living space to be gained at the price of a neighbour's liberty or even life. They have made basically honest citizens into habitual givers and takers of bribes because it is the only way to get petty services and things which are self-evidently available to the man in the street in other countries. The object of such a transaction is often no more than a roll of toilet paper or the repair of a clogged sink. They have made gifted writers into prostitutes (not really the right word, because some of these women are honest professionals, capable of giving pleasure). They have transformed the trade unions into all-powerful employers, merciless corporations exerting organized intimidation, themselves slaves to the Party but slave-drivers with the right to designate every would-be striker as an enemy of the State. They have turned scientists into slogan-mouthing scribblers, always carefully in tune with the day's or the hour's telex directives from Moscow. They have turned our children into habitual liars and hypocrites, though with luck this may be only outside the home. They have made whole nations into a trembling mass of wretches with human communication reduced to whispered rumours, jokes and hints exchanged when the telephone is safely covered with pillows and the radio switched on high enough. They have reduced intellectuals to passionate coveters of privileges and infantile hunters and smugglers of THINGS. (I remember sitting in a café with a fine translator and a well-known poet, both just back from short trips abroad, and all they talked about was how best to get plastic raincoats, cosmetics and pullovers.)

Whatever the price in human lives, for all of its murderous

record, socialism has killed more souls and minds than bodies; and it continues to kill them far beyond the range of its iron fist, in places where souls and thought are free if only they so choose. But who can make a western fellow-traveller understand that the Russians have been living for half a century under all-powerful, unassailable, unremovable McCarthies with the right to kill? That what they condemn as corruption and incompetence in their governments is the norm in ours? That what they see as the unjust privileges of their rich are – relatively – far smaller than those enjoyed by our upper class? How can one make them see that status hunting and the obsession with consumer goods is no less disgusting when the object is a pink plastic toilet brush, a trashy pop record or a rasping transistor radio than it is when the object is a sports car or a suede sofa?

All through 1955, both my husband and I continued to address letters to party, government and legal authorities. Only one was answered. Encouraged by rumours that a party committee was being set up in Prague for the revision of possibly incorrect sentences in certain exceptional cases where mistakes could have been made, I asked for an audience and was promptly granted one. I was to appear on a certain day, at a specified hour at the Central Committee, where a female comrade by the name of Kunstadt was prepared to hear me out. This, I think, was the most humiliating of all the humiliating experiences wished on me by the Party. I made the trip to Prague on borrowed money and entered the sumptuous building not full of hope but not entirely without a spark of it. After presenting my identification papers and the letter making the appointment to the man behind the giant desk in the huge marble-lined lobby, I was given a number of forms to fill in, then told to sit down and wait. The man then telephoned the lady. Instead of being directed to the floor and room where I expected to be expected, I was again ordered (not asked) to sit down and wait. After a good half hour I finally saw a well-dressed but untidy middle-aged spinsterish woman coming down the stairs and approaching me. In applying for the interview I had described my husband's case in detail, but now she asked why I was there and what I wanted. I was so disconcerted at being interviewed in this public place, and in this brusque, impatient tone that I only managed to stammer a few words. The woman's expression was one of disgust and her stance made it obvious that she might turn on her heel and leave at any moment; and I felt myself becoming a trembling, incoherent idiot, a worm waiting to be stepped upon, even hoping to be crushed since it would stop me feeling what I now felt. I was wrong, the woman said, if I thought that the committee had been set up to deal with a clear and justly handled case like my husband's. There was nothing to revise. She expressed the wish that hysterical, pushy women would stop taking up her time when she had so much to do, turned around and left me standing there.

In the summer of 1955, on my husband's insisting, I engaged a lawyer. Like every lawyer in the state, he was an employee of a Juridical Advice Centre. He was openly cynical and so was I, but he went through the motions I was paying for. He demanded the reopening of the case, and applied for official annulment of the deportation and confiscation decrees and for the return of at least half of the money in the bankbook seized during the search. None of this did any good, and as far as the decrees were concerned it had no purpose. It was clear by then that our presence in Bratislava was tacitly tolerated and that I owned nothing worth confiscating. I did not even succeed in getting a permit to send Oscar parcels, although these were sometimes issued. The only parcel I sent, hoping that it would get through somehow, came back two months later, a stinking mouldy mess of what had been a cake, a few precious lemons and some chocolate bars. Nor did any of Susie's first records get through.

However, in August we did receive a permit for a second visit, this time to Leopoldov prison. Paradoxically enough, his having been transferred entailed certain advantages. He no longer had to work with uranium, he was in Slovakia, only a couple of hours away, and we could exchange more, longer and more carelessly censored letters now. Not that they helped much in bridging over more than five years of separation.

'I too see the mistakes' – he wrote – 'but I know that they are temporary ones which the Party will overcome, and that they are outweighed by the good the Party has done. I understand that you felt lonely on the first of May in the midst of happy, celebrating crowds . . . Please don't use drastic expressions that lower the standard of your letters and often sound worse in Slovak than what you perhaps think in Hungarian slang . . .'

This referred to a letter in which I had written: 'You are probably right that no mistakes are made only where nothing is being done. However, in certain cases quantity changes not into quality as we are being taught, but rather into a bigger quantity of shit. I have engaged a lawyer, and the results are likely to be the same . . . Much as I admire your political and moral strength, for instance when you devote half a letter to your joy about the new housing project for the miners, I think you ought to be able to understand that I, considering everything, am not ideologically staunch enough fully to share your joy . . .'

I did not translate what I wrote out of Hungarian, and meant every word of it in any language, but naturally these bitchy passages were exceptions, and so were his ideological lecturings. We both tried hard to keep up each other's courage with mutual assurances of love and hope (basically true, although they became monotonous with time), with detailed stories about the children from me and often amusing descriptions of fellow prisoners from him, and by recommending and discussing books now that he had access to a library. In spite of this good will, however, we were separated by more than time and space.

Leopoldov prison looks like a prison in a nightmare. It is a giant fortress surrounded by forbidding walls, standing in the middle of nothing. This time there were only a few people waiting on the dusty road, at about a hundred metres distance from the first high wire fence behind which there was a huge bare yard with two more fences, and behind them a great, heavy iron gate. Two uniformed guards came marching all the way down to where we stood to summon visitors as their turn came. No place to sit, no roof for protection against sun or rain, but experienced as we now were we had a vacuum flask and a few sandwiches with us. We didn't need them though, because after only two hours we were escorted up the road, let through two wire doors and after crossing the yard, the big iron gate was opened and immediately banged shut and locked behind us. In the dark medieval stone hall we went through the procedure of identification and then were ordered to deposit our bags, and Tania her teddy bear, on a shelf. Which left us without a handkerchief, without the family snapshots we hoped to show and the bits of sweets we hoped to slip through the wire mesh. However, as a first sign of destalinization and the humanization of socialism, this time there was no wire.

We were led into a large, well-lit room where we sat on a long bench at a long table beside a row of other visitors. My husband was then led in and sat across from us with his guard standing behind him. This was the first time after five full years that we got a full view of each other. He looked very thin, very pale, his hair had thinned and gone grey, but he was freshly shaved and when he smiled in his characteristic, shy, hesitant, somewhat lopsided way, revealing his perfectly preserved teeth, I suddenly saw before me the boy who had approached me in a Vienna hotel lobby at our first secret meeting after two years of correspondence to ask whether I was the girl he loved.

This visit was without the half painful, half joyful, almost fainting excitement of the first one, and was undertaken more as a self-evident duty and to show the children than out of a deep desire to meet. But this unexpected physical nearness, the fact that we could touch hands across the table, and my picture of him from the past, melted all hardness and estrangement into an almost unbearably hot surge of compassion, a great wish to understand and love again, and tearful thankfulness for the miracle that in spite of all he was still here. He was alive, thin and pale and greyed, but neither insane nor ill. The father of my children, my husband. At that moment I felt sure that after all he had gone through and with my deep desire to love and understand, if only we could be together and touch and talk again, there was still time to make up for everything, time for a new and better common life, for at least growing old together in peace and gentle tolerance.

While writing this I ask myself whether Novotný's fall and what's happening now under Dubček would justify Oscar's faith and fulfil his hopes. Whatever my own doubts and fears, it is a dreadful thing that he was not allowed to live to take part in today's events. A few weeks ago I found the copy of a letter he wrote two years before his death to Dubček who then, in April 1963, became First Secretary of the Communist Party of Slovakia. I sent the letter to an editor friend to help Oscar contribute at least posthumously to what he would now so enthusiastically support, and it was reproduced in part in an article entitled: 'A Touching Voice from Beyond the Tomb'.

'In this year of 1968 we wish to remind those who did not know or who have forgotten this splendid man, this pre-war communist, formerly a leading figure in our economy, then known throughout the State as a "Zionistic, cosmopolitan, revisionist conspirator and spy", who sat in Novotný's prisons for ten years, that he did not live to see and take part in our process of rebirth after all the suffering he was made to endure. He passed away three years ago. We quote from a letter he wrote five years ago: "Dear Comrade Dubček! It is rumoured (if Vienna radio is telling the truth) that you have been nominated First Secretary of the Central Committee of the Communist Party of Slovakia. Although we don't know each other personally, allow me to wish you good health and much success in your new function. I should be sincerely glad – and millions of others with me – if your taking office would bring about a change as against the past in the sense that honest people could feel safe from despotic rule and persecution. This is indispensable for the future of both our republic and of socialism. I say this because I am one of those who have paid a dreadful price for the lack of this sense of safety in the past. I consider it my duty to express the conviction that the real initiative and potential for cooperation of all strata of the population can be mobilized only if freedom from fear is definitely established and the backbones of the people are straightened out again. Forgive my unconventional tone, but I ask you to accept my wish that when finally you lay down your function you will be able to do so knowing that people respect you, don't avoid you, don't hesitate to invite you to their homes, and that they think of you as of a man who did not misuse the trust placed in him, was never a phrase-monger and had nothing to hide or embellish as regards his time in public life . . ."

'We think that Oscar Langer would be satisfied with Dubček now. Truly, a prophetic vision of the man our now firmly united brother nations know that Comrade Dubček is.'

This article appeared in July. It is early August now, and although I do not much doubt Dubček's integrity and I am myself carried away at times by the great wave of hope sweeping the whole nation and the small waves of honesty in our public life, I am more often afraid than happy. Why is my husband said to have sat 'in Novotný's prisons'? Why not in Gottwald's, in the Russian adviser's prisons? Dubček was making his career in Stalin's and Gottwald's party, and Novotný was nothing when all this started. Is a new set of lies needed to rid us of the old ones? Husák, who is in the foreground again at Dubček's side, is a foxy old Stalinist and even more of a chauvinist. He wouldn't give a bloody damn about the innocent victims if he did not happen to be one of them. Dubček is probably honest and, no doubt, charming. But is personal honesty and charm enough to lift a desperate nation out of the great morass? Lift it where to? Surrounded as it is by greater, deeper, menacing morasses?

The truth is that if my husband were alive today, he would put all his soul into the fight on the side of the Dubček people, even though they include many who would have hanged him with a clear conscience 'for the Party's good' a few years back. And the other, the old fight between the two of us, would be going on at home.

Västerås, Sweden, November, 1978

To continue, I must go back from a cold dark December day in
Sweden to summer in Czechoslovakia almost two decades ago
when I got my first job after having lived for years as an outcast.
How can I convey to anyone in this place, at this time, what
tremendous significance the most ordinary events, the smallest
improvements, then had? Who can celebrate with me what a miracle of justice it seemed to be when an innocent man like my
husband got his twenty-two-years' sentence reduced to twelve? Or
the great event it was when at last I could afford to have the chimney rebuilt so that we no longer had to decide whether to suffocate
or freeze? Who can appreciate with me the incredible step towards
destalinization which made it possible for us to visit my husband
every second month, and instead of standing in the road we were
able to wait in a little house with a toilet and a sink with running
water? The place was lavishly decorated with posters showing
dimpled babies held high (towards what?) by their working mothers, their eyes gazing upwards with ecstatic enthusiasm (to
whom?), and bigger children sitting in the laps of their tractor-
driver fathers, allowed to rest their fat little hands on the steering
wheel, smiling into the happy future, following their father's bold
revolutionary gaze. These masterworks of socialist realism were
boldly captioned: 'The children are our future, let us treasure
them!' Or: 'Our love for our children can be realized through the
eternal love that binds us to the Great Soviet Union!' Since the
little house was always full of real children, the sight of these

posters in that place was hard to bear; but the shelter over our heads and the toilet were deeply appreciated.

Can I explain here what is so marvellous about a greeting in the street from someone whom you had known intimately for decades, who for the last five years or so has been making himself invisible whenever you appeared? Or what it meant to get a job with a newly founded newspaper, even if – for cadre reasons – I was employed only as a typist, doing a bit of editorial work on the side? How can I convey what it meant to me to begin to belong again? To work with a group of people with whom I could laugh openly about the rubbish and the lies that went from their desks through the censor to the printing shop? The elation of smuggling in a word of truth or a spark of humour here and there, and seeing it in print?

From my Swedish window, as I write, I can see tidy rows of box-like houses, the well-lit parking place and the shopping centre against a patch of virgin forest with a scatter of primaeval rocks, all of which constitutes the typical suburb of a modern Swedish industrial town. Swiftly falling snow is silencing and immobilizing the silent and the immobile. If peace, well-being and liberty are blessings, we are truly blessed. What was it that Jesus said? Are we blessed for what we are or the other way around? Does man need punishment to come alive and think? Oppression, to know what freedom is?

The branch library in this suburban shopping centre contains more useful information and spiritual food than we had access to for twenty years. Can I explain to young people sitting between rows of books and long shelves of papers and magazines from all over the world, with a bunch of comics in their lap, what it meant to me to be issued with a little card entitling me to enter the special journalists' institute where I could read *The Times* and *Le Monde*? I am afraid I can't.

The paper where I worked was a novelty in many ways. The editor-in-chief, to whose civil courage I owed my employment, was not a party member, only an experienced and efficient newspaper man, a novelty in itself in such a job. This new Slovak evening paper had tacit permission from high up to be lighter and slightly more boulevardish than were the official morning papers. Our most popular column was the one in which citizens could vent their gripes, mostly about the lack of services and the absence or demented distribution of consumer goods. The early morning news from Vienna, London, Paris and Rome was played in on a tape recorder from the radio, and from my rough translations the editors picked bits of information and gossip not contained in the Czechoslovak News Agency and TASS material. Nothing controversial of course, but still it made our paper more colourful, a bit more lighthearted and interesting than the official press. People stood in line for it as though it were meat or oranges. We were constantly trying to smuggle information through, there were clashes with the censor, a few serious warnings from Party Headquarters, but the paper continued to come out and was a huge success.

Why should anybody in his right mind stand in line to buy a paper because it contained a few little drops of what overflows the news-stands here? You have to live for years on a diet of *Pravda* in order to relish the humanity of a bit of gossip about Lollobrigida, a story about a faithful dog sitting at his dead master's grave or one about a husband who shot a man not because he was an imperialist or a Trotskyist but because he was his wife's lover. You have to be surfeited with photographs of heads of states embracing at airports and of joyous workers behind machines in order to experience the photograph of a pretty girl with a daring décolleté as a gift bestowed by a new liberty . . .

Liberty? How much? Not even censors are always capable of following the paranoid train of thought of party higher-ups. Once, on the occasion of an industrial fair, a small sailing boat was set up in the square in front of the National Theatre. During the night an unexpected storm turned it upside down, and thanks to our alert photographer we had a little picture of it on the first page, captioned with a few words about the wind. A small item of local interest. The consequences were frightening. The sale of copies was stopped very early in the afternoon, the editor-in-chief was summoned to Party Headquarters to be reprimanded and the censor who had let the picture through lost his job. The reason?

I give it here fully aware of the risk that I won't be believed. It was that the picture of the overturned boat happened to be on the same page as the official announcement of the arrival in Bratislava of Minister Široký from Prague, on that day.

A brilliant young girl who had joined the staff straight from the university, where she had studied journalism for five years, was summarily fired after a year's good work in our cultural department. Why? Her boss was at home with a cold when she wrote a mildly disparaging review of a miserable radio play by a Soviet author. It slipped through editorial control and censorship, but somewhere higher up, probably on the initiative of the Soviet Consulate, the wheels that were to crush her started rolling. In our system this wasn't just the loss of a job but the end of a career.

And yet, in 1956 there was something new in the air. Khrushchev had revealed what – at least in Czechoslovakia – everybody in his right mind had known for years, and although his speech was called a secret one, it was widely discussed and hopeful guesses were made at its implications. At the writers' congress in Prague a few voices were raised expressing disillusion and even a degree of disgust. Even to the most faithful and the privileged it began to be clear that something had gone horribly wrong. It was of course Stalin's fault. Then Novotný's.

My husband, too, pinned his hopes on Khrushchev. 'The man who has stood up at last to speak is an honest and humane one. The times and circumstances that made people into cowards are now at an end,' he wrote from prison. As usual, I had my doubts. With the censor in mind I answered in a sentence smuggled in between news about the family and the weather: 'If the humane and honest people you refer to are really such, why so late? Whether a person is basically honest or not is usually revealed and comes to expression in his life shortly after puberty and only rarely if at all in very late middle age . . .'

Soon it was to become evident how far the honesty and humanity of the man filling Stalin's place could reach. The news about the beginnings of protest in Poland and subsequently in Hungary was ignored by our press. No paper in Czechoslovakia mentioned Imre Nagy's memorandum which he sent in February 1956 to

Khrushchev and to the Hungarian party leadership, setting forth his ideas for a reform of the communist régime. In this document he pointed out that what was morally wrong could not be politically right, and outlined 'Communism which does not forget the human being'. When the time came it was the honest, humane man who had him hanged.

The Hungarian uprising has been described much better than I ever could by people who were there. I talk of it only as it affected us in Czechoslovakia. When events reached a point where they could no longer be ignored, things began to happen so quickly and official news from wavering Moscow became so scarce that the gentlemen in our information-manipulating machine lived through a short but intense period of fright and confusion of which I was a maliciously delighted witness. This is how I happened to be there.

News, or rather that part of it which was selected for distortion and publication by the morning papers, was already out of date by noon. At Party Headquarters it was known, of course, that we had a telex machine and were taping the latest news from foreign capitals through the radio. I don't know how it was in Prague, but in Bratislava they used our editorial offices as the quickest source of information. This meant that I had to run from telex to tape and back, writing out little bulletins every hour. Being the only Hungarian there, most of the time I kept in telex touch with Budapest. I shall never know who was at the other end, but the conversation we carried on through that – for me – incomprehensibly miraculous machine remains one of the highlights of my life. I received a constant flow of information that seemed to shake the world, interspersed with highly personal and emotional comments, and I sent fervent congratulations in reply. The great outcry for truth and human dignity going up over there, which was the essence of it all, was in our throats as well. If there was any hope for us, it was being fought for there . . . Between questions, answers and news we exchanged greetings, jokes, endearments and rows and rows of exclamation marks.

Our authorities were so impatient to hear the very latest news that I had no time to write it out. They sent a black limousine for me, and I was driven to the Party building to report what had just come through. For the first time I stood – or rather sat, for once – face to face with a couple of the almighty, and it was not I who was pale with fear, but they. I told them the news about Rajk's solemn funeral procession and the Hungarian leadership's official confession to the great trial's infamy. It was from me they got the story about how Stalin's giant statue was pulled down, and I it was who gave them Kádár's speech where he talked about 'the great popular movement' and promised to cooperate with Nagy. In November I could still quote Kádár calling it a 'glorious uprising'.

The pale functionaries knew, of course, whose wife I was and hurried to assure me that it was now only a matter of days before things would be cleared up here, as well. Not a word of my little bulletins appeared in our paper, nor in any other.

Then the telex fell silent for longish periods and the few words that appeared from time to time in answer to my calls were enigmatic or sad. From the radio I knew why. The last message came through after a day's complete silence, and, since it came from Budapest, it had to be a joke. It must have swept the bludgeoned city like wildfire, as such jokes do: 'Workers of the world, unite, but not in groups of more than three . . .'

When the telex came alive again it started to pour out streams of the familiar old jargon about the shameful counter-revolution, the fascist and reactionary elements who had launched an armed attack on the forces of law and order with the help of imperialist agents, the CIA and so on. My clients at Headquarters got back their rosy cheeks, my services were no longer needed, the news material came straight from Moscow again, and we began to publish articles about the counter-revolution. My husband and other criminals of his ilk had to rot in jail for four more years and wait another four for their rehabilitation.

After the bloody end in Hungary, our first reaction was horror and disappointment. Gradually the mood changed into a sense of vague resignation and after a while most people were mainly glad that the whole thing had happened somewhere else. Under the constant bombardment of propaganda, sharply focused on hair-raising photographs of mobbed and hanged state security men and on the doings of the small but loud band of real fascists that emerged in the final phase, the real cause, ideas and purpose of the uprising were more or less successfully erased from the population's consciousness. But what had happened in Hungary was a godsend to Novotný. The first feeble moves that had been made towards the revision of false trials could now be stopped. The guilty ones could raise their heads again and life went on. Visits to the prison and marriage by way of letters which we found more and more difficult to make remotely meaningful became a matter of routine. Another empty routine was the lawyer's activity and our continuing one-sided correspondence with legal and other authorities. After Hungary they could afford to keep silent and do nothing.

I liked my work, and now I could get translations to do in my own name. I could afford to make our basement a bit more livable and I was tacitly acknowledged reliable enough to get a telephone. Tania was doing well at school, and in her miniature, fragile way was as pretty as a doll. Living in a single room as we did, she knew and understood much more than other children her age, and too soon perhaps, for better or for worse, we had to become more than mother and child. Totally dependent on each other, we became friends. How else could it be? Most evenings we were alone together, out there in the sticks. If Maria and her crowd came with a few bottles of wine to spend an evening, they came as much for her sake as for mine. After she had sat with us for a while, everyone collaborated in undressing and washing her, reading to her and putting her to bed. In the winter I could make a fire only in the evening, so she came straight to the editorial office from school. There she did her homework, drew pictures in the telephonist's little room, ran errands for the staff and learned to work the telex. It was warm there and she was made to feel welcome and important. After work she came with me wherever I went in town: to Jucka, where we were pampered with a hot bath, much love, a good dinner, a drink for me and sweets for her; to the library; to Magda's, a faithful party friend of Oscar's whom I had inherited, and who remained faithful to us. Or to Bronia's for a chat and for the English books she used to lend me. In short, we were constantly together and wholly dependent on each other. Probably too much. As she grew older I gave her the liberty she needed, but then again her friends began to accept me. According to all modern theories of family psychology we should both be full of complexes. Perhaps we are. I tell myself that in that case they do not come from the excessive love between us but rather from the circumstances that forced us into it.

At the very top of our hill, about half an hour's stiff climb above us, stood a little house built long ago by its owner, an old carpenter who was so disabled by rheumatism that he never moved from home. His wife was not much younger, but healthy and although she was big and fat, she moved with a certain grace and her face was unlined and beautiful. I saw her almost daily passing by, descending the steep narrow road and then ascending it again late at night. Intrigued by her courage, her appearance and her regular comings and goings in all sorts of weather, I asked the neighbours about her.

They said that she was supporting her husband and herself, and helping her married daughter who lived in town with two children and a mostly drunk husband, by washing, mending, ironing and cleaning in the neighbourhood. I was told that she would gladly come in if I needed help. Out of loneliness and curiosity, one winter night I opened the window and invited her in for a cup of tea. That was the beginning of a long relationship between two women who were as different from each other in every respect as two people can possibly be. It lasted for years and was very near to what I would call friendship. She has now been dead for years, but I shall never forget her, nor will my gratitude to her ever die.

It turned out that when I saw her go down to the streetcar so regularly in the evenings it was not to work she went but to rehearsals with a little Hungarian amateur theatre group of which she was a member. At that time they were doing a play by George Bernard Shaw. She adored talking, she talked too much, she gossiped a lot and often bored me half to death. And yet, all in all I heard more wisdom from her than from my educated friends. She had innate intelligence, realistic views on public life, a passionate love for the theatre and the little literature she knew, a deep faith in God, inexhaustible vitality and a practical way of doing things which I lacked. Although she was not nearly old enough to be my mother, she acted like one to me. She asked us to call her 'Auntie' but insisted on calling me 'Missus' to the end. Long before I got my job and could pay for her services, she took charge of my hopeless household. She turned out and rearranged the suitcases and cartons stacked away in the woodshed, aired and brushed my husband's suits, chopped wood, scrubbed the floor, and brought us home-made cider. For a good chat she would do anything. In the late summer she would disappear on her own all day, to return loaded down with baskets of fruit and all sorts of flowers which she knew how to dry expertly so that she could sell them to a dealer in medicinal herbs. She also taught me about mice. My first encounter with a live mouse, outside a picture book, had charmed me – its shiny black eyes were so trusting. But soon the little beasts were waking us at night by scuttling all over us and I found their droppings everywhere. So I went and bought the sort of trap that catches but does not kill the mice, and every morning I took them across the road into the woods where I let them out. This did not seem to help, and it was Auntie who told me that they were not only coming back out of the woods to grow fat on our cheese, but were also spreading the good news to their friends. I don't know what I would have done without Auntie, who bought a whole arsenal of guillotine-type traps and then discreetly removed the carnage I could never have faced. She was rewarded by her terrific success everywhere she went with the story of my methods. It was also Auntie who started watering the mushrooms that sprouted along our kitchen wall. In the hope of having me placed at least on the waiting list for a flat, the gripe column of our paper got the Housing Department to send a couple of officials to inspect our place. A week before their scheduled visit Auntie started watering the mushrooms so that when they arrived we had an admirable crop. Although the idea was good and a statement was written out confirming the absolute uninhabitability of our habitation, and the men got their bottle of plum brandy each, the whole procedure failed to bring us one step nearer to a flat. But it

160

was good for laughs. Our cat kept on getting kittens, and it was Auntie who found homes for them. Of course, when I started to make a living I paid her like everybody else when she washed, cleaned and mended things for me, but I could never pay her for what she taught me about accepting life. Nor for her encouragement in my darkest hours. I was unable to share her belief in God, but I gratefully accepted the comfort she herself got out of it and so generously shared with me.

Tania was away from me only when Susie took her along during vacation time to where she and her future husband were singing in the Tatra Mountains, in Carlsbad or at some other spa after they had left Prague. Why they decided to move from the capital with all its advantages is a story in itself.

Nobody I ever knew in my whole life was as bad at lying as my daughter Susie. When her cheerful, chatty letters suddenly began to sound strange to me I knew that she was holding something back. Her reassurances over the telephone that everything was fine and that I was imagining things sounded unconvincing. The ads and little articles in the Prague papers testified to the fact that she was well and working, and I knew that she was at last happily and firmly in love with her future husband, a member of the band whom I had already met and whose greetings appeared on her letters. Seemingly all was as it should be. And yet I knew that something must be wrong. I weighed possibilities and finally, during a sleepless night, I came to the conclusion that she was perhaps pregnant and afraid to let me know. I had no personal objections to her friend but was not especially enthusiastic about seeing her forced into marriage so soon, right at the beginning of her career. I decided to visit her and reassure her that I could take it and that she could stop her useless efforts at pretending and needn't worry about worrying me.

When I arrived in Prague I found that I was both right and mistaken. She was indeed in great trouble, but her secret was far from being so natural and innocent as being pregnant by the man she loved.

When she welcomed me she looked strained and pale. I had to wait until we were alone in the safety of her little room before she dared to whisper to me what she could not write or tell on the telephone. For the past month the Secret Police had been making repeated attempts to make her work for them. It started with a summons to the Ministry of the Interior, a frightening event in itself. At first she was only questioned in a general, quite friendly manner about her family, herself, her feelings for her father, her work, and then allowed to leave after having signed a paper acquainting her with all the dire consequences she would have to face if she breathed so much as a word about her visit. She signed and left without knowing why she had been there. It was not long before they called her in again, and this time they told her what they wanted her to do. This was in 1957, the Hungarian bacillus was in the air and heightened vigilance was the order of the day. Every visiting foreigner, whether tourist or businessman, was considered a potential enemy. Susie was asked, or rather ordered, to sit around in the afternoons in the posh lounge of the Alcron hotel, strike up acquaintance with men, get out of them whatever information she could and then report on them to a 'contact man' who would be waiting for her at a fixed hour once a week at a certain café. When she tried to refuse, saying that she was by her very nature and way of life absolutely unfit for this role, they produced a thick dossier on all her movements. They read out to her the names of every foreigner for whom she had ever sung a song on request, they told her who had sent her flowers and when. They told her from whom she had once accepted a little bottle of French perfume. Singing where she did, with her looks and all the languages she knew, it was useless to pretend, they said, that she could not attract the attention of and get confidential with the people they were interested in. They read out data from only a few pages of a frighteningly thick dossier and made threatening hints at the rest of its contents. They went on bombarding her with an intimidating mixture of appeals to her patriotic feelings and dark threats, impressing her all the time with their evident omniscience and omnipotence. When she brought up the argument that she was engaged and never went anywhere without her friend they said that this was a problem for them to solve. Anyway, they added, they knew very well that the young man's divorce hadn't come through as yet, and if they chose to do so, they could prosecute her on moral grounds for sleeping with a man who was still technically married.

Susie says that the pressure was so great that she could not avoid signing but she clung firmly to the thought that she would somehow manage to do nothing. As an unexpected reward for her signature on the paper pledging her to cooperation and absolute secrecy, a few days later her 'contact man' called to tell her that her father was at that very moment in Prague, that she could visit him at Pankrác prison that very day and give him any amount of food she chose to buy. She went, of course, and what she brought him was the first and only gift that reached him in six years.

While she did not dare to write or say anything over the telephone, she confided in her friend. Or rather he told her first, because it turned out that he was in the same position with another contact man in charge of him. After they had met their respective 'friends' once or twice and had nothing to report, the security people made a few efforts to separate them. He was shown faked photographs of Susie in compromising situations, she was told about his secret meetings with other women, and so on. However, since they were constantly together day and night and were in no way open to further blackmail, they were soon judged to be useless. After a few subsequent summonses, threats and promises the whole thing petered out, but it was enough to make them leave the band and Prague. They continued as a singing duo travelling to spas. One of the security men made a last tentative appearance in the High Tatras, and that was the end of it.

After having blocked out my own fear of the secret police, I was shaken by Susie's adventure. It kept me in a state of worry for quite some time, especially since we did not meet for several months after she left Prague, and in her letters she could not inform me about the relatively quick and painless way the whole thing had ended. Also, I had new reasons to feel unsure of my employment. Soon after what was so diplomatically called 'the Hungarian events' we got a new editor-in-chief. He was a provincial apparatchik who knew as much about journalism as I did about Chinese calligraphy and made up for his lack of education and experience with heightened vigilance and discipline. The atmosphere changed and our little paper turned into an abbreviated version of the official morning press. We were joined by a new colleague who drove his own car to Vienna at weekends and was known to be an informer. The tape-recorder was discarded and a couple of members of the staff hurriedly became candidates for party membership. The very young reporter, who was the only Jew at the office besides me (a fact known, at least seemingly, to no one else but me), increased his pathetic efforts at dissimulation by toeing the party line and diligently contributing poisonous glosses referring to the Middle East. I never let on that I knew his story from a friend who had known his mother well before the war. It was a miracle that he was alive. As a little boy he had crawled out from beneath the corpses of his parents in the mass grave they had been forced to dig in Eastern Slovakia before being shot. It was by no means out of gratitude to the Gentiles whose bullets had missed him that the boy was so eager to be considered one of them. It was simply because for a young man wishing to make a career in our brand of socialism it wasn't expedient to be a Jew.

When I was young in Budapest, in our circles, being a Jew was nothing to be either proud or ashamed of. In fact, it was so unimportant that my generation didn't even read Jewish history and we were quite unaware of the fact that only a little more than half a century had passed since the Jews had attained full emancipation in Austria-Hungary. Only after the Holocaust, and after our trials, when those who had been most zealous in forgetting their origins were the first to be hanged for no other reason than for being what they tried so hard not to be, did I begin to feel Jewish. So, although I understood the boy's motivation and never breathed a word, I felt contempt for him. In my eyes he was identifying himself with his parents' murderers. After Hitler and after what socialism turned out to be, dissimulation was just that.

I can't read Hebrew, I don't need a synagogue to communicate with God, I don't know Yiddish, I believe that if Jewish religious fanatics have never done much harm it is only because – thanks to the nature of their God – they never had the power of a Pope or a Torquemada. But I have found my Jewish identity. I could not explain what makes a person like me, who to the best of her knowledge does not represent any specific race, religion or nationality, a Jew. Perhaps I want to belong to the powerless because if I have learned one thing in my life it is that power corrupts. Perhaps I am just haunted by the sad old story of the man who says that he is proud of being a Jew, and when asked why, answers that he might just as well be proud of it since not being proud of it would still leave him being one.

I think I found my own answer when I visited Israel for the first time in my life this spring. From a Tel Aviv sidewalk café I was scrutinizing the faces of the incredible variety of people in the passing crowd, unable to evoke any special feeling of being finally among my own, asking myself what it was I had in common with them when they themselves didn't seem to have much in common with each other. Suddenly the truth came to me. Our unity was in the gas chambers of the extermination camps. All through history the nations of the world have hated, fought and killed each other, but they remained united in one thing: their treatment of the Jews. Israel was the outcome of two thousand years of martyrdom in a sea of hate, it has saved hundreds of thousands of would-be fervent German, Hungarian, Polish and Russian patriots. If the Jews had to become a nation it was because of the nationalism of others. If they had to become fighters it was in self-defence, to survive. Considering the odds against which this miraculous survival took place I am tempted to see a purpose behind it which I could only grasp if I could grasp God. If I could pray I would pray for Israel, but I would begin with the words: 'Please, God, let them live in peace, prosperity and governed by humane common sense, but don't give them too much power . . .'

Reverting to my original self I would prefer the words: 'Please, God, change the world and its inhabitants so that no Israel should be needed, Amen . . .'

But the world my original self hoped for does not exist, I can't pray, God does not seem to listen to those who can, and against all the expectations of our youth, the world is becoming increasingly one where Israel must exist.

During 1967 I heard that a second cousin of mine was about to visit Czechoslovakia, and this visit seemed to offer a chance that I must not refuse. Somehow or other my Great-Aunt Tiny's favourite granddaughter Kiki had grown up to be the great French film actress Simone Signoret. Her husband Yves Montand was to give concerts in Prague and Bratislava on his way back from a visit to Moscow, and she would be with him: an honoured guest of the State to be wined and dined by our highest functionaries, because the Montands were leading members of the French Communist Party.

I felt sure that whatever Simone's convictions were, if I could talk to her privately about Oscar's imprisonment she would believe me and try to help. After Hungary, and what she must have known about the trials there, she must surely recognize the ring of truth in my story; and I would not be asking her a great deal. A single, seemingly casual, enquiry about my husband's fate from these distinguished guests might well be enough to shame the authorities into quietly releasing him.

The concert in Bratislava was sold out, and the Montands would be staying in the posh hotel where Susie and her husband happened to be singing just then. It would be natural for me to invite my cousin to listen to my daughter, and it would provide an inconspicuous occasion for talk. I decided to telephone her at the Alcron Hotel in Prague and make the appointment in advance.

As Simone Signoret describes it in her autobiography, I sounded so eager over the telephone that she concluded I must be one of those bores who wish to impress their friends with having a famous relation, so she was quite relieved to be able to tell me that the concert in Bratislava would probably be cancelled. It was, so I called her in Prague once again and this time she was more friendly and allowed me to explain our relationship. I must have sounded very disappointed because she assured me that she, too, was sorry and that she sincerely hoped we would meet some other time.

I took the first train to Prague, went straight from the station to the Alcron and sat down in the lounge. I had as yet no clear idea of what I was going to do, but the Alcron is so planned that anyone entering the hotel, or coming downstairs to go to the dining-room, must pass through the lounge, so I felt certain that I would see her sooner or later and I was waiting for the circumstances of her appearance to dictate my action. At the table next to mine there were two young men who didn't look right against the plushy background, and I became convinced that they were watching me. I went over to the reception desk to buy cigarettes, then sat down at a different table in a far corner. Soon afterwards the two men changed tables too, so that now I was almost sure, and very nervous. Then Simone appeared in the entrance, beside her tall husband. They crossed the lounge towards the dining-room, closely surrounded by a crowd of eagerly smiling officials. I had a fleeting glimpse of an extremely elegant, queenly figure, evidently in a hurry, her head held high so that I could clearly see the expression on her beautiful face, which was one of impatience, annoyance and boredom.

I could not move. Two visions flashed through my mind: the two men, or some of Simone's followers, grabbing me and holding me back, or – even more humiliating – reaching her, speaking to her, and being snubbed in public as a pushy poor relation. She looked arrogant enough for that. I went back to the station and took the next train home.

We were to meet ten years later in London, when a German refugee couple whom we had befriended in Bratislava before the war made it possible for me to travel. By 1966, if you could pro-duce an invitation you could get a passport with a limited exit permit, and three pounds-worth of currency from the National Bank. It was the husband of the German couple who was gen-uinely anxious to repay our hospitality of the thirties. His wife felt that the whole thing was a nuisance. Having found a family with whom Tania could work as an *au pair*, she installed me not in her own sumptuous and roomy flat but in an expensive hotel which supplied bed and breakfast, and she obviously felt that one dinner at her home and one sight-seeing trip was as much as she need offer. I didn't want to let on that my only spending money was three legal and three illegal pounds, and was thankful that English breakfasts are what they are. The hotel management must have been surprised at my gargantuan morning appetite.

It turned out that Simone Signoret was in London, preparing to appear on the stage as Lady Macbeth. This time I had nothing to ask her and felt that she could not suspect me of wanting to show off, so I called her and we arranged to meet. She asked me to bring Tania to have a drink with her in her room at the Savoy, doing it at such short notice – she was very busy – that I had to invest my third but last pound in a taxi.

I was anxious to explain why I had appeared so eager ten years earlier, and I was also longing to take this unique opportunity of talking with a representative of that (to me) incomprehensible species, the French intellectual left, and seeing for myself if they really did not know, or just preferred to ignore, the truth about the régimes still so staunchly supported by *l'Humanité*. So after a drink and a little small talk about our families, I plunged into the story of why I had wanted so desperately to meet her in Bratislava, the Alcron incident, and Oscar's imprisonment.

I could not know it, but I had hit on a bad time for this meeting. Simone describes in her autobiography how exhausted she was, and how tense. Perhaps for the first time in her life as an actress she was feeling unsure of herself (and in fact her Lady Macbeth was not to be a success), and she could spare little thought for anything else but her part. I had hardly started when she cut me short by saying: 'But if you had stayed in New York your husband, as a communist, would have met with very much the same fate.'

I fell silent. When she asked me to go on with my story I said it was useless. I excused myself, gave Tania a sign and left. I did not say it in so many words, but she must have known that I considered it pointless to talk any further with her. I felt very sad after that meeting, partly because of what her remark had revealed of the blindness of people in her circles, and partly because during the first part of our chat I had taken a genuine liking to her.

After the Alcron incident I knew that something was terribly wrong with me. My normal self would never have panicked and given up like that. The two men in the lounge were quite possibly innocent guests, secret policemen only in my sick imagination. All right, they had been watching me – but I had been quite well dressed and I was wearing make-up, all for Simone. Perhaps they just liked my looks. It was true that Simone had seemed arrogant, unapproachable and bored . . . So what? Famous visitors can well be annoyed and bored by the solicitous flock of people at their heels. Why didn't I go into the dining-room? Or leave a message at the reception desk? Why did I run? That wasn't like me. I had talked with her twice over the telephone, I had made the expensive trip to Prague, I was sure that given the political situation at that moment there was a chance that she could help. And yet I ran away. What I had done was illogical, absurd and shameful. Simply not normal.

But then, everything around me was illogical, absurd, shameful and abnormal. Was it logical, so long after Khrushchev's speech and the unmasking of political trials elsewhere, that our Stalinists should still be in power and their victims still in jail? Wasn't it shameful that my colleagues felt they must take the openly cynical decision to join the Party in this its most despicable phase of existence? And wasn't it a shameful thing that terror, having become less bloody, was now taken for granted and its still-suffering victims were forgotten, simply because a few consumer goods were beginning to reappear in the shops?

Even my job had become shameful and absurd. The new editor-in-chief had a habit of commandeering me into service as an interpreter. I had to go around with visiting groups of western and exotic progressives, mostly members of the International Peace Organization, and I would be depressed days ahead of the scheduled arrival of these 'pigeons', as I called them. They came from Italy, France, India, and once a whole big family arrived in two shiny Cadillacs from Iraq.

It was always the same round. We would visit a perfectly

equipped nursery with one nurse to almost every baby where I had to translate that this was our usual standard, knowing that it was the only one of its kind, newly built for the privileged, while other nurseries were overcrowded and employed one sour, untrained old woman to every twenty or thirty children. We would be shown round one particular agricultural co-operative where everything was in good order and even the chickens cackled Marx by heart, and where by an incredible coincidence we always happened to stop for a chat with the same smiling, buxom, talkative milkmaid. We always went to the same modern factory, where the manager spouted heroic production statistics while normally unavailable ham was served and glasses of export brandy were clinked for Eternal Peace; and we always ate the same lavish lunch at the same hotel. There was a last-minute panic only once when the Iraqi guests politely refused to eat pork and asked for veal instead. It was rushed to the hotel in a black limousine from the State Hospital, the only place that received a small ration of it. The guests assured us that in their country such meat was only for the rich, but that after they, too, had enjoyed a victorious revolution like ours, veal cutlets would certainly be made available to the Iraqi working masses.

On one of these excursions, while going through the usual factory with some Frenchmen, I suddenly felt crushed and suffocated by such an avalanche of revulsion that I had to run to the nearest toilet and throw up. Afterwards my face was so green that the functionary in charge allowed me to go home.

The doctors found nothing wrong with my stomach. Nor with my throat, my eyes, my head, my heart or any other part of my body although they had all begun to hurt one after the other, or all at once. In the end I was sent to a psychiatrist. He told me that it is a well-known phenomenon for a person who has stood up well under the worst conditions to break down just when things begin to improve and pressure eases. Under our régime no such thing as a nervous breakdown could be officially diagnosed. Pavlov was God, Freud anathema and every sort of psychotherapy developed after Freud was capitalist hogwash. Since the psyche is formed by the material conditions and the society one lives in, and our conditions and society were good and on the way to becoming perfect, there could be no neurosis. You could be run down after an illness, or overworked, in which case you were sent to a spa, put into a tub of bubbly water, given showers and massage and told to go dancing in the evening. Or you could have something wrong in the mechanism of your brain or with certain glands, whereupon you would be sent to a clinic for diagnosis, medication, shocks or the latest Soviet cure which was said to produce miraculous results: the sleep treatment. They put you to sleep for several weeks with interruption only for eating and using the toilet, and then you woke up wholly regenerated, ready to function like a perfectly repaired machine.

I was terrified of going mad, so I tried to believe this doctor when he assured me that if I really were going mad I would neither know nor fear it. But soon I began to envy the really insane for that very reason. They did not know, but I did.

Fainting with starvation, I could not touch food. Completely exhausted, I was terrified of going to bed because of the visions that inevitably came to haunt and torture me, and to wake me a dozen times a night, bathed in cold sweat. Two grey sparrows trying to fly away, their brittle feet entangled in a ball of wire. Should they go on struggling vainly or should they tear themselves away, leaving their little bloody feet behind? It was for me to decide but I couldn't. I could only watch and suffer their agony. Healthy people have nightmares too, and besides, what's so terrible about the fate of two sparrows in which you yourself are not involved? Only a person who has had a nervous breakdown could answer that. The unspeakable horror of it, when the sparrows come back every night, the decision is always mine, and I could never make it . . .

Or the simultaneously frightening and desirable man with eyes of pure gold who appeared and came nearer and nearer . . . When he moved his lips to tell his name there was no sound, but his mouth kept opening and opening and opening until it changed into a cloaca spouting green slime. Which I felt sticking to my body all day, while knowing that it would be back, and so would the sparrows, if I dared to lie down and shut my eyes.

I had an overwhelming need to make somebody understand how dreadfully ill I was. The doctor was not interested in details: he gave me sleeping pills and recommended rest, perhaps a vacation in the mountains. Terrified of the night, dreading the day, I went on working and playing the role of a sane person. This I found easier at work than in private life where human relations and emotions were, or rather should have been, involved. To my horror I found that I had none. Except for the unbearable pity I felt for my child who had only me and didn't know that I was turning into a stranger who was going through the usual motions of love and interest only to hide the awful truth from her. My friends noticed, of course, that I was evidently run down. Who wouldn't be, after all I had gone through and such constant overwork? Sympathetically they advised me to 'pull myself together' and cheer up. After all, they said, the conditions of Oscar's imprisonment had improved a bit, and there was every reason to hope that he would come home on some sort of amnesty quite soon. How could I tell them that I didn't care, that all I could think of was that I was unable to live or die . . .? Whose husband were they talking about anyway? I did not have one. I would have given the world to exchange whatever was causing me this unbearable suffering for a disease that other people recognized, for a big festering sore, or for two broken legs. All I could say was yes, of course I must try to pull myself together. Gradually I gave up meeting my friends because I felt that I was becoming a burden instead of good company and because it was impossible to make them understand.

The only person who knew how to give me a measure of comfort was 'Auntie' from the hilltop, who had probably never heard the word 'psychology'. Some wondrous instinct made her act in just the right way. Instead of telling me to pull myself together she let me know that she believed that I could not do so and that it was not my fault. Only with her did I feel that I need not display a sore in order to prove that I was ill. While others enumerated all the reasons I had for hope, and made me feel even crazier by pointing out that my depression was irrational, she said little and listened much. Noticing my estrangement from the child, she made no comment, but played with her, prepared food, put her to bed, and somehow made her understand that her mother was not angry, just not well. Often she forced me into taking long brisk walks with her. After such a walk, which I would never have taken by myself, I could sometimes cry, eat a bit and sleep a while. When Auntie was there to assure me in her quiet way that with God's help this too would pass, I almost believed it.

But Auntie had no diploma, and the doctor sent me for a thorough examination and treatment to the psychiatric clinic. By then I had lost about fifteen kilos and was unable to read or hold a pen, so I agreed. In fact, I was longing for the hospital. It meant escape. Above all, it held the promise of sleep. In my mind I saw myself lying in a white, silent, peaceful room. A kind nurse was giving me something to drink and I did not have to hide or explain that I was ill, since that's why I was there. When she left, she closed the door behind her so carefully that it made no sound. Then came quiet, peace, no thoughts, no pain, no fear, no responsibilities, no more effort to pretend that I was myself, nothing – just sleep. When I opened my eyes a kind doctor was sitting there who encouraged me to speak, listened patiently and then reassured me that there was hope and that I was not really going mad. After that I could sleep again.

But first I had to hold out for one more week, so I could be there when Susie got married. I felt that a wedding with both of the bride's parents absent, one in jail and the other in a madhouse, would have been too much for my children. From what I was told afterwards, it was a beautiful wedding, but if we didn't have a picture showing me in a new dress, and apparently quite sane, I wouldn't know that I was there. To get me through it I was given an injection at dawn and another at ten o'clock. After the reception the young couple left for an engagement at the venerable Hotel Pupp (now the Moskva) in Carlsbad, and I took a taxi to the hospital. Only my friend Jucka knew where I went from the wedding, and it was she who took Tania to her home.

The old State Hospital was probably built in the city's outskirts, but now it stands on one of the noisiest corners and its garden consists of two benches and a few square metres of grass between parked delivery trucks. The psychiatric clinic was on the fourth floor but the elevator was reserved for stretcher cases and deliveries. Somehow I managed to climb the stairs and I gave the papers from my doctor to a nurse who sat behind a small window. She nodded, let me in and then carefully locked the door behind me. I was led down a long corridor where men and women of all ages, all dressed alike, were sitting at small tables, leaning against the wall or lying on the stone floor. I was shown a bed in a room with two more beds, given a striped garment, told to change and to lie down and sleep. I tried to explain that that was exactly what I could not do, but the nurse said I must. It was too late to start anything else that day. She was going to wake me for supper.

The rest of that afternoon I spent walking up and down that corridor, trying not to step on anyone. The quiet, and therefore least frightening, patients gave me empty stares, but the loud, seemingly gay group at the card table invited me to sit down. They were eager to point out the most interesting cases and to give me hair-raising descriptions of lumbar punctures, electric shocks, brain operations and so on which I was likely to undergo. A man with a bandaged head told me exactly where he had a hole in it and insisted that I feel it. Then they showed me the elderly lady and the young man who were going to be sent away next morning although they did not know it. They never knew, said the man with the hole in his head; they were told that they were going for some special examination at another place. But away it was, haha!! I learned that 'away' meant the big insane asylum near Bratislava where patients were taken as incurables if several months of treatment at the clinic brought no results. After that, whenever I was led somewhere for an examination I was sure that I was being taken 'away', a horror which could easily have been dispelled if only one single doctor had talked to me during the two months I was in the clinic.

Everything in this place seemed calculated to aggravate my state. One of my symptoms was an inability to eat, and here I was faced with greasy messes which would have nauseated anyone. I couldn't sleep, and the cleaning women started clattering their pails at five in the morning, while the delivery trucks never stopped unloading just under the window. Each evening two burly male nurses appeared in a little room at the end of the corridor, and when a bell rang we had to line up, lean over and receive an injection against insomnia; but this assembly line method resulted, more often than not, in the needle hitting some nerve so that even though one was drugged, the pain woke one up. My third symptom, even worse than not being able to eat or sleep, was terror at the thought that I was going mad. In this place we were given no knives or forks to eat with, but only spoons, so clearly we were dangerous, and none of the staff would listen to me or talk to me, so clearly they thought I wasn't making sense. I was given all sorts of examinations and tests, always in silence, and the dossier which accompanied me everywhere grew thicker and thicker – frighteningly thick – but no one would tell me what it contained.

Finally they started giving me insulin injections, which put me into a state of blissful half-sleep so that I felt sorry when a mug of sweet tea and another injection brought me back to reality. About ten days later I began to feel hungry, and somewhat reassured at not yet having been sent 'away'. Friends and relations were telephoning me, and although visitors could be received only in a room downstairs or in the yard, one day little Tania managed – I still don't understand how – to cajole or fight her way right up to my room. After that they let her in every day and she brought me fresh vegetables, fruit and pieces of cake from Jucka's table. She also brought me a light blue dotted housecoat which she had chosen and purchased herself, convinced that looking pretty would make me feel better. I was so moved that I almost did.

As soon as I started to eat they stopped the insulin and put me on a combination of injections and pills of various colours which had frightening effects, about which no one warned me. I was so drugged that I can't remember much about the next six weeks, only that my longing to escape from that place became stronger and stronger. Finally I told the usual silent doctor that I was now feeling well enough to go home, and to my surprise and relief he agreed. I was told that I had been suffering from 'reactive depression', now cured, and that it would be a good idea to spend a couple of weeks at a spa. So off I went to a sanatorium in Marienbad, and two days after I got there I was collapsing, totally unable to eat or sleep, twitching in a sort of delirium. The house physician telephoned the clinic in Bratislava and discovered that while there I had been on heavy daily doses of a then entirely new, imported tranquillizer – incredibly enough, after a month of stuffing me with this heavy drug, they had sent me out without a single pill. The doctor wanted to pack me off to the nearest hospital in an ambulance, but I refused and telephoned Susie, who was working in Carlsbad. She and her husband took me in and spoon-fed me like a sick child, not only with food and drink but also with comforting words, kindness and infinite patience. Without them I do not think that I would have made it back to health.

My husband knew from Susie that I was exhausted and spending some time in a 'sanatorium'. I took up my correspondence with him again when I came home supposedly cured. In fact I wasn't, except that I could work. To live, to exist still seemed to me an insurmountable task for months to come. The only thing that saved me from a total relapse was the terror I felt at the thought of having to return to the clinic, which was infinitely worse than my own private hell at home. Twice a week I went to fetch my ration of pills and once I was recommended to submit to hypnotic treatment. The doctor was so kind and tried so hard that I closed my eyes and pretended to fall into the deep sleep he told me I was in. He must have noticed that I was wide awake, twitching and trembling as I always did, because after two sessions he gave up. I don't know how, why or exactly when I got gradually better and then well. The whole thing lasted for about ten months, and I suspect now that my depression would have passed of its own accord, without any of the treatment I received.

When the next permit came to visit Oscar, I was glad to have an excuse not to go. Only two adults were allowed, and this time Susie's father was to meet his new son-in-law. Oscar was now reading the papers, listening to the radio and was occasionally allowed to watch television. So he was writing mostly about having heard, seen or read about Susie and Zdenek. I didn't know what to write.

In late 1959 we heard at last that a committee was going to hear him and re-examine his case. He asked me to write dozens of letters to various legal and political authorities, to former coworkers, functionaries, etc., all of whom were to send character reports on him to this committee. I did so. Then I received a letter from my husband saying that this whole procedure was arranged with a view to possible release on amnesty, and he was not interested in amnesty. Nothing short of a new trial resulting in full rehabilitation could make him want to return to the outside world. If he had known that the committee was concerned only with amnesty, he would have refused to appear. Besides, it was only another farce. The first question he had to answer was exactly when he had made the decision to become an enemy of the state. He was reproached for having worked as a young man for a stock corporation and thus for capitalism, he was told that he married not for love but for money, that he was known to have been a nightclub-crawling womanizer and wide open to corruption when in public life. All of which meant that at least for the moment he could not be considered a case deserving release on amnesty.

In the course of that year many other people were sent home quietly, one by one. They were no less innocent than my husband, but they were glad to be let out and they kept silent. They could not understand why Oscar did not realize at last that he was no exception. The more fuss he made, they said, the longer he would be there. Didn't he know that he was only a pawn in the big dirty game, and that he could not turn over the board all alone . . . ?

To me his attitude meant that he thought it more important to be rehabilitated by a gang of criminals than to come home. He wanted to stand clean. In whose eyes? Every decent, thinking person knew that he was innocent. Those who were still accusing him knew it too. His expectation of justice from these very people meant that he still had some sort of respect for them, that the Party meant more to him than everything else life had to offer.

By then the political situation was such that they couldn't keep him in prison much longer, whatever his attitude. He was sure to be free before long, and I was naturally eager for it. But I was beginning to have doubts about our future common life.

Susie and Zdenek now had a steady engagement at a theatre in Bratislava and were travelling only when they sang at concerts in Prague, Budapest and Moscow. Living as they did, and had done for years, in a hotel room, they were desperately longing for a home. And Tania was getting too old to continue sleeping with me on the only couch we had in our den. It was hopeless to apply for an apartment. There were none. But the Trade Union Organization, owner of the paper I was working for, was building the first of the so-called co-operative houses, in which members could buy a flat, and I was lucky enough to learn about it at an early stage so that I could get my name on the waiting list. Later on these queues for co-operative flats that cost a fortune became so long that the waiting time was many years, but this was in the beginning, and if we could raise the money we could count on moving into a new three-room flat in the spring of 1960.

What we needed in cash was about three years' average salary. Susie and Zdenek, who were earning well, had some savings. I took in all the translating work I could get, and swallowing both pride and fear of the censor, I wrote to America. Through 'Tuzex' coupons sold on the black market the three hundred dollars our cousin sent me made a nice sum. At the last minute the children managed to complete what we had with a small bank loan. We made it! And high time too, because when we moved in Susie was already expecting a baby.

There was a small room for Tania and myself, a bedroom for the young couple and a living-room in between. The crowning glory of it all was the bathroom with a toilet. The first in nine years! Who cared how long it would take to furnish the place if one could sit in the bath tub, get up in the morning without freezing, cook real meals on a real stove . . . We were in seventh heaven. And full of hope, because according to ever more convincing rumours a general amnesty was due either on Mayday or on the 9th, the Day of Liberation.

On Mayday nothing happened except that I took special pains to march briskly and to look joyful because the boss was marching beside me, and only a day before he had announced that the Communist Party of Slovakia was taking over our paper. For him this was good news, a step up on the ladder. For me it was fraught with danger. In fact, next day I was summoned to the conference room where Trade Union representatives from both the office and the printing shop were waiting for me. They were sorry, they said, but the Party wasn't going to take me over with the rest of the staff. I had to understand that as the wife of my husband I could not possibly be employed by the party press.

Why hadn't anybody warned me? The editor-in-chief must have known long ago, and my colleagues had known too – that was why they had suddenly started applying for membership. Were they too sorry for me or too ashamed of themselves to tell? If I had known in time I could have taken the initiative, handed in my notice and found a job elsewhere, any job! What chance did I have now, thrown out like this, an outcast again . . . ? Humiliating as it was, I begged them to keep me on at least for a while. I was willing to do anything in the printing shop or to pack papers for distribution, just until I found work. I was a member of the Trade Union, paying my dues. Weren't they supposed to be on my side? I knew very well what they were, I was asking only out of pure desperation. The answer was embarrassed silence, and when I left the room I wasn't sure if I didn't pity them as much as myself. If they hadn't been representatives of the Trade Union they would have been decent fellows. It was small comfort to learn that there were two others who shared my fate. One was a chauffeur who had once had trouble with the police when his wife reported that he was sleeping with one of their daughters. The other was a middle-aged printing technician in whose cadre dossier the new owners discovered that he had been active in the scout movement before the war.

On the Day of Liberation the telephone started ringing early in the morning. Did we know that Husák had reached home? Then another call: Loebl was back! Amnesty!! A wife rang to ask if my husband had arrived, because hers had come in on the ten o'clock train and said that mine should have been on the same one. Three, four, five calls. Trembling with fear, hope and excitement, we studied the timetable. The next and last train from Leopoldov was due late in the afternoon. We didn't know what to think, we did not dare to think. Then the doorbell rang and when the children

179

opened my husband came in. The police had driven him straight home.

For the first half hour we did nothing but cry, laugh, kiss and run around him in circles. Did he want to drink something? Eat? Rest? Talk? Where does one begin, after almost ten years of this sort of separation? We kept telling him that he looked fine, and he really did in his old suit, the one they took him away in. He kept telling us that we looked fine, that the flat was fine, and after that we didn't know what to say. He wasn't hungry and he didn't really want anything except perhaps to lie down for a while.

While he was resting in my room, we were feverishly active. Zdenek ran out to buy him a pair of shoes, Susie was preparing something special in the kitchen, Tania and I were moving things around and discussing where to make a place for him. We had to decide on the living-room.

During the past ten years my feelings for my husband had passed through many stages. There had been love and desperate longing, burning compassion, later on resentment and anger, indifference at times, estrangement in the end, yes, but passionate loyalty always. After the initial paralysing shock and during the first years of false hopes I was even physically faithful. Which was more than we expected from each other. We got married in the thirties, when our notion of life in the Soviet Union – our Utopia – was not based on the current reality but on an idealized view of what it had been like in the early twenties. So, besides freedom, social justice, equality and respect for human rights we also believed that free love prevailed in Utopia, and was therefore right. Not promiscuity, but the principle that no two people were to own each other. Sex was all right, but it was much less important than everything else we had in common. We were not going to live for each other, but together for something more. The body was a secondary thing, liable to become jaded after a while, open to temptation. Withstanding such an occasional temptation for one's partner's sake could easily give rise to unconscious resentment and spoil a human relationship which was so close and so perfect that no purely erotic adventure could harm it. We wasted little thought on the possibility that one of us might fall seriously

in love with such an occasional partner; but if – against all expectations – this should happen, we were free to part. Sexual
possessiveness was nothing but bourgeois baggage. Such were our
principles, and for quite some time neither of us felt the need to
put them into practice; not until it became gradually clear that
aside from the great common ideas that had brought us together
we had very different tastes in life.

In the days when my husband felt that he could not possibly live
without me he knew perfectly well that I was more interested in
poetry than in the kitchen, that I loved nature, animals and sports,
that I laughed at dirty jokes if they were good and drank a glass or
two in company. He must also have noticed how careless I was
with things, because whenever we met the hotel room and my
suitcase were a mess. Nevertheless, it was not long before he
started expecting me to be someone else: a woman not unlike his
mother and sisters, whom he loved but would never have fallen in
love with. And it wasn't just a matter of wanting me to be more
efficient about the house. He wanted me to change my tastes.
Sport was a waste of time, keeping a dog was a rich man's whim,
poetry without a social message was a sentimental trick to take
people's minds off real problems. Off-colour jokes made him
blush, ordering a drink was not worthy of his wife, smoking and
wasteful ways with things and food were irritating. Going out of
an evening made no sense – he used to visit nightclubs, he said,
when he needed to find a woman, but now that he had one whom
he loved, what was the use of dancing? As for my wanting to bring
a baby into a world where millions of children were dying of
hunger, this was foolish obedience to a primitive instinct.

When I fell in love with my husband and then, after a passionate but intellectually unsatisfying affair with someone else, decided
to marry him, I too knew almost all I was to know about him later.
But I felt that he was so much better, wiser and purer than I that
I tried hard to live up to his expectations. I really and truly wanted
to be the wife he needed. But one cannot change entirely, and after
a while one stops wanting to.

According to the second-hand Soviet ideology of those days, in
our circles it was considered good to have sex because a physically

frustrated person was unlikely to be fully fit to devote his capacities to the cause. It was the old 'glass of water' thing. There was nothing wrong with my husband's thirst, but the time came when I lost my taste for water. Besides, that ubiquitous Chinese coolie was spreading guilt feelings not only at our table, where he hungrily reproached us for our food, but also in our bed. Anything slightly better, more beautiful or more enjoyable than absolutely necessary for survival was tacitly branded as wicked. I myself have been haunted by this feeling all my life and I am to this day, but not to the degree of becoming a killjoy, especially not when I was young and full of life.

I went to meetings, lectures and seminars with my husband, I read all the books we discussed and I did typing, folding, mailing and money-collecting work for the Party. Together we watched and were deeply moved by all the Soviet films. We lodged, clothed and fed German and Hungarian political refugees at our home and some of them left us to go and fight in Spain with their photographs stuck into Czechoslovak passports conveniently 'lost' by people of our acquaintance.

While I found much of the demagogy and intolerance in the correspondence and polemical writings of the 'classics' quite offensive, these feelings were quickly repressed by my reaction to what was happening on the opposite side of the political scene. What doubt could one have about where to stand between Hitler and Franco on the one side, of whom we knew a great deal, and Stalin on the other, of whom we knew only what he and we wanted us to know? In all this my husband and I were completely at one, with a single exception that gave rise to our first marital discord on the political level. At that time every self-respecting leftist subscribed to *Die Rundschau*, the organ of the Third International. I fully agreed with every opinion expressed in this paper, but its style offended against such standards as had been bequeathed to my literary judgment, and ultimately to my critical faculties, by my earlier reading habits. So when the postman came I used to say to my husband: 'Your bulwark has come.' That made him furious, not only because I was making fun of such a very serious thing but because I called it 'his'. There was a bulwark in every headline and dozens of bulwarks on every page. Every one of these bulwarks stood to defend some positive social phenomenon ranging from peace and progress through art, freedom and good morals all the way to total perfection – this last bulwark being, of course, the Soviet Union with its great Helmsman. My slowly ripening suspicion was that nothing written so badly could possibly be wholly good and true. Perhaps it was this that started me on the way to doubt, of which I became fully conscious only later, when the Nazi–Soviet pact was signed and *Die Rundschau* and my unqualified belief in my husband's superior judgment crumbled simultaneously.

However, at the start of our marriage ideological and intellectual harmony between us was still perfect. It was our attitudes to pleasure which clashed, as was demonstrated during the first holiday we shared. Swimming and lying in the sun for hours made me happy and brown, but fifteen minutes on the beach made my husband impatient and red. On the train, while I was swapping food, accepting wine from a common bottle and using my hands or making grimaces where I lacked words, he sat politely sulking in the corner, feeling ashamed for me. Never having visited a Mediterranean country before, he ascribed the admiring glances and insinuating gestures which Italian men so generously distribute to foreign and often quite undeserving women to the indecency of my dress. He was not jealous, but he hated to be noticed, and I was part of him. When a group of young people invited us both to join them on a boat trip he preferred to stay at the hotel, but generously told me to go ahead if I wished. I did, of course, and I also went dancing with the crowd in the evening and played tennis in the morning. My husband seemed grateful that I didn't insist on dragging him along, and I appreciated his tolerance, but I was also hurt by his not being at least a bit jealous. He seemed perfectly satisfied with his rest and his papers and books, so long as I came back not too late, reasonably sober and willing to give him his glass of water. But even if I came in late it seemed to bother him less than a single bulwark-type joke. He probably didn't even know that I considered this holiday a disaster. Whatever it was, it set the pattern for our future married life.

Incredibly enough, I never loved any other man as I loved Oscar in the days when I did love him, and I know that although he was sometimes interested in and slept with other women, he was never in love with anybody else but me. Which does not necessarily mean that our marriage was a good thing in spite of its shortcomings. Often I wonder whether both of us would have had a better life if one or both of us had fallen in love with someone else, deeply enough to make us see that we hadn't much in common apart from the initial bond, and to make us end our marriage. Instead, as that initial bond weakened it was gradually replaced by other ties, the stronger for being painful. Those of shared suffering, of my defiant loyalty in the face of injustice and persecution, and finally of approaching age.

Although a prisoner released on amnesty was still a non-person so that the only work my husband could get was shifting lumber in a warehouse for wages that would not have paid for a room, and although I had no job, our reunited family had much to be thankful for. My husband was in relatively good shape; Susie was happily married and expecting a child; Tania was a good pupil, healthy, no more moody than other girls her age and prettier than most; and I, for better or worse, was myself again. It ought to be possible to say 'we lived happily ever after', but it is not.

If someone had asked my children if they loved their father, they would have been surprised at the question; but if they had been asked why they loved him, they could not have answered. Why should one love a person one does not know? He was a total stranger to Tania and no more than a childhood memory to Susie, they had never had a chance to develop a genuinely loving relationship with him. They very much wished to learn to love him, that was certainly true, particularly Susie, who was old enough to understand what he had been through, and on this wish he could have built if he had been patient and understanding.

Instead he failed to see that his daughters were no longer the children he had left behind a decade ago, but were individuals whose habits, tastes and views had been formed by hard experiences. Much as they wanted to please him, they were unable to submit to the sudden imposition of a strict and ascetic régime, patterned on prison life. They could not accept the campaign of re-education on which my husband launched as soon as he had expressed his appreciation of what he approved of.

Susie, a married woman, was not so much exposed to it directly, but was much discussed in her absence. Did she need to wear all that make-up? How could I know that she was really good and that her public was not applauding her exaggerated décolleté? If she was as gifted as she was said to be, why hadn't I insisted on her studying to be a 'real' singer? Even now it wasn't too late – or rather it was, because I had let her marry so soon. Zdenek seemed all right, but couldn't she have waited for her father? Stuck as she was now with marriage and light music, she should at least improve her repertoire in a more serious direction. Was it wise to have a baby now, before they had a flat of their own? (A flat of their own? This was the man from Mars speaking.) How come Zdenek's father, a railway worker all his life, had never been in the Party? (This question came from the man not from Mars but from Marx.) Susie heard only a little of this, and what she heard she knew how to answer with patience and understanding for her father's long isolation. She has a kind heart and a wonderful gift for keeping silent and disappearing from the scene of a possible conflict. Zdenek was behaving respectfully and with male solidarity. The atmosphere between Oscar and the young couple was sometimes a little tense, but nothing worse.

Not so with Tania, who as a child was not considered to be beyond radical re-education.

She is as warm-hearted as her sister, but has a more militant nature, ready to stand up both for herself and for others. Because of what she had seen, heard and lived through, she was much older in many ways than most twelve-year-olds, very independent, but not mature enough to be tolerant. A girl her age does not easily submit to constant nagging and admonishments, even from a father to whom she is accustomed. Tania was expected to adjust to an alien lifestyle imposed on her by a newcomer, some of whose habits and idiosyncracies must have seemed strange to her to say the least (bottles of milk were warmed next to the radiator to save electricity. Hard crusts had to be consumed before fresh bread could be served). Tania had too many dresses, too many toys and too many opinions of her own. She was a spoiled brat. When she talked with disrespect about members of the family and other grown-ups who hadn't been 'nice' to us she was told that we had probably given them good reason to behave as they did. To this she answered with outcries of indignation and used what her father considered unpardonable language. When she helped herself to fruit before making sure that none of the visitors wanted more, she was humiliatingly told off in public. She was summarily sent to bed. I was reproached for letting her enter Susie's room in the morning when Susie was still in bed with her husband. Her friends were noisy and her love birds a messy nuisance to be got rid of. Once, when she was ordered to eat up a left-over potato which she was going to throw out when clearing the table, she shouted back at her father that he could eat it himself. This was when she got the first beating of her life.

Needless to say, she had her faults. I did spoil her in an attempt to make up for everything else, and perhaps, according to the standards of those days, some of her father's objections were well-grounded; but more often they were unjust and humiliating. However, what ultimately broke down the relationship between the girls and their father was not so much this nagging about their behaviour as his lack of interest in their lives, his inability to listen to them when they spontaneously tried to speak about their own joys and problems. He didn't have the time for them – or for me. All he needed was a place corresponding to his idea of an orderly home where he could receive his friends and then devote the rest of his free time to the fight for rehabilitation. I was there to keep the children out of his way, to take care of the household and to pay for it. We needed every crown I got for my translations, but since my husband never did any shopping he had no idea what things cost and failed to understand this. To him it seemed that I could keep the house in better order if I took in less translating work, and that I could have achieved this if I wished by being less extravagant.

The first person he visited after his return was the man who had been the Minister of Justice when he was sentenced to twenty-two years and dozens of other people were hanged. This visit gave rise to our first really bitter row. He was unable to forgive the pecadillos of his wife and daughters, but towards those who had truly sinned against him he was more forgiving than Christ himself. He resented the slightest criticism of such people: their behaviour was justified by historical reasons which I was too petty-minded to grasp. He refused to make a trip to the village where we had spent two years. He made Maria and the rest of my friends feel so unwelcome at their first visit that it was also their last. They were not his kind of people and what I felt about them did not count. He was fighting for justice and was unjust himself. He called me irresponsible in money matters, and never asked how I had managed to keep us going against such heavy odds through all those years, nor did he seem to notice that we were now living on my earnings. Not a word of praise did I get for having brought up the children single-handed, nor for my courage. I was merely the little woman who had to be told what to do, how to do it, and what not to do – and above all how wrong I was in whatever I had done on my own.

With Tania disappointed and obstinate, my husband nervous, miserable and unjust, myself angry and overworked, and the house constantly full of admiring comrades whom I despised but had to feed, the days were pure hell. In the evening, when the guests were gone, the dishes had been washed, the long letters to the Party had been written and Tania was asleep, my husband called me into his room. While going through the motions of the sedate love-making of a happily reunited middle-aged married couple, we kept reassuring each other of our unchanged love. We were lying.

I am inclined to believe that he thought he was sincere. On that secondary level to which all personal life and private feelings were relegated, he meant it when he said that he loved me. He just did not seem to like anything about me. And in a way I was sincere too. I did love the husband for whose return I had been waiting, the one I had built up in my dreams. And the dreams had not been very wild ones. Remembering only the good in Oscar, it had not been unreasonable to hope that after his ordeal he was going to find a new taste for the things in life he'd had no time for ten years ago. Nor had it been unreasonable to suppose that, even if not disillusioned with the ideals of socialism, after what he had gone through he would come back less dedicated to dogma, less religious, less ascetic. I had imagined us enjoying nature together, reading books, going to exhibitions and the theatre, being friends with our children, looking forward to having grandchildren, making the best of what was left of life and then growing slowly old together. No doubt we would often be sad, but not bitter. We would be resigned to the fact that we were unable to remake the world. I had also assumed that because I had remained loyal to him for a long time in difficult circumstances, and had proved strong enough to bring myself and the girls through it all, he would have a new respect for me and would be less impatient with my faults. He was going to find that a frivolous, dreamy, untidy and – by his standards – vulgarly bohemian wife who smoked was better than no wife at all, particularly as she genuinely wanted to please him and was now too old to think of dancing and ski-ing and wearing dresses with very low necks. Simple personal freedom, a home and the absence of terror were in themselves such wonderful gifts; surely we had both changed enough to be able to enjoy them together?

I don't know what picture of me Oscar made up while he was in prison, but I do know that he was as disappointed as I was. While we were both sincere to start with when we said the word 'love', the object of our love existed only in our own imaginations. It was not long before the word started to sound hollow, and in time it was no longer spoken. True, the years had changed us, but instead of bringing us together they had torn us irreparably apart.

I was made to feel dreadfully guilty because to his family and many other people my husband was a hero: a man of impeccable character, great talent and much personal charm (and all this was true) who had come through a terrible ordeal unbroken and was now leading a valiant fight for justice, and was working out in his mind ideas of a kind which would bring about the Prague Spring two years after his death. Who would have believed me if I had said what I gradually came to think: that the years of humiliation and brutality had left their mark on his innermost being, and that deep down he was totally disillusioned, and sick because he could not admit it even to himself? He was sick both in body and mind, and so was I. At any rate, not well enough to heal him.

After the birth of Susie's baby he began to spend less and less time at home, and I was sincerely glad to know that he could find elsewhere what he could not find at home: peace and quiet with his papers at his own table at the coffee house, political talk on walks with his friends, rich dinners and sympathy at his sister's house, and among the comrades one or two admiring and willing youngish women.

In a last bid for domestic peace we sacrificed the money we had invested in the co-operative and exchanged our modern flat for an old one with one more room. This transaction involved eight families, a black-market operator well paid by all, a housing department officer paid by the black-market operator, and a great deal of nervous waiting because the whole intricate chain might have broken at any time, right up to the last minute. But it worked, and although the kitchen was small and cold and the bathroom water-heater was temperamental, we were less under each other's feet and on each other's nerves.

When rehabilitation came at last, so overdue that it was not very dramatic, it was not as a result of my husband's fight. The party handed it out wholesale to a particular group of amnestied people, no more innocent than anyone else, but slightly more prominent. With rehabilitation came the Party book, an apartment, a fairly large sum of money, a ration card entitling its owner to purchase a car without the usual four years' delay, and a fairly good job. Rehabilitated people and their families could also get health care at the State Sanitarium, an institution for higher cadres with its entrance well hidden in the backyard of the Lenin Museum, which also ran a luxurious rest-home in the woods near Bratislava. There apparatchiks splashed about in the pool along with their former victims, some of whom I saw placidly and respectfully playing chess with retired Police Minister Karol Bacílek, who had recently been replaced as Secretary General of the Slovak Communist Party by the little-known Alexander Dubček.

By that time I had landed a job with a popular science magazine, so we were well-off – which did not prevent a great deal of quibbling when we furnished our new flat. My husband did not finally decide to buy a car – a light blue Skoda – until long after all the others had done so. He drove it for only a few months before he fell ill with what proved to be hepatitis.

A friend took me to the isolation hospital in the Skoda every day, but I was not allowed upstairs. On the fifth day Oscar went into a coma and specialists were called in. Two endless days later I was sitting downstairs when a woman doctor came to tell me that my husband had regained consciousness and I could see him if I wished. I had to undress and change into a white coat. My husband was sitting up in bed, smiling at me as if we had met the day before. He said that I made a good-looking doctor in that coat and I said that he already had a better-looking, younger one right there, and that he had better hurry up and come home. He did not know that he had been unconscious for days and I did not know that these silly words were the last ones we were to exchange. A few hours later he was dead.

The specialists said that it was a light case of hepatitis, but ten years of prison fare, stress and repeated hunger strikes had robbed the organism of its normal capacity to resist. They comforted me by saying that after a long coma it was a blessing that his heart failed, because he could have lived on only as a very very sick man.

The funeral was a solemn political affair with speeches by functionaries and by friends who were not my friends. I felt like an outsider, or rather a guilty intruder. It was as though the speakers, Oscar's relatives, and all the rest of that great crowd of people were accusing me of having failed to give him the happy home and the understanding he deserved after his dreadful ordeal. Everything said in the speeches was true: it *was* a cruel loss to society to have to bury a man who had every civic virtue. He *was* a man of talent, a steadfast, courageous fighter for what he believed in. He *was* unselfish, helpful, frugal, and he *had* emerged from hell as pure in heart, thought and deed as they had known him to be before.

I was bewildered, bereaved and horrified at a sneaking sense of relief at no longer having to live up to something I could not cope with. Oddly enough, the person who seemed to know and understand what I myself was afraid of knowing and understanding, who took charge of my house, of the endless stream of condolers, and of all practical matters, and then became my closest friend for the next years, was the young woman whose home had been my husband's refuge in the last months of his life and with whom he had been quite obviously in love.

In trying to describe what my children and their father felt, or should have felt, for each other, in talking about our marriage and now about this woman, I have used the word 'love' quite freely, as though I knew what it meant. I don't think I do – or rather, I do only if I don't think. At least where physical love is involved the word has been used and misused so much that it has lost its significance, and to me it does not seem to fit completely anything I ever felt for a man.

If I say that I never really loved any other man than my husband, I am truthful on the generally accepted level, but as soon as it is said it rings false. But then, what do we allow ourselves to feel? And how much dare we admit to *not* feeling what we should feel, according to others? We jot down the word 'love' as a convenient shorthand, one we can hardly decipher ourselves. It is a hopelessly inadequate abbreviation where a thousand words would be needed to give an approximate definition of a single facet of the innumerable shapes into which this emotion crystallizes, only to disintegrate and recrystallize into a new and again only transitory shape

Of course I have loved other men, but none of my loves resemble any of the others. It was love when I was thirteen and sat trembling, waiting for a telephone call. It was also love when I was eighteen and went to meet my husband in secret to make love for the first time in my life. But during the two years before we got married I had an affair with a man whose body and touch enraptured me, but with whom I found nothing to talk about once we were dressed, and this too was love, full of passion, tenderness, gratitude and deep regret when I left him.

Does any woman ever meet the one man who fills all of her needs? I haven't. I seemed to want another man for every one of mine, and today I can say so. I couldn't in the past. In those days I had to keep my idea of a perfect love affair a well-guarded secret, or I would have been considered a moral outcast. I wished to make love when I was in the mood, and only then. When I felt loveable, and only then. I wanted to share with a man only what was best in us, and to do this detached from the past and the future. To know about him only what he cared to tell and to tell him only what he wanted to hear. To know little enough of him so as to be able to invest him with dreams. It was only under these conditions that my body was capable of total response. Some people need alcohol, others mirrors, some need complicated gymnastics; I could make satisfactory love only if I was left to be myself and was loved for what I was. Of course, a woman looking for this sort of encounter lays herself wide open to advances from the wrong sort of men, she is often alone and even more often in company she no longer wants. But this is part of the game, and looking back I would say that on the whole it was worth it over and over.

I was almost forty when I happened to meet a man who was prepared for such a relationship, and the reason it lasted for fifteen years (with a decent interruption when my husband came home) was that we were together only on weekends and holidays. That he was many years younger and that I was married excluded any plans for changing this perfect perpetual adventure into something else. We had delicious waiting, beautiful letters, flawless meetings, sad partings as if for ever, sweet remembering and waiting again. Above all, there was the total absence of claims on each other. Whatever was then given and taken seemed purer than it could have been in a marriage. When we met we were perfectly sure that we wanted each other and that we had no other motive for meeting. It was perfect physical love, and for the rest, we had a thousand things in common, but where our tastes, opinions and beliefs differed, we could afford to listen with interest and tolerance knowing that we would never be forced into giving up our own for each other's sake.

To happy couples and unrequited lovers this may sound like

selfish frivolity which has nothing to do with real love. Perhaps that is what it was: circumstances allowing, we might very well have ended up as a miserable married couple. I am thankful to fate that we did not.

It was a sign of the times and the place that, bad taste or not, most of the visitors who came to express their condolences used the occasion to make inquiries regarding my plans about the flat. No mother of an almost marriageable daughter would consider moving to a smaller one, they said, I had to think of Tania's future needs; but while she was still single, three rooms plus the cubby-hole next to the kitchen were more square metres than we could keep. Everybody had someone near and dear in desperate need of living space. This started an era of boarders: a sequence of young couples in my husband's room and of girl students, occasionally with their lovers, in the cubbyhole.

After a couple of months I realized that I now had access to the money in the bank which had been untouchable hitherto for moral reasons, and I decided to spend some of it on formerly imper-missible luxuries. I had a gas radiator installed in the otherwise arctic kitchen, bought a vacuum cleaner and – perhaps as a belated protest against years of freezing – sheepskin coats for Tania and myself. Then I bought a few totally superfluous things such as potted plants, pale yellow curtains for Tania's room and a number of useless colourful objects. The light blue Skoda was standing untouched in front of the house and reminded me every time I passed it of the hospital, which was the only place to which I ever rode in it. I wasn't allowed to sell it for four years, nor could I drive. In the summer I exchanged it for a tiny Fiat and decided to take lessons. According to my teacher I had a natural talent, and in fact, considering my age, I learned fast and became quite an effi-cient driver. Except for getting lost, which I do even when I am walking, and for avoiding certain intricate crossings, especially the ones with a policeman in the middle. I never know which way to turn, and when I move to a new flat it takes me months before I reach in the right direction for the light switch. And I am still scared stiff of policemen.

Long before we heard about the sociological experiments of the alienated young in the West, we made our home into something very near to what they dreamed of. Except that we washed, ate meat when we could get it, didn't use drugs, didn't cut people into pieces to better the world and restricted our promiscuity to the meals, we functioned as a very informal, very warm collective. Having to take boarders, which had sounded like a nuisance, turned into a blessing. The student girls kept coming back after they married to mix with Tania's friends and to be mothered by me. My old friends reappeared and so did Auntie from the hill, whom I could now pay for her help. The place was constantly full of people of all ages, including my grandchildren, of whom I already had two. When their parents were singing abroad, sometimes for months, they had to leave the boys in charge of an old woman under my supervision and with Tania as their substitute mother. Whoever stayed too late for the last bus was welcome to sleep over on the extra couch. I helped the young woman boarder with her English thesis and her husband did what was considered man's work around the house. A frequent late guest was Bronia, Bronia of the unforgettable loaf of bread, with whom I was doing technical and agricultural translations. Much of the time we did not know what the texts were about, but with the help of dictionaries, some imagination and many bloody marys we managed, certain as we were that nobody was ever going to read the stuff. It was an open secret that while Slovakia had little to teach American scientific institutes on such subjects, these papers were being sent out to get their literature in exchange without having to pay for it in hard currency. Anyway, we laughed our heads off at the intricacies of the love life of Slovak pigs and chickens.

Owning a car was a rare privilege and I thought I should share it with as many as possible. Besides, I still felt quite important driving, so that the little car was more often than not crammed with people on the way to a nearby lake or out into the woods. I used it alone only to drive to work and to the cemetery. There I had long conversations with my husband, remembering both the good and the bad and asking him to forgive me for not missing him too much. Perhaps it was the quiet and the lovely smell of the flowers that instilled into me the peaceful hope that he forgave me as I forgave him and that he didn't dreadfully mind being dead. While sitting there I wouldn't have minded being at rest myself. Cemeteries attract me. Not in a morbid way but rather because they hold the promise of an ultimate refuge from fear and homelessness. I visit them even in strange countries. I sit down at a grave, preferably one without too many angels and pigeons, with an agreeable name and a more or less acceptable life span on the stone. Then I imagine it is my father's which I cannot visit, my mother's who doesn't have one of her own, my brother's who is lying in a Russian mass grave, and finally mine. Rest.

But rest and peace were something I could not find during the night. The days at work and at home among my children, grandchildren and people I liked or loved, and with the first morally and intellectually intoxicating signs of the coming Prague Spring in the air, were good. But my nights were once more beginning to loom as a menace. No nameless nightmares this time, but compulsive communication with my husband's image and with my own as a failure. In daylight I thought of us simply as of a badly matched couple who should have had the courage to part in time, but the twilight of disturbed sleep brought tormenting regrets, the memory of love lost and feelings of guilt. Panicked by the threat of relapse into depression I saw a doctor, and when no medicine helped, he advised me to go to one of our famous spas for a cure.

Once there, I drank the waters, took the baths and swallowed the little pink pills they prescribed against whatever they thought was wrong with me. The spa's prospectus listed an imposing choice of ailments its waters were good for, but mine was not among them. None of the local mineral springs was a fountain of youth. Surrounded by flocks of bored, tired, lonely, mostly unattractive women of my own age and older it suddenly dawned on me that I was an ageing woman myself. I saw them as pathetic figures who seemed to have lost everything. Especially widows like me. I listened to the monotonous complaints of my table companions, watched old peasant women undress for massage revealing mountains of flabby flesh or poor skeletons covered by folds of dry skin, I took a sober inventory of their material and spiritual reserves and found that fate is even more unjust than usual to women when it comes to growing old. The elderly man can openly remain a receptor for the erotic emanations of young women, he can still father a child and nobody cares how he looks. A woman his age bears no more children, she has ceased to radiate attraction, and if she feels attracted, she must keep it a secret. She is tacitly reproached all the time – or feels so – for defacing the scenery. Even for a very 'well-preserved' matron the day comes when she realizes that in a very important sense she has ceased to exist. She has become invisible.

One gets used to it, but for quite a while it does hurt. Where is the woman, however decent, who does not need her share of appreciative glances from strange males and in whose ears a truck driver's whistle doesn't sound like sweet music? And what about the rest of life while it is still there to be lived? What was it like for these women? Most of them slept in a corner of a flat that used to belong to them, acting as unpaid household help and nursemaid for their married children. Daily, they spent hours on aching feet in food queues, and often they were doing a job on the side, since few of them had a pension worth mentioning. Before the war housemaids had a room of their own, their salary, their days off, the right to change employers. Not these women. What did they have? Past generations of grandmothers were loved and respected and usually in nobody's way. Age used to bring status, not shame. Even those who were not loved could count on a measure of consideration from offspring who hoped to be remembered with an estate, a house, a bankbook, a gold brooch or a good cooking pot. After two world wars and twenty years of socialism few grandmothers own anything to bequeath. In our country, the maternal urge to give something to one's offspring can best be satisfied by disappearing and making the family a gift of a few precious square metres of living space.

The women at the spa were not only ugly, bitter and boring but they talked about nothing except their miseries and the food. The few nondescript male patients kept to themselves, to their cards, their sports pages and their beer, and they looked no better.

This was the year 1967 and things were beginning to happen in our country which had been unthinkable only a few months ago. Bits of truth started appearing in print for the first time in two decades, ideas were taking form that held out the hope for a change which could have shaken the world. None of these people seemed to know or to care.

Finding nobody to talk with I fled into the woods, asking myself whether age would rob me, too, of everything worth living for. Was I becoming like them? I sat down on a rock, and looking down into the beautiful valley I remembered the girl I had been. A girl who once sat on a rock like this one, looked down on a lake and thought that she had discovered the secret of happiness. A girl who believed that she could and had to make something out of her life, something that would make sense in relation to other people because people were good and ready to make the world better if only they were told how.

When I returned home from this 'cure' I took out my old diary to see what was left of that girl.

***

Velden am Wörthersee, July 14, 1929. I don't quite understand what made them send me for this summer holiday to this place. It's a villa with an old lady in charge of twelve girls, mostly from Budapest, and we are supposed to enjoy it. I for one don't. Last summer in England was not so good either. A convent in Worthing with crazy discipline, dreadful food and the nuns tried to convert me. But it had a purpose at least: I was supposed to improve my English. All the rest of the girls came from France and therefore speaking French, like almost everything else, was strictly forbidden. So I learned to smoke and improved my French. But why Austria? What was the big idea? Daddy hasn't been feeling too well lately, and perhaps they wanted to get rid of me.

After lunch we must stay in our rooms and rest. Today I managed to sneak out with my diary. I am alone in the woods up the hill. It's a marvellous feeling. Among the girls and at home I feel often alone. That is bad solitude, but this is a good one. Here I can afford to do nothing else than to just simply *be*. I am listening to sounds I would never hear if I weren't alone. Right above my head a bird has just hopped from one twig to another. Now there was a short sharp chirp of a cricket. I can even hear the fall of a single prematurely dead leaf. Two tiny slender golden wasps are performing an intricate buzzing dance around me. All sorts of insects are crawling in and out of the hole below the rock I am sitting on. Anywhere else I would find them disgusting; here they are beautiful. Perhaps because they are where they belong. Wouldn't the whole world be a more beautiful place if everything and everybody could be where they belong? Yesterday I swam all the way across the lake all by myself. I should like to write a poem about that – I mean about one's need to try and prove one's strength. Of both body and spirit. I do write poems, but then I find that somebody else has already written a much better one about the same thing. Now I wish I could write one about being so perfectly happy at this moment for no special reason. Last year when I was in love for the first time in my life I thought I would go crazy with happiness if he would only start paying attention to me. When he finally did, it was sort of a luke-warm satisfaction, nothing as hot as happiness. Happiness should perhaps never be set as a goal. It must come just like this by itself, or rather brought on by something that promised nothing. Like a surprise. I'd better stop writing about it. Thought kills feelings, and I want to keep this one alive for a while . . .

Budapest, July 19, 1929. I have just come back from my father's funeral. Don't think, don't start to think now! Dear God, why can't I believe in you, why can't I ask you now to grant this one favour . . . please help me . . . All I am asking for is that you help me stop thinking. Please don't let me cry! I must write.

When my mother's friend arrived to fetch me she said Daddy was ill and I was to come home on the night train. From the very start I sensed something queer about her. She acted too friendly, almost like an equal. When she offered me a cigarette on the train, I already knew.

(Daddy, please forgive me that I am writing now. It would be more natural and decent to cry. But for me it's easier to write. It's awful of me to do what's easier now when I ought to do what's hardest. But why? Never mind . . .)

When we arrived home I was led to my mother who was lying on a couch. I felt everybody watching me, like on a stage. After the show Daddy was going to tell me like once at the National Theatre: 'Stop crying now. It didn't really happen. Romeo and Juliet are having a nice cup of coffee, and Mercutio, having been killed off in time, is probably sound asleep. And you are going to eat a nice chocolate ice-cream on the way home . . .'

They even bought me a black straw hat. I never put on a hat before because I think they are ludicrous things. In the taxi I sat next to Mother, who wore a thick black veil. I envied her for having it over her face. I wanted to comfort her but didn't know what to say. I had never been to a burial. We gathered in a little low-ceilinged house and I stood on a platform, very near to the coffin. At first I was afraid to look, then I was relieved to see that Daddy wasn't there at all. He was at home, sitting in the big grey armchair, smoking and whistling softly as usual. There were several speeches and the last speaker had jug ears. I had to think of my friend Dudu whom I met on a vacation in the mountains and with whom we spent a month laughing. We played at collecting people with ears that stuck out, and in the end everybody's ears, even normal ones, seemed unbearably funny. I bowed down my head and tried not to think of Dudu and ears.

Three days later. I am writing this in the pantry. The rooms are full of black people. In here, there is a strange mixture of smells. Onions, bayleaves, but also chocolate. It must be hidden. I could eat heaps of it now. I won't look for it or eat any, but I do want it. That's awful. But what if writers would start writing like this, I mean put down everything one really feels, not what one is supposed to?

It was *angina pectoris*. Lovely Latin words. The only subject I really cared for at school. He was forty-nine. I never thought of his age.

Now I must be very good and kind to my mother. Does that

mean that I shall have to say yes to everything? Already I have heard them making decisions about me. When I finish school I don't need to (in other words, I am not to) work. We have enough money to live on and to have my brother finish his studies in Germany. No hope for me to study abroad. With the *numerus clausus* for Jewish children (do all Latin words mean something bad?), I have little hope of being accepted at the university here. They probably won't even let me try. They don't think it matters for a girl.

I want to love her. She needs me now.

September, 1929. This is my last year in high-school and it's about time to start cramming for the maturity exam. The flat is empty. The great armchair is empty. Six rooms are too much if one constantly looks for someone who isn't here. It's also too expensive. We will move to a smaller flat.

October, 1929. Today I helped Mother to go through things in the attic. There was Daddy's old army outfit, our toys, law books, stamp collections, embroideries. How can one be so attached to things? I am unjust.

An uncle whom I don't like has been appointed my guardian. He is speaking in Daddy's name and telling me that I must stay at home with Mother. How can he speak in his name? I know that Daddy would understand that I am unhappy enough about not being able to study and that if I want to work it's not because of the money. For me it's a question of becoming a real person or not, I shall feel useless, imprisoned. It's got so that we quarrel every day. I am terribly sorry for Mother, but not sorry enough to erase myself for her sake.

November, 1929. I am tired. Perhaps they are right. I am wicked, selfish, thankless. What business do I have thinking about wanting to be useful to others when I refuse to be useful where I am wanted? They ask: why do I want to work if I have everything I need? I can't make them understand that I don't want to work to make money for dresses. I want to become part of the world so that I can understand more about it. If I can't explain something I feel so intensely I am probably no good anyway. If I were right, I could.

Now Mother needs me at home, but I bet, in a couple of years they will want me to get married to make things easier for her. If I take my coat to go out because I want to stop fighting, she says: 'So you are leaving me alone again . . . ?' If I stay I must fight back. If I try to explain things nicely I notice that she stops listening where she does not want to understand. How can I make her grasp that I must make myself entitled to life? It may be a crazy notion, but I keep telling myself that if I work I can learn enough about people and things to become a journalist, perhaps a writer. If I do no more than awaken the conscience and the compassion of a few people I shall have earned the right to live. I may not succeed, but I shall have tried. At least let me dream, let me hope, let me want to do it !

It's very late and I can't sleep. I try to be very just. One of us must be wrong. It may be me.

December, 1929. Last night I was sitting in my bath and I heard a funny hissing sound from the stove as if gas was escaping. I meant to look, but I didn't budge. What if I were to die now? I thought. What would it mean to me and to others? I have lived seventeen years and so far I haven't really hurt anyone. Nor have I spoiled anything of importance, and I was seldom bored. I haven't done anything to better things but neither am I responsible yet for any of the sorrow and misery around us. Shall I be able to say this in ten years from now, or twenty or forty?

To disappear just like that. But right now, at this very moment, now when it doesn't seem to hurt, now when Daddy is gone and I don't love anybody or anything too much. One must die anyway, why then not now when it seems easy? Will God punish me for not having turned to him? I am not afraid. If there is a God it's him who made me what I am. Let it come, whatever it is. It can't be much worse than life without a meaning.

When Mother called me for dinner I opened my eyes and was amazed that I could hear and see. The water was cold. I got out of the tub and stood shivering in front of the mirror, glad to be alive. I got absorbed in the study of my breasts. I tried the visual effect of cupping them in my palms. I wondered how it could feel to have somebody else's hand on them like that. And if I don't sleep now it is this thought rather than the thought of death that keeps me awake. Could it be that I simply want that? I do. But not only that . . .

. . . For some reason I miss Father more than right after his death. It's a snowless winter, the trees stand bare. Is it like this to grow old? Losing things like the tree its leaves, one by one and then suddenly in heaps? No promise of spring for man. From my window I can see a rag on the pavement. From time to time it flutters in the wind as if it were trying to fly away, but it's stuck and keeps falling back. It's only a dirty shred of cloth, but I feel such pity for it that I could cry. On the windowsill across the street a sparrow is picking away at a paper bag. It picks and picks with its little beak, but the paper is stiff. That's how I keep picking and picking without ever getting at the bread, the meaning of it all. A hungry little sparrow. That's me.

Daddy, they say I am not mourning for you. I wonder whether you would blame me for hating to wear black for a whole year. It means nothing to me. Nothing connected with you and with my love for you.

March, 1930. At the graduation celebration we are planning I am to recite two of my poems. One of them is about our teacher of Latin and one is dedicated to Ju. Eight of us are always together and we have abbreviated our names like this: Vi, Do, Ju, Gu and so on, and that's how I became Jo. I don't know how the whole thing started, but we have a theory that it was necessary because we have so much to say to each other that we must save time on the names.

It's still cold and mostly rainy. The only sign of spring is that men are accosting us in the streets.

The phantom of the exam is approaching. I was afraid of it for eight years, but now I don't care. What the hell do I need to graduate for if I am not to study. I can't work up any enthusiasm for

Boyle-Marriott's law about the volume of gaseous bodies (or whatever it is). Every morning I take my books and notes, and full of good intentions I go to sit on the stairs that lead from the Parliament down to the Danube. It's the traditional place for undisturbed study. I sit down, arrange the papers. Just then the sun comes out really warm, the sky, the water, the hills across the river are shining. I can smell the lilac in the far-away gardens, or I think so. Out of each thesis I know the first sentence by heart, and that's about as far as I get. 'Taking a historical view of the development of Hungarian jurisdiction . . .' While repeating this for the seventh time I am thinking of running away from home. 'Taking a historical view . . .' There is a sweet little puppy down by the river. It's too young to know which leg to lift when it wants to pee. It tries this one and then that one, it even tried lifting a foreleg. At last it squats down, and that's it.

May *19, 1930*. Today we did our test paper in literature. I drew 'The Hungarian people's soul as reflected in its folksongs'. I made it so long and put so much soul into it that they must have fallen sobbing into each other's arms, moved to the very depth of their patriotic hearts.

May 20. Tacitus. I was finished at ten, and then I wrote three more compositions for others. There is a loose brick in the lav for this purpose. At least for one of these I ought to get the mathematics in exchange tomorrow.

May 21. Mathematics. I got it. For the sake of credibility I put in some errors. Now I am safe.

I spent a wonderful afternoon with Ju by the Danube. We had to walk on a stretch of rail, and if we didn't fall off, anything we wished would come true.

June. It's all over. I mean school. I am what's called *bene matura* which is more than I deserved. The banquet was a big bore. The professor of Latin, the only one I really cared for, was ill, the women teachers were ridiculously trying to be matey. It was depressing how I couldn't be angry at the ones I used to hate. I am not as relieved as I expected to be after the exam. On the contrary. While I was learning, we had a sort of armistice at home, but now we are discussing my future again. They say I am thankless. I got a gold watch and Mother ordered a grey suit and a couple of summer dresses for me. What more for heaven's sake do I want? I don't give a damn for pretty clothes and such. I have only a single all-consuming desire: to lead a life that makes sense. Zoli says it's the Great Love I need. Rubbish. Although of course I agree that it's about time for me to fall in love.

Why can't I cry? If I can't, why am I choking with tears? Why must I write poems if I am not a poet? It's not fame or personal importance I am after. How can I express it? Let's say that I am a teacher and I am a better one than the ones I had. I might succeed in helping a few children to think. Among them, there might be just one who would grow up into somebody who does something great for the people. This would be more than enough. Nobody would have to know even that I had any part in it.

To me, Romain Rolland is one of the greatest writers, or rather, I think he is the greatest human being among the writers I know. He has more moral courage and he has done more against hate among nations than any other. There simply can't be any more wars after him and after Remarque. Not if people read and think. But do they?

July 1930. It's hard to describe the past day because I lived through it like through a dream or rather a nightmare. I had one of those hopeless quarrels with Mother and then I tried to write her a letter. A last attempt at making her understand. When I realized the futility of it I was seized by panic like a trapped animal. I went out and wandered aimlessly about town. Soon I was standing on that lonely strip of pavement behind the warehouses by the Danube. The lazily rolling waters seemed full of promise of peace and I seriously considered jumping into the Danube. Then it occurred to me that I could swim too well. I ran around the warehouse onto the highway and almost under the wheels of a truck. The driver was swearing at me and I hid in a doorway. There I stood trembling, ashamed of not daring to either live or die. That's when I remembered that I left the unfinished letter on my desk and that Mother must have found it and was now probably frantic. That made me hate myself even more. Shaking all over I somehow managed to go to Lucy's who is the only grown-up I know who listens. She put me under a cold shower, made me lie down and telephoned my mother. Lucy teaches Swedish gymnastics. She is divorced and Mother doesn't like it if I see her and her friends because they are 'Bohemians'. This time she must have been glad to hear her voice.

Lucy sat down on the edge of the couch and I talked and talked, and then, for the first time in a long long time I could finally cry. She gave me a drink and a cigarette and then I felt relieved, hopeful, at peace, and I fell asleep.

August 1930. Lucy has done it. We are on a holiday in Austria with Mother and Grandmother, and when we go home I can look for a job.

I swim every day. There was a boy from Berlin who didn't mind the rain either and we swam across the lake together five times. That's almost three kilometres one way. He left yesterday, and when we went to the garage to fetch his car he asked me whether I would let him kiss me good-bye. I hoped he would. We kissed, and if he hadn't left I could have perhaps fallen in love. A year or so ago I would have written a lot about this, after all, kissing like that is an event. Now I can only say that it was lovely and I can't feel as guilty as I should. According to current notions I 'let him take advantage of me' and I didn't behave as a nice girl should. But why? Why not the other way round? I didn't give more than I took. What's immoral about that?

. . . I have been working now for over a year and I like it. Tacitus and Horace are of little help, but at least it doesn't matter here that I never grasped equations. Only the mood is bad this week at the office. It's the general crisis. About five of us will have to go, and I feel guilty that it won't be me since I got the job through my father's friends. Now it would be logical for the others to hate me.

Half of my salary I give to Mother, and every time I feel like I bought myself a new piece of independence. Now I can stay away through weekends for ski-ing and rowing and I am saving money for a trip to Italy. I have met a group of young people who meet regularly to talk politics. These are allegedly social gatherings, but in fact meetings. They promised to take me along if I don't talk about it. It's dangerous.

Last week two of my poems were published and it was nice to see them in print. Also translations of three Verlaine poems.

Needless to say, I should also find a boyfriend. It's strange that I can't fall in love. I need boys to swim, hike, row and ski with, boys who make me feel alive and let me know that I am a woman, but nobody to belong to.

I am eighteen. Much happier than on my last birthday. Oh yes, and still a virgin. I don't seem to have the patience to fall in love. Or what is it? At times I feel my blood burning through my skin.

Last week we went for a three-day skiing tour. We slept in peasant houses and got sour milk and hot bread for breakfast. In the morning we washed in a frozen brook. Can anything make you feel better? In the evening we stuck burning torches into the snow and danced around them and yelled. I fell into a ditch with a boy and there we laughed like mad and kissed. He has eyes like a sweet puppy, he is handsome, strong and just eighteen like me. It would have been an ideal chance to get rid of my virginity without obligations, lies or involvement. But how could we in a snowy ditch? This sounds cynical, I know, but I don't mean it that way. What I mean is that this was a very special moment that will not come back. I wouldn't do it today, and if I did, we would both feel obliged to pretend all sorts of non-existent feelings and get involved in what would be really immoral: in lies for decency's sake. I wonder what he thinks of me now. Or do I really? Do I care what a bunch of grapes thinks of me? I loved the warmth of his cheeks, the touch of his hands under my sweater, his smell, not him. It was wonderful, but when he rang me up today I was at a loss what to say.

Lately I seem to have contact with the world by way of my

senses only. I am catching snowflakes in my mouth as I walk and that too is a pleasure I feel all over, right down to my toes.

It's still snowing, big wet flakes are falling into my soul and they are shining out of my eyes. A little vase with the first bunch of snowdrops stands on my desk. Spring is almost here.

I have been to one of those meetings and everything I hear there makes sense. I wish I could read more about Russia, but such books are forbidden here. One of the boys was arrested and sat for two weeks just for having had a brochure.

1931. A friend of mine who has been transferred to a country town and with whom we keep exchanging long letters is also interested in politics and corresponds with a friend he has in Prague. This young man is coming now and I am to show him around in Budapest. Should be interesting.

. . . He was quite nice. In Prague they have a group called 'Links Front', they have a legal communist party over there and they can quite openly read and discuss Marxist literature. I asked him a thousand questions but he gave me the address of a friend of his who, as he says, knows much more than he and will be glad to write me about everything I want to know. I wrote and he answered, and I answered, and now I wait for his letters and the clippings he sends at least twice a week. His name is Oscar, Oscar Langer. Our letters are becoming more and more personal and he would like to meet me.

The old bunch of girls from school still holds together. The one I love most is Ju. That's a very special friendship and it started in a special way. Across the street from our school stood a red brick building. When the morning sun shone on it at a certain angle, for a quarter of an hour or so it was surrounded by a trembling luminous haze and took on a mysterious pink hue. Once, during a physics lesson, we both looked out of the window and when our eyes met afterwards we instantly knew that we had seen the same thing. When tightly rolled-up slips of paper flew from desk to desk we found that we had written almost word for word the same: 'Let's meet in that pink house. We know that it is enchanted.'

The deserted strip of pavement between the warehouses and the river was to become our enchanted house. There we spend long afternoons sitting on dirty timber. We see miracles in every chance incident and read promises out of the water. Towards evening when the lights go on on St Margaret's Island we are alone in the world. It is understood between the two of us that nothing real is to be mentioned. We have worked out a plan for a common trip to Italy. We know exactly what her future child is going to look like, and what cover my first volume of poems will have. We also decided what to spend the first prize of the state lottery on (we have of course no tickets, that would be real and against the rules.) We also speak about the miracle drug Ju will invent as a children's doctor. And about my career as a brilliant, adventurous international reporter. I let her read some of Oscar's letters, she likes them, but she is not interested in politics. She is much gentler than I, more of a woman.

Västerås 1978

Ju was killed in Budapest during the war. They found her frail body crushed under a heap of bricks. Her husband was gassed in a concentration camp. They had a daughter. During the uprising in 1956 a bullet hit her in the belly. I never met her, but I am told she survived and somebody took her over the border. I don't know whether it was a just or unjust, a revolutionary or counter-revolutionary bullet.

Vi of the lovely legs who had such incredibly long eyelashes and much-envied dimples in both cheeks managed to be happily married for a whole year before she was deported. She never reached the camp. A woman who came back after the war was in the same wagon as she. They threw her out on the way, but the woman swears that she wasn't quite dead.

Li, who had the most envied breasts and for whom we used to model in the nude because she was studying to become a sculptress, married a fascist and they escaped to the Argentine in 1945.

Eva lives in America. One of us simply disappeared. The survivors discovered others from our class and they still meet once a week. I saw them when I came home from America in 1946, but when my husband was in jail I couldn't cross the border into Hungary for years. But we kept in touch, and I met them last in Budapest before the Russians came. Now, as an illegal emigrant, I am sentenced to imprisonment in Czechoslovakia and I am afraid to enter Hungary. But we keep in touch and write each other funny letters about getting old.

The magic that pervaded Czechoslovakia in the years 1967–1968 was such that it captivated even me for a while. At last, the audible part of the nation was awakening to the fact that something was dreadfully wrong with what went under the name of socialism in our country, and that it could and had to be changed. Into what? Into real socialism, of course, into the sort of socialism we wanted when we were young. Students and intellectuals began openly to demand things which should have needed no demanding: the end of the inane and ruinous cadre system, the right to choose members of Parliament, an end to the privileges enjoyed by the few – which were relatively much greater than those of a rich man in the West as against a worker. They demanded access to papers and books of their own choice, the right to travel, the release from jail and rehabilitation of innocent people, the punishment of the investigators and torturers of the fifties. They wanted the national flag displayed without the Soviet flag beside it except on special occasions, and they wanted to hear less of the Soviet anthem. They demanded that press and radio report news honestly. The morally and politically bankrupt Novotný régime refused to grant these things, but truth began to appear between the lines and the nation learned to read it. Simple citizens began to protest against spending hours in queues for food and other everyday needs while being told how well they lived, and to question why culture palaces were being built instead of apartment houses, and why when flats were built they were not given to ordinary workers.

Then, at last, Novotný fell. So much has been written by political scientists about the intricacies surrounding his fall and the events that followed that I want to recall here only my own personal experience.

On the day of Novotný's fall I happened to be in Prague. I went to a pub with my friend and a bunch of young people, and we got drunk: not on the little wine we consumed but on the heavenly drink of hope. For one evening we firmly believed in the essence of fairy stories: that finally evil has to succumb and good prevails.

Then Dubček took over. Nobody knew him but everything was expected from him. Censorship was abolished or rather restricted to self-censorship, and voices were raised expressing disillusion with the system. Different groups wanted different things, but none asked for a return to capitalism.

It is difficult if not impossible to explain to a westerner why we sat in front of the TV in a trance of gratitude, with tears in our eyes, when we heard things said that we had known for years; why Vaculik's '2000 words' were an event that shook Europe, although nothing new was said, only what ninety-nine per cent of our people had been saying silently and in secret for decades. Or why we marched to sign this and other proclamations in solemn groups with pen in hand, approaching the paper to be signed like devout Christians about to receive the Host.

It is difficult to describe how Czechs felt when they could bring Masaryk's picture down from the attic and explain to their children who that nice-looking uncle was; when they could tell them that before the German occupation and the Russian colonization their country had been the most progressive and fully developed parliamentary democracy in Europe, a country to be proud of in spite of its shortcomings and the world economic crisis, quite unlike the feudalistic hell they had been taught about.

We were enchanted to hear Professor Sik tell us on TV that we were on the brink of economic ruin. This was incomparably better than to be told day in day out that we were just about to surpass the American standard of living when we could buy only three eggs with an hour's wages, and one or two of them were sure to stink.

The alienation from each other caused by fear came to an end. Our friendly home was only a miniature reflection of every place where people met. Total strangers exchanged smiles, listened to each other's transistor radios in the streetcar and discussed events. Millions of people who had become indifferent and resigned now played the role of citizens for the first time.

I felt the charm of all this. I wanted to rejoice so much that there were times when I almost did. But in the past years I had been too deeply involved to become indifferent, and now I couldn't help noticing the false notes which kept creeping into the hymn of hope and renewal, and the identity of the people who sang it loudest. Just as Oscar had attributed his victimization to 'mistakes', so did the new prophets ascribe murder, unbearable living conditions and the system's shameless dishonesty to the same source. Mistakes had been made; and mainly – most conveniently – by Novotný. And we still had slogans. 'Violation of socialist legality', for example. What socialist legality had been violated? Where did it ever exist, except in our dreams? Another was 'The Party has to return to the Leninist norms.' The norms of the man who rubbed out all parties but his own, which he made into an instrument of terror? Would it have been much different if he had lived? Lenin never tried to convince his opponents within the Party. His methods were ridicule and slander, he called those who disagreed with him mercenaries, lackeys, imperialist hirelings, agents, and once he was firmly enough in power he delivered them to the Cheka. The Kronstadt rebellion and the Petrograd strikes were 'organized from abroad'. Reading Lenin in the thirties one could believe that this was the price to be paid for the future. Reading him in 1968, having seen this future, was a different thing. Every rebellion against unbearable conditions and terror was 'organized from abroad'. Why, in 1968 we could hear from Moscow and from Ulbricht's radio and read in *Das Neue Deutschland* that our whole protest movement was 'organized from abroad'. As for those 'mercenaries and lackeys', I had seen too many of them hanged, and I had lived for many years with an 'imperialist agent'.

Another slogan that was being used as an incantation and an excuse for all crimes was 'The Cult of Personality'. This was an inane phrase. As if Stalin hadn't been dead for fifteen years! There had been no cult of Novotný when the horrors and bungling were going on. I recognized too many voices among our new intellectual prophets. I had read their odes to Stalin and their rantings during the trials, so that now, when they were busy celebrating a new socialism with 'a human face', I couldn't help hearing it as just one more incantation, and a dangerous one at that, since the Russians must inevitably see it as a provocation.

I felt increasingly that this 'new socialism' was only skin deep. The Party remained infallible. The old Stalinists were still there on the Central Committee. Gottwald was still a saint – most of our prophets had worked with him. The report on the purge trials which a commission had been working on for years was never published. True, some of the master torturers of Ruzyně jail were brought to justice – the trial, confession and punishment of one of them was widely publicized. Less publicity was given to the fact that subsequently he became the manager of our State Travel Bureau, and evidently found our Spring so pleasant that he did not take advantage of his enviable position in order to flee over the border. Dubček was riding on the crest of the nation's hopes, not on any policy of his own. And either everyone was still as deluded as ever about the nature of the Soviet Union, or they had all forgotten their geography.

With the best will I was unable to forget it, and I decided to take advantage of the mobility now allowed us by the 'Spring'. Tania had gone with a group of youngsters to work on a kibbutz in Israel (their visas were issued in Vienna on separate sheets of paper so that their passports remained 'pure'; this was considered a wise precaution although their destination was an open secret). Susie and Zdenek were in Yugoslavia on a two-month engagement and had been allowed to take their children with them. In early August I told friends that I was driving to Yugoslavia to spend a holiday with them, and only my boarders knew that I planned to leave the country for ever and to persuade my children to leave with me. I sent a wire to Tania asking her to join Susie instead of coming home, sent a suitcase of her clothes to Vienna, packed as many of my own things as I could, and was ready to leave.

On the fifth of August my lodgers gave me a fond farewell with much hugging and laughter, in spite of thinking me mad. Less than a full week later they welcomed me home, ironical this time, though no less fond. I had spent five days with old friends in Graz, swinging back and forth between going on and going back. My friends were eternal refugees and when I listened to them it seemed right to go on; but I also listened to the radio from Bratislava, and that made me feel like a mad Cassandra. Finally the radio prevailed. I sent another wire to Tania calling her home, and life under socialism with a human face went on; for not quite a fortnight.

On the twentieth of August I dined out at the posh restaurant near the Castle. There was an elderly white-maned American professor à la Russell, on his way to give lectures in Russia; a couple of foreign journalists, both seasoned Kremlinologists, who were there to feel the pulse of our Spring; and my friends the Loebls. The animated discussion was tinged with some criticism of Ulbricht, but otherwise optimism was so great that I felt even more of a fool than they would have thought me if they had known how little of an optimist I was. For once I kept quiet, and did no more than exchange some thoughtful glances with Fritzi Loebl.

At about eleven I got home and let out Tania's boyfriend who was in uniform because he was on leave from his military service. We were in bed when we heard stones hitting the window. I jumped out of bed and saw the boy in the garden, asking with excited gestures to be let in. When I opened the gate he stumbled in breathless, green in the face. Shortly after leaving us he had run into a man who had shouted at him to hide for God's sake, uniformed as he was, because tanks were rolling up our hill. There was no need for explanations. We could already hear the rumbling quite near and a few shots from afar. Then telephones started ringing all over town. 'Is it true?' – 'Are you mad?' – 'You must be drunk!' – 'It can't be!' Many who got the news thought it was a bad joke.

Soon came the solemn radio announcement. The nationwide cry 'They wouldn't dare!' changed into a panic-stricken 'They are here!'

The Soviet consulate was housed across our street in a former rich man's villa. Nobody thought of attacking it, but after several bus-loads of Russian families had been brought there during the night, intermittent preventive fusillades came from their windows. The bullets reverberated on the pavement, some hit the trees in the garden.

The following five days were a mixture of fear, useless heroic gestures, listening to the admirably organized secret radio, rumours, great promises of resistance, a number of tragic deaths, hunting for food, radio batteries and petrol, kids hunger-striking in our street, youngsters arguing with the dumb and seemingly deaf boys in their tanks, desperately funny graffiti on the walls, street signs torn off and exchanged to confuse the troops and above all, a great feeling of brotherhood.

I wasn't surprised and therefore I was less shocked than the others. What made me tremble with fear were the names of our own old guard that kept coming up in the warning messages of the secret radio: names I knew only too well from the fifties, bloody-handed criminals still at large all the time, and now backed up by tanks.

This time nothing could make me change my mind. A newly furnished flat, money in the bank and my present comparatively easy life weighed nothing against what the return to power of these men would mean. This was no place for my children to live in, for my grandchildren to grow up in. Now that I had proof that I was the sane person when everybody else called me mad, I had confidence in my own judgment.

Oh the fifth day after the invasion I packed a few things, put the little money I had at home into a hole I made in a plastic sponge, told my lodgers who was welcome to what of my things and wished luck to whoever would win the fight to keep the flat. The evening before, a refugee had told a reporter in Vienna that he was probably the last to get out and that cars were being shot at. Tania was very much afraid so I gave her two pills, and we drove away. At this farewell there was no laughter.

I drove between rows of tanks but the stunned and bored soldiers didn't pay any attention to us. When we reached Vienna we found that we were neither the first nor the last, but rather part of a refugee crowd which was to grow into a flood of well over a hundred thousand.

Tania and I were given wonderful friendship, hospitality, help and political asylum in England. That only two months later I ended up as a refugee in Sweden – a country I knew nothing about except that it was cold and had Lagerölf and Strindberg – is a story which I must keep short.

Susie, Zdenek and their two little sons were there. After the invasion, sympathetic Yugoslavs had prolonged their engagement so that instead of returning to sing in Bratislava during September, as had been planned, they were able to drive directly to Västerås in Sweden where they already had a two-month booking. Friends were now trying to persuade them to go home and when I spoke to them on the telephone they sounded undecided.

I became obsessed with the need to tell them what I thought about the future of Czechoslovakia. I was not going to tell them what to do, but they had to listen to me before they decided; it was not, I told them, a question of my own future, but of that of their children. If they still wanted to go home after hearing me out, I was ready to go with them in order to help with the boys (they themselves might be allowed to travel outside the country with the band, but they certainly would not be allowed to take the children out again).

When I kissed Tania goodbye in London I thought it might well be for the last time. I shall never forget that bleak October day: this was easily the worst dilemma that I had faced in my far from problem-free life. On the boat I thought quite seriously of ending it all by jumping into the sea – that would persuade them, I thought. It sounds over-dramatic now, but that is how I felt. Ludicrously enough, what kept me going was my manuscript. I told myself that even if I had to go back to Czechoslovakia with Susie, I would finish it first so that I could leave a piece of the truth behind me, a document telling people in the West what they so obviously didn't know. Had I known then that I would one day meet people who branded Solzhenitzyn a fascist without bothering to open his books, I would probably have jumped; but at that time I was still convinced that leftists in the West acted as they did because they did not know the facts.

So I arrived in Västerås alive, although I don't know to this day how I made it without getting lost, and so quickly. I drove in a daze, and the only thing I remember are the signboards at the innumerable petrol stations on the way with the big illuminated inscription (it was October, and dark almost till noon) saying INFART. This is the Swedish word for 'Entrance', but I read it as INFARKT, the word for heart failure in several languages I know. Every time I saw it I both hoped and feared to drop dead.

In Västerås I was given a room with the grandchildren at the hotel where the band was playing. The Christmas season was approaching and there was a constantly replenished smörgåsbord in the dining room, where the musicians were free to eat. During the day we discussed politics and emigration, in the evenings I listened to the band and danced with Swedes of all ages in various stages of drunkenness, and at night I lay awake. Almost daily there was a telephone call from Bratislava. The Russians were packing to go, Dubček was fine, and Susie and Zdenek were mad if they didn't come home. When I asked Zdenek whether he was prepared to sing in Moscow again he almost bit off my nose, and when I said that he would have to sooner or later, we stopped talking to each other for days. Then we drove to Stockholm to get our transit visas. It was a snowless, dreary, very cold winter day, one of those days when Sweden is at its worst. I watched the bundled-up people in the streets and told myself that I felt sorry for them. They had to live here in the dark and in this dreadful climate while I was going home to where spring was around the corner. It did not help.

The end of November, and with it the end of their engagement in Sweden, was approaching. At the thought of having to face Czechoslovak uniforms at the border I felt sick. Susie was giving me secret reports about her husband's reactions to the latest news. By then I had become resigned. Nobody, least of all I, a rootless, wandering Jew, had the right to talk a native Czech into abandoning his country for my pessimism's sake. Nor could I abandon the boys. One early morning I met my son-in-law in the hotel corridor still in pyjamas, and I said that I needed winter tyres for the long, snowy drive home. Would he please help me to buy good second-hand ones? To which he said that I wasn't going to need them.

Whether it was my influence, or that of the news, or of other personal factors that made him decide I shall never know. We stayed in Sweden, and as far as the children are concerned, everything turned out well. If I myself am asked how I like life here I usually say: 'For me, it is not a question of where I am but rather of where I am not. So I am satisfied.' And this is, in fact, part of the truth.

It's the end of April, and it's snowing. But soon the miracle will happen. We will go to bed in the winter and wake up to see that summer has exploded overnight as it does only in the North. I can't think of anything more beautiful than a Swedish summer (when it isn't cold . . .), nor do I know whether I experience it so intensely because it really is more beautiful than elsewhere or because – in this – I too have become Swedish after all.

I am getting old now and it sometimes happens that when I lie down to sleep I almost wish it were for ever because nothing seems hopeful or important enough any longer to wake up to. But then comes a day when I can look at this country as if I had arrived yesterday, but with the knowledge I have now of its resources and of its past. Then I see my old belief confirmed after all. Society *can* be improved in a humane manner, life *can* be made better for the masses without their having to pay for it with hecatombs of lives and with all that makes life worth living. Here it was done with common sense, some good will and with work. It's far from perfect, but it's a good attempt in many ways. That I see much discontent around me only seems to prove that want, suffering, hardship and struggle are an intrinsic part of life and indispensable stepping stones to a measure of maturity which alone enables man to enjoy what's good in life.

Then comes a Music School concert when – in the midst of a flock of angel-faced and wholly dedicated young Swedes – my younger grandson plays his brother's composition and Susie, pretty as ever, sits hand in hand with her husband, and I know that they love me, musical idiot though I am. Or I spend a few days with Tania who has made a big mistake and has now nobody to hold hands with, but who has a little boy who can't read yet but loves books and wants to be read to for hours. I see my child who, in the midst of so much fashionable 'alienation', has not been spoiled, and I know that although it's not *in* to like one's mother, Tania is still my best friend, and that we can laugh and cry together.

After such days come mornings when an overnight miracle has happened to me like that which will soon be happening to the northern landscape. It would be too much to say that I feel young, but I feel engaged in the future, grateful for freedom, curious, loving, thoughtful – alive.